Governance
and
Development

Towards
Quality Leadership
in Kenya

Edited by Kimani Njogu

TWAWEZA
COMMUNICATIONS
"Working Towards a Better World"

First Published in 2007 by

Twaweza Communications Ltd.,
P.O. Box 66872 - 00800 Westlands,
Twaweza House, Parklands Road,
Mpesi Lane, Nairobi Kenya
email: info@twaweza.org
websire: www.twaweza.org
Tel: +(254)020 3752009
Fax: +(254)020 3753941

Design and Layout by Catherine Bosire
Cover Design by Patrick Thirimu

With the support of The Ford Foundation, Office of Eastern Africa

ISBN: **9966 9743 5 0**

Printed in Kenya, East Africa

Dedication

This book is dedicated to the youth of Africa who must work hard to revive the spirit of Pan-Africanism and facilitate the rebirth of the continent.

Contents

Acknowledgements   *ix*

Foreword   *xi*

Introduction   *xiii*

1   Leadership, Youth and Culture   1
Kimani Njogu

2   Constitution and Leadership in East Africa: The Crisis   25
PLO Lumumba

3   The Law and Leadership – The Post-Colonial Experience in Kenya   50
Kibe Mungai

4   Leadership Challenges in the African Diaspora   104
Macharia Munene

5   Politics and Alternative Leadership in Africa   120
Eric Masinde Aseka

6   Women And Leadership in Africa: A Case of Deviate or Die   139
Njeri Kang'ethe

7   "Bodily Contrariness": Some Preliminary Questions on Disability and Leadership in Kenya   163
Mbugua Wa- Mungai

8   Religion and Leadership: The Creation of a Just Society   176
Philomena N. Mwaura

9   Leadership and Economic Development in the Informal Sector   195
Mark O. Ogutu

10   Leadership and Economic Development: What Type of Leadership Facilitates Rapid Economic Advancement?   215
Sunny Bindra

About the Contributors   *236*

Index   *237*

Acknowledgements

This book has a collection of articles presented and discussed at a Leadership Workshop held in August 2005 in Nairobi and organized by Twaweza Communications. The workshop was funded by the Ford Foundation Office of Eastern Africa and we are immensely grateful to Dr. Tade Aina for making it possible to address leadership issues in Kenya in a rigorous manner and supporting the publication of this book. Equally, we are thankful to the participants who provided valuable input into the presentations by raising questions and suggesting options.

We are also indebted to the contributors who took the time to think with us about the leadership question in Kenya. They raise key questions about leadership styles and priorities and suggest ways in which matters could be re-arraigned so that leadership is more responsive to the needs of the public. We hope that the issues raised in this book can become points of reference in examining how leadership work ought to be undertaken in Africa.

The hard working team at Twaweza Communications deserves gratitude for not only organizing the Leadership Workshop but also for carrying forward the leadership agenda. Thank you all for being patient and understanding. I am grateful to Catherine Bosire for typesetting the manuscript and designing it and to Richard Wafula for the index.

Without you, the reader, this book would not have been possible. The contributors had you in mind as they put their thoughts and words together. We hope that you will find something of value, between the pages, and that you will continue the discussion in your own interactions.

This book is part of the leadership work being undertaken by Twaweza Communications. Whether it is to develop cultural leadership through *Jahazi: The Arts, Culture, and Performance Journal,* the interactions between academicians and art practitioners, the development of Kiswahili, networking with the media, mentoring younger scholars, or the work with political parties in Kenya to assemble viable platforms, Twaweza Communications is surely making a difference in the conceptualization of leadership in Kenya. We would like to thank all those who make our work possible.

Kimani Njogu, Ph.D.

Foreword

Quality Leadership: The beginning of an important conversation

This book is an important contribution to the debate and the imagining of what it means to have an alternative and transformational mode of leadership in East Africa today. It is an important contribution because it transcends the self-flagellation and Afro-pessimism that have characterized previous analyses and discussions on contemporary leadership in late 20th Century Africa. Through presenting us with a set of critical but optimistic and affirmative contributions, the book unravels the bases of the current sorry state of leadership in Kenya in particular and East Africa in general. Proceeding from the analyses, one finds that the book then moves on to affirmatively examine and declare the many possibilities embodied in the emergence of new and alternative notions, practices and agents of leadership in East Africa. The authors demonstrate a concern with leadership that goes beyond the conventional tired and often monolithic terrain of leadership, that of the formal political domain. Appropriating a notion of the 'political' that encompasses wide regions of the public sphere, the authors challenge the conventional wisdom in much of social science and management literature discourse on leadership by examining leadership that touches on religion, women's rights, youth and people with disability.

What we have in this book is an exploration of leadership beyond the focus on the conventional elites and extended to those groups that are normally excluded, marginalized and often times made invisible by the dominant political structures and intellectual discourse in Kenya and East Africa. There is also the challenge to the fixation with place bound and nativist discourse on leadership through the examination of the conditions, place and role of the African Diaspora. Through these contributions, we find in this book, a freshness, courage and vitality that are missing in the conventional literature on leadership in Kenya. We also find the beginning of a new kind of imagination and vision around leadership driven by implicit and explicit affirmation of social justice, rights and democracy. Leadership begins to take on value and depth beyond managerialist and technocratic orientations and belief. All of these of course do not deny the need for training, expertise or the building of the necessary capacity for demonstrating and ensuring leadership.

The contributions are therefore of great significance in the search for alternative paradigms and generations of leaders and leadership in contemporary Kenya. This body of work resonates with the efforts of the Ford Foundation office for Eastern Africa's Governance and Civil Society portfolio. The portfolio has made grants over the past years to support the understanding, formation, and promotion of alternative and transformational leadership thinking, practices and agents across the East African region. Our support has also sought to break the boundaries of generations, gender, ethnicity, religions, nationalities and disciplines. Rejecting a limited patriarchal conventional notion and practice of leadership located in an often authoritarian definition of power relations that are self-perpetuating, exclusionist and self-serving, the Foundation in Eastern Africa has made efforts to support fresh, vigorous and in many cases transformational thinking, training and practices in the field. We have emphasized rigor and discipline in thinking and the adoption of the necessary kills and behavioral traits and have attempted to promote visionary thinking and action and a sense of stewardship and social justice as inherent elements of leadership.

This body of work by Twaweza Communications which is just one of the many products of year's of focused and diverse work in the emerging field of alternative leadership in Eastern Africa, is a strong statement of the concern with and commitment to alternative and transformational leadership. Although the expression of a diverse group of authors with strong convictions of their own, the underlying thread is the collective recognition of the role and importance of this kind of leadership to good democratic governance and development and the very strong need for all parties and stake holders in Kenya and East Africa to invest in and promote the debates and practices that this book represents only a beginning.

Tade Aina
Nairobi, May 2007

Introduction

The topic of leadership has become of critical importance, globally and locally. This interest results from a number of events that call for informed interpretation, resolution and direction. At the global level terrorism, war in the Middle East, HIV / AIDS, environmental disasters resulting from global warming, glaring inequalities between poor and rich nations, religious fundamentalism, trafficking of drugs and so on have made it imperative that a global leadership, committed to the human values of integrity, trust, and dialogue across cultures and nations, be given a space in which to bring sanity back into the world.

Global challenges play themselves out in a number of ways in Africa. For instance, the culture of consumerism and individualism that defines the elite in the West guides the behaviour and lifestyle of the political and economic elite in Africa. Indeed, most of the money looted by the political class in Africa is stashed in the West, with the direct support of individuals and institutions based in the developed world. Moreover, global tensions and wars resulting from the intolerance and the excesses of the ruling class in Western countries occasionally blow out in Africa, to tremendous loss of life and property, as was so clear in the Nairobi and Dar es Salaam bomb blasts of August 7, 1998. Indeed, the editor of this book almost lost his life, and that of his son, as they queued outside the American Embassy in Nairobi to get a visa on that fateful day. With regard to HIV / AIDS it is unbelievable that in a world that has made huge strides in technology and that spends billions of dollars in unnecessary wars such as in Iraq and Afghanistan, we are unable to marshal resources to combat the pandemic: there are still HIV positive people who cannot get ARVs and enough food around the world. Why is it that the political class is unable to pursue, with the same vigor and determination used in the accumulation of power, matters related to the health of citizens? The quality of life of the majority of the people is far from being satisfactory and this will continue to be the case unless another value system is injected into leadership in all sectors of life.

There are a multitude of ways in which leadership could be imagined. For instance, it could be conceptualized in terms of *power relationship, between leaders and followers*. In such a case, leaders wield power which they use to bring about change. Alternatively, leadership could be imagined as *transformational*, allowing the transitioning of followers from one state of being to another. It could, moreover, be defined from *a knowledge and skills perspective* such that certain skills and capabilities that make good leadership possible are invoked. All in all, it could be claimed that *leadership is a process in which an individual or individuals influence others to achieve a common goal.* As a process, the relationship between leaders and followers is dialogic – leaders influence followers and vice versa. It is also *distributed* across individuals so that each has the potential of playing a leadership role. The tendency to locate leadership only in certain individuals and domains of life, such as the political arena, has constrained our understanding of the dynamics of societies and social change. This can be corrected through a broadening of the concept in order to incorporate leadership in all individuals and arenas of existence. This is what this book seeks to do.

The trouble with most African countries can be located in the type of leadership that guides it at the national and community levels. Because that leadership has failed to dismantle the political and economic system inherited from the colonial experience and has instead used it to consolidate power and perpetuate a dependency syndrome through occasional rewards among sections of the citizenry, new ideas have not been given a space in which to flourish. Attempts to come up with alternative ways of running countries have often been criminalized and suppressed. Nonetheless, citizens have always sought to assert and inscribe their rights.

This book interrogates the phenomenon of leadership in Kenya , within and without the political domain. It raises major issues related to constitutionalism, economic development, religion, the rights of women, youth and people with disabilities. Whereas Kimani Njogu is concerned with the role that the youth play, and can play, in shaping leadership trends, P.L.O Lumumba and Kibe Mungai revisit the politics of constitution making in Kenya. They show ways in which the political class manipulates the process to keep their grasp on power and the efforts of the Kenyan people to assert themselves in the pursuit of good governance, accountability and transparency in the conduct of public affairs. Drawing on a wide range of experiences, the two lawyers show that the *process* of constitution making and the *final document* itself are key to containing the political class.

In his chapter, Macharia Munene discusses the interaction between continental Africa and the diaspora and shows ways in which for decades the diaspora has engaged, through solidarity or distancing, political leadership on the continent. Drawing on events in three phases: pre-independence, after independence and in the post-Cold War era and the intensification of globalization , Munene shows the complexity of the relationship between continental Africa and the diaspora. And taking the discussion further, historian Eric Masinde theorizes the duality of politics and alternative leadership in Africa and argues that the moral well being of leaders is key in building a new political and social dispensation. Behaviour change among the political class is, for him, of critical importance. He urges the citizenry to consider sharpening the personality traits, aptitudes and competencies of those who might lead them. In the final analysis, Aseka's chapter suggests attributes that good leaders may need to have if they are to contribute in social change.

One such quality is commitment to the cause of society, to which Njeri Kang'ethe turns when discussing leadership and women. Njeri argues, convincingly, that for the women of Africa to be relevant in this dispensation, they must create space within which to exercise their leadership abilities in order to have an impact on their societies and communities. This they can do within politics or in other domains of life. She draws on evidence from pre-colonial, colonial, neo-colonial and present day experiences, to show that women have occupied leadership roles despite the hurdles in their midst. In "Bodily Contrariness: Some Preliminary Questions on Disability and Leadership in Kenya" Mbugua wa Mungai discusses disability, a matter to which his own subjectivity is implicated. In his view, the lack of an agentic role for people with disabilities is a consequence of institutional structures–political, cultural, linguistic, economic, social - inscribed in everyday forms of exclusivist behavior. He shows that people with disabilities in Kenya are often, mistakenly, associated with marginal social spaces and viewed as 'scars' and diseased. Mbugua problematizes this perception of people with disabilities and shows the tremendous abilities they have.

Faith based organizations have played a major role in political and social change in Africa. But from where does their legitimacy emanate? Philomena Mwaura shows that religion is mandated to participate in the creation of a just society. Her evidence comes from Christianity and African religions, principally, but could be applied to other faiths, including Islam and Buddhism. Mwaura says that religion can be a catalyst for change because it could be used to provide leadership in times of social upheaval, though it may also be used as an oppressive tool. Maybe by injecting *spirituality* into leadership work, we may contribute in growing better quality leadership.

One of the critical challenges facing Africa is, of course, economic development. How can leadership be marshaled to facilitate economic transition? How can we learn to increase productivity and facilitate growth? That is the subject of the chapters by Mark Ogutu and Sunny Bindra. Whereas Ogutu discusses the culture of entrepreneurship and the informal sector, Bindra draws on the experiences of Asia to suggest ways in which Kenya can make an economic breakthrough by encouraging an informed and focused leadership. The book raises important questions and suggests ways in which leadership work could be done. Kenya is used as a case study to mirror other African countries.

Kimani Njogu
Nairobi, May 2007.

1

Youth, Leadership and Culture

Kimani Njogu

...if the democratic system is based on election, the public has to be more conscious as to who they elect because their vote is sacred. And that capacity to mobilize the population towards participation is a very broad avenue, which we have not pursued, which we have not managed to travel. Hopefully there are young people now who are going to motivate others so they might go down this road... It's one where the people arise and vote and elect a person who will leave a precedent in the histories of native peoples. There is a key thing we must cultivate aside from our participation, and that is to take pride in our successes. There are successes... on the part of young people, and by women. (Rigoberta Menchú Tum –Quoted in Zajonc 2006)

Introduction

The continent of Africa is faced by a wide range of challenges which have a direct relevance to the youth who constitute the majority population: communities are threatened by the struggle for power and limited resources; rural-urban migration has led to the mushrooming of poverty ridden informal settlements in the cities; unemployed youth are desperate and some have resorted to drugs and crime; weapons proliferation is leading to urban violence and cross border conflicts and insecurity have become rampant in urban and rural areas; dictatorships have muffled the voices of citizens who have lost trust in national leadership; Western nations have continued to loot the continent's natural resources without giving anything in return; ethno-linguistic differences have been manipulated by internal and external forces to a point of exploding into ethnic cleansing and genocide as was evident in Rwanda; racism and the control of oil rich Darfur has led to incidences of rape and the killing of millions of innocent people in that region; and the HIV/AIDS pandemic is destroying the continent's workforce at an alarming rate.

When these events are taking place, African countries are struggling to uphold the principles of liberal democracy and pay their debts to international lenders, even if those debts only benefit the ruling class with the aid of global partners. This is at a time that transfers of Africa's wealth to the developed countries of Europe and America have been expanding annually in value (Davidson 1992: 9). Moreover, the institutions and instruments of national leadership inherited from the colonial experience have also not been liberating and the state in Africa has not delivered to its people mainly because it has avoided mass' participation. Yet mass participation was at the heart of governance in those African societies that were stable and progressive before the onslaught of the slave trade and colonial dispossession (Davidson, 1992: 295).

Strategies that have been used since the early 1960s in many African states have tended to be inward looking, insulated, constrained and limited the participation of citizens in the management of national affairs. Linked as they have been to the colonial political and economic systems, they have been only minimally creative and innovative. This has led to frustration and disillusionment with the ruling elite and its tendencies of consumerism and glorification of materialism, in an environment of high incidences of poverty and other deprivations. Citizens have been, at times, apathetic and not demanded better performance from leaders. Even when such demands are made there are no sufficient and enforceable constitutional structures to hold leadership accountable to its people. The manipulation of ethnic difference, within a context of poverty and illiteracy, has ensured that the political and economic elite keep their hold on power. Can this be changed through a greater focus on the quality of leadership generated from the continent? Do the youth provide an avenue to ameliorate the suffering of ordinary people?

The political class that took power at independence betrayed the dream of the nationalist struggle, which in the case of Kenya is captured eloquently by Ngugi wa Thiongo in *A Grain of Wheat*, and could not come up with policies and sustainable programs to build national infrastructure and eradicate disease, ignorance and poverty. In the words of Bujra (2005: 20):

> "The nation-building project was the first casualty because it was replaced by ethnicity as a primary unit for mobilising political support and for using public resources to improve, in the ethnic areas of those in power, the infrastructure, economic investment, education and health services."

This ethnic insularity continues to this day. This is not to suggest that all the ethnic areas of those in power benefited! Far from it. What emerged were pockets of riches amidst poverty. In fact, a cross-ethnic economic and political elite has been solidifying in most of Africa.

The difficulties that came with the nationalist project of the 1960s led the youth to lose their status as the 'national hope' and lifeline. Their needs were not prioritized. Hence, educational institutions, health facilities and recreational centres deteriorated and more and more young people found their way into the streets, garbage dumps and the underworld. Because they are excluded from the arenas of power, health maintenance, relaxation and intellectual pursuits the youth have had to construct alternative spaces of socialization and to redefine themselves as simultaneously victims and agents and to adopt a posture of defiance (Mamadou Diof, 2003:5). Most have become actors in a performance orchestrated by globalization and its instruments. They participate in engaging and, where possible, uprooting the symbols of postcolonial munificence. They carry with them media images and attitudes especially from the entertainment industry of the African diaspora. They are searching for an identity different from that assigned by the nationalist project. The search is, however, neither coordinated, nor systematic. It is not ideologically driven because it is not based on reflection, inquiry or dialogue. If the youth in Africa are to search for an alternative direction for the continent they must participate in knowledge creation through reflection.

In *Leading Through Conflict*, Mark Gerzon (2006) invokes two important concepts important for all leaders in Africa: 'presence' and 'global leadership.' To be 'present' is to be fully conscious, mentally and physically, in order to be able to undertake the task at hand. 'Presence' is a key ingredient in bringing about social change because it requires the total engagement of individuals and communities through a clear understanding of the issues at stake and what it would take to resolve them. Global leadership, on the other hand, is to step out of polarities and to engage in an understanding of other positions and viewpoints. It is to see value in the most unlikely spaces and to see the 'whole'. Global leadership requires that we reexamine the prevailing tendency to polarize the world by rebuilding trust in our collective humanity and anchoring tolerance of other viewpoints and interpretations (Njogu 2006). It requires that we see value in things that are good not just for ourselves but also for others. This is the calling that is being made with reference to the youth in Africa: that they need to be fully 'present' and to transcend those things that seek to limit their potentiality. These actions are deliberate, conscious and consistent; they cannot be incidental if they are to make a difference. If the youth in Africa are to contribute in pushing the continent forward they will need to be fully conscious of their historical responsibility and to identify areas in which they can make meaningful interventions. They would need to think globally but act locally; to embrace the spirit of pan-Africanism and refuse to be constrained by narrow considerations of ethnicity.

Reigniting the Spirit of Pan-Africanism

The spirit of Pan-Africanism espoused by Kwame Nkrumah, Patrice Lumumba, Julius Nyerere and other leaders of decolonization in Africa is gaining new impetus under the auspices of the African Union and its various instruments including the Pan-African Parliament, NEPAD and Africa Peer Review Mechanism (APRM). There are also a number of Pan-African research institutions, such as the Association of Public Administration and Management (APAM), the Council of Economic and Social Research in Africa (CODESRIA), the African Association of Political Scientists (AAPS), among others, which are involved in generating and disseminating knowledge. Youth dominated outlets for a reconceptualization of Pan-African leadership have been mushrooming within the continent and a discourse of greater solidarity between African nation-states is in vogue. Unfortunately, the political class, which has significantly contributed in the disintegration of the continent, has been given a major role to play in Pan African institutions, as well as in the process of concretizing this envisaged integration and solidification of African concerns and interests. In spite of this situation, the new continental solidarity and spirit of rebirth does provide an opportunity for African leaders, within and without the political sphere, to reconsider their role in the economic and social development of their countries. Just like in the process of decolonization, African unity could be mobilized to push the continent's economic and social agenda. But for that to happen the youth ought to occupy their rightful place in the current pan-African discourse. As the 'continental hope' they need to pay particular attention to good governance as well as other challenges facing the continent.

When addressing the Sixth Ordinary Session of the Pan-African Parliament on 13th November 2006 in Midrand, South Africa, H.E Nelson Mandela reflected on the importance of good governance for democracy and economic prosperity to take root. He celebrated the birth of the African Union, NEPAD, Africa Peer Review Mechanism (APRM) and the Pan-African Parliament and said:

"The future and deepening of real democracy in our continent rests firmly on the pillars of good governance. I am, therefore, happy that African countries have recommitted themselves to these ideals of democracy, good governance and economic prosperity for our peoples. Too many lives were sacrificed in the liberation struggle across Africa for us not to ensure that we create transparent and accountable systems of government on all levels.... Poverty, illiteracy, unemployment, lack of shelter and clean water and HIV/AIDS remain some of the biggest challenges confronting our continent. (Mandela Speech to Pan African Parliament, Midrand, 13 Nov. 2006, p. 1-2)

The presence of an energetic and youthful population in Africa does point to an opportunity for the continent to resolve some of its most pressing challenges. But for the youth to play their role to completion, they must be fully present to the tasks that face the continent and be committed and courageous enough to engage the problems selflessly. They will need to be crusaders on a liberating mission. We recognize that the youth themselves are not homogenous; they are shaped by the political, economic, cultural and social contexts in which they find themselves. They have a wide range of contradictions some of which are a consequence of Western individualism, materialism and decadence perpetuated by Western media. They cannot undertake the tasks if they allow themselves to be driven by forces that seek to tear the continent apart. This situation can be reversed and the youth can become genuine engines of change in Africa if they engage in internal and external inquiry. They must become 'seekers' of knowledge about themselves and the destiny of the downtrodden, so well exemplified by the Ghanaian novelist Ayi Kwei Armah in *The Healers*. Through systematic inquiry, they will be able to question political trends in Africa, as discussed in this volume. In doing so, they will also pave the way for the growth of a more visionary and responsive leadership in Africa.

I believe that the youth can play a major role in reenergizing the continent through their creativity and ability to adjust to new situations. But it would be necessary for spaces to be deliberately set aside for intergenerational dialogue so that the wisdom of the past and the ingenuity of the present can be mobilized for the political, economic, social and technological advancement of Africa. Considering that younger people can be more inventive and daring in their activities, they need support and resources so that they can harness information, science and technology in the service of Africa. Given their ability to navigate new technologies and to venture into new spaces, the youth can breath new life into the continent. But they need to be fully present: to be awake to the realities of the contemporary world and to see their role in social change. They can redefine Africa in the eyes of its inhabitants as well as in the eyes of others. Moreover, they need to 'know themselves' and see themselves as part of the solution. They need to be global and have particular interest in the continent and, like the youth in India who are using knowledge and advances in Information, Communication and Technology admirably, extract the best from the West and East for the benefit of the African people. As the youth reach out to other domains, it is equally critical that African households, communities and governments invest in them and give them the confidence they need to bring about much needed social change.

Youth in Civil Society

The term 'civil society' is used generally in reference to a heterogeneous range of formal as well as informal organizations which occupy a space as non-state and non-profit making actors. Whereas the formal organizations are visible and legally recognized – foreign and indigenous NGOs, business groups, trade unions, community based organizations etc. – the informal ones are made of alliances that are less visible and may be based on gender, age, kinship, etc. There is no doubt that it is within civil society that the youth can initially situate themselves most effectively in order to bring meaningful change at the community level before venturing into elective politics, if that is a desired goal. But what is 'civil society' in the African context? As suggested above, the term 'civil society' is used in a variety of ways but principally to refer to the presence of social actors and new patterns of political participation outside of formal state structures and institutions. Civil society provides possibilities of economic and social development not significantly linked with the state or governing elite. However it is not necessarily de-linked from its influences, contradictions and aspirations. The term has certain historical connotations in Western political thought, notably in the writings of John Locke and John Stuart Mill. In the Western tradition it is rooted in ideals of citizenship under law; in freedom of speech; in the protection of minority rights within the context of majority rule. Moreover, it is linked to the differentiation between public and private interests and the emergence of the bourgeoisie. In the 1780s, prior to the French Revolution, concepts related to social and political change were floated in intellectual, scientific and literary salons and coffee houses in France. Civil society grew out of a response to monarchical and semi feudal structures and institutions which treated the political space as if it was the private property of the monarchy. In Europe, patrimonial rule was challenged through a popularization of the notion that political authorities ought to be held accountable to the public. Social groups sought to curve a public arena in order to interrogate the operations of the state and its organs. 17th and 18th century thinkers, such as contract theorists, developed concepts and limitations of civil society currently in use such as 'internationality.' To transcend the vicissitudes of the 'state of nature', Thomas Hobbes and John Locke propagated the view that people set out laws to govern relations of power. Locke went on to argue that national power resides in the individuals making up civil society – those who give power to others to govern them and power is given so long as the governors use it to fulfill the protective function. But this power is not absolute because the governed have residual power which they can use to challenge the governors.

Taking the discussion forward, Antonio Gramsci argued that civil society is the arena in which class and national identities are formed and is indicative of the struggles over the imposition of norms and economic interests. For Gramsci, 'hegemony' suggests the attempts of the dominant class to use its political, moral and intellectual leadership to establish its values, systems and view of the world as all-inclusive and universal, and to shape the interests and needs of sub-ordinate groups so that domination is viewed as consensual. Because the dominant class does not maintain its hold solely through the use of the state machinery but also through mediating institutions, a critical way of undermining the ruling class is the development of a counter-hegemonic position through mediating institutions. This view by Gramsci points to the importance of social associations in shaping and directing societal norms.

In Africa, the emergence of a social space separate from the state and kinship groupings is related to the process of urbanization during the colonial era. Voluntary associations grew out of the needs and demands of the new migrants. There were ethnic, cultural, class and intellectual associations in the emerging urban areas. African intellectuals rooted in their communities and working together with Asian migrants and sympathetic missionaries played a key role in providing a normative framework for associational politics before independence. They mobilized against colonialism and created an alternative vision of a post-colonial state distinct from that envisaged by the colonial onslaught. The youth were key in that venture.

The associational activity of the 1920s and 1930s in Africa provided the critical foundation for the growth of nationalist parties of the 1940s and 1950s. Unfortunately, the instruments that made colonial domination possible were not dismantled during the struggle for independence and there was no real change for ordinary people when colonial rule was brought down. The state continued being "totalistic in scope, constituting a statist economy. It presented itself as an apparatus of violence, had a narrow social base, and relied for compliance on coercion rather than authority"

(Ake 1996:3). The political class used the state to consolidate its hold on power and civil society, in countries such as Kenya, was forced to reorganize in order to deal with the emerging dictatorship. Indeed, with the rise of the one party state around the 1970s, the trans-ethnic associations (trade unions, women's movement, youth groups) key to national integration, were targeted by the ruling class. Thus in Africa, civil society, be it formal or informal, has sought to challenge power and to agitate on behalf of the people.

Communities in post-colonial Africa have been looking up to the youth and intellectuals to once again provide leadership against oppression. In Uganda, the youth and intellectuals were key to the removal of Idi Amin Dada. When Amin took power in the 1971 coup he was internally supported by the coalition of traders, southern kulaks, and the Catholic petty bourgeoisie. That was the social base that he was later to consolidate with the expulsion of the Asian commercial and petty bourgeoisie. But these were not the only supporters. Externally, the British and the Israelis were the first supporters of Amin's 1971 coup because they were unhappy with Milton Obote. Obote had broken relations with Britain over the Rhodesian Unilateral Declaration of Independence (UDI) and had moved ahead to mobilize towards the formation of a 'progressive block' at the 1971 Singapore Commonwealth Conference. That soured relations between Britain and Uganda (Mamdani 1982: 129). But the students consistently opposed the dictatorship of Idi Amin. In neighbouring Kenya, whereas the Asian business community and Britain supported the reign of Daniel Arap Moi, students and intellectuals stood up to him to agitate for multiparty democracy. According to Mamdani, this role is historical. Mamdani says:

> In the history of revolutions, students have often acted as the catalysts of a movement. On the one hand, having no articulate class interests, on the other, threatened by unemployment and an adverse economic situation once they complete their studies, the radicalization of student action is rapid. Their political significance, however, is defined by the demands they advance and the classes with which they objectively ally (1982: 131).

In Kenya, the universities took up the task especially in the 1970s and 1980s to engage the state in rethinking the direction it had chosen to take. Amutabi (2002:158-159) delineates five situations to show that student activism has been informed generally by a democratic agenda. First, they have resisted the presence of state agents in universities. Second, their demands have included freedom of assembly, speech and association. Three, they have questioned governance of universities as students seek more representation in management committees. Four, they have galvanized the country in contesting national policies such as Structural Adjustment Programmes. Five, they have stood alongside critics of government. The University of Nairobi and Kenyatta University have especially been visible in keeping the political elite on its toes and their activities have in the past led to the deregistration of student bodies and the blacklisting of academic staff unions. It cannot be contested that despite the lack of strategy and ideological direction, students in Kenya, especially in the 1970s and 1980s, pushed the democratic agenda forward. This positive contribution is often destroyed by the occasional acts of thuggery, stoning of motorists and the destruction of property. Also there has not been unity of purpose and on many occasions in the past the state infiltrated the university, detained lecturers and expelled 'rebellious' students.

The universities have not acted alone in democratic pursuits because religious organizations, workers unions, pressure groups, farmers cooperatives, and the media also created the space needed to argue the case for democracy and good governance. Despite these efforts, the solid leadership exemplified by African youth and intellectuals during the colonial era in mobilizing and shaping public opinion has not in reality been replicated in the post colonial phase. They have not given communities original conceptual tools to transform their political and economic situation. Except for a few isolated cases in which positions have been taken against abuse of power, the excess of state instruments and misappropriation of public resources by the ruling classes, African intellectuals of the post-independence era have generally tended to be opportunistic and half-hearted in providing direction to the masses. In certain cases, they have provided the fodder for dictatorships to flourish.

Mazrui in an article titled '*Academics Have been Advocates of Major Changes in East Africa*' (Sunday Nation September 03, 2006 p.13), argues that academics in post-colonial Africa have contributed to political but not economic changes. Young African intellectuals, linked to the needs of their society and reaching out beyond their borders, were key to the process of decolonization and were connected to the pursuit of freedom for the majority. Mazrui says:

> The speed of political decolonization of the three East African countries was spectacular but the second phase of nation building was truly in fits and starts. Previously because African intellectuals and academics could not come to grips with viable strategies of economic development, nation building was difficult to sustain in the post colonial era.

Why did the young postcolonial leaders not provide guidance for economic recovery? Among other reasons, they cut links with the societies which had given them the task of transforming their countries at the onset of independence and succumbed to the trappings of power. Instead of serving their societies, they used the new opportunities to accumulate personal wealth and perpetuate a culture of patronage. Others were caught in the Cold War battles between Marxism and capitalism, paying little attention to the role of context specific trends in production, technology, and culture in social transformation. Home grown political and economic solutions were not given the chance to blossom individual creativity was muzzled and there was no deliberate effort to curve a niche for the emergence of more youthful leadership that would propel the continent forward. Dissidence was criminalized and governance was personalized and ethnicized. Peter Kagwanja (2000: 30-31) captures this scenario as follows:

> From the early 1970s, the African hegemonial elite grew increasingly autarchic, undemocratic and repressive. In turn, African intellectuals became vocal critics of the authoritarian tendencies and misconceived policies of the ruling elite. The latter responded by severely restricting academic freedom, expulsion, detention, and even liquidation of intellectuals. This brought the era of cooperation and interface between academics and the state to an end. The widespread adoption of SAPs by African governments from the mid 1970s brought the problem of barren interface to a head and policy dependence to its acme. The World Bank's claim to superiority of its knowledge over that of the African thinkers and the acceptance of this claim by African policy makers opened the floodgates for the marginalization of indigenous knowledge in favour of externally formulated policy frameworks.

> By maintaining a repressive labour regime in the universities and research institutions, the African-elite managed to pay scandalous wages to the academics and other professionals without any fear of facing industrial action. In this regard, the state's action of keeping down intellectual labour costs by fostering repressive labour regimes was not different from the general objectives of multinational corporations in the Third World economies. Cuts in educational budgets, particularly university funding, as a result of pressure from the World Bank, devastatingly undermined the productivity of intellectuals and starved universities of resources to undertake research. Moreover, spiraling inflation and devaluation of the national currencies increased costs of foods, school fees, medical services and so on. The hardships

created by SAPs set in motion the twin process of *pauperisation* and *proletarianisation* of academics.

Despite these setbacks, some workers, small scale farmers, students and intellectuals have over the years played an important role in criticizing the ruling class and have brought to the fore the issue of human rights and the need to increase public participation in national issues and to limit personalized rule. Equally, certain faith based organizations have taken positions at variance with the state and defended the rights of citizens to express themselves freely. On occasion, faith based organizations have tried to present themselves as encapsulating an identity that is acceptable to the African people through indigenization of its structures and the development of a metalanguage for democracy in Africa. But ethnicity and an unarticulated economic direction continue to challenge the continent. There are gaping inequalities between regions and socio-economic classes. In the urban areas, the economic elite is defined by a lifestyle incomprehensible in a continent that continues to suffer starvation and poor health. How does one articulate the economic differentiation and engage the particularism of ethnicity, constantly manipulated by the ruling class? Interestingly, most progressive civil society organizations are pushing for liberal democracy in a continent already replete with gross socio-economic inequalities and lacking in the conditions that existed in Europe and USA at the onset of liberal democracy. Alternative models of political and economic organizing that pay particular attention to rural areas as well as cultural and ethno-linguistic diversities have not been sufficiently investigated. This is an area that youth leadership can explore; first, at the level of civil society and later in national politics.

An important function that leadership in civil society organizations can undertake is the creation of norms that address ethnic particularism in politics and inject a new search for creativity in knowledge at all levels. In the case of Kenya, 'the institutional expression of multiparty politics, whether in terms of political party formation or informal political alliance and lobbying, expresses itself purely on ethnic lines' (Omollo 2002:217). Political parties organize around patron-client relations. Civil society can change this though it is not immune to schisms and the challenges of ethnicity in the larger society which serves to weaken its solidarity as change agents. Quite often, civil society groupings, when not serving the interests of personalities and ethnicities, are too conscious of donor interests to be innovative and daring. In the process because oppositional civil society is non-autonomous and listens too closely to promptings from external funding agencies and foreign interests, it tends to compromise principles that would guide the nation. Moreover, the patrimonial state has the resources and ability to compromise pockets of civil society by penetrating them and using them to advantage. These situations have served to weaken reflection and inquiry in civil society leadership as it waits for external guidance on crucial national issues. Again, youth leadership can break from this tendency.

But the youth would also need to reflect on the relationship between Africa and Western countries. Is there a way in which they could extract knowledge from the North for the benefit of the African continent? Instead of engaging in external trade which is, in any case, skewed to the benefit of the West, can they strategically extract technological knowledge and then domesticate it? Walter Rodney (1976: 115) argues:

> The European slave trade was a direct block, in removing millions of youth and young adults who are the human agents from whom inventiveness springs. Those who remained in areas badly hit by slave-capturing were preoccupied about their freedom rather than improvements in production.

In the recent years the social, economic and political challenges facing Africa have led to unprecedented urge to migrate to the North in search of education and more opportunities; a situation neatly captured by Said Ahmed Mohamed in his Kiswahili novel *Dunia Yao* ('Their World'). In that novel, the cultural ramifications of globalization are enunciated and interrogated. What does a parent do when, over dinner and for the first time, the daughter excitedly announces that she is off to Britain the following morning to run away from the squalor of her neighbourhood? He is left wondering how she had kept the secret of a passport and visa to herself and to marvel at the absence of intergenerational dialogue.

Nonetheless, there are signs that the migration to the North, while denying the continent skilled people and intellectuals, is beneficial, to a degree, through repatriation of financial support to families. But again this repatriation is random and not well thought out due to a number of factors including the 'non-registered' status of Africans in the diaspora. It is not also sustainable. A deliberate technological transfer in which African youth are facilitated to become the key players in industrializing the continent might be the way out. This is because the youth are inventive and inventiveness is key, as is borrowing of technology. To paraphrase Rodney (1976: 115) again, 'when a society for whatever reason finds itself technologically trailing behind others, it catches up not so much by independent inventions but by borrowing.' That is what Japan did. It borrowed effectively from Europe and domesticated it. Because the Japanese were not enslaved or colonized, they had the independence of mind and a cultural base on which to situate their development. In Kenya, the *jua kali* informal sector is an important engine of development. Though curtailed by limited sources of energy and capital, Kenya's small industries are sources of employment and have the potential of making the country industrialize. The *jua kali* sector is evidence that the youth can play a major role in creating new knowledge and direction for Africa by interrogating the reasons for the continent's current sorry state. They would need to passionately and diligently study the cultural terrain in which they are working, mobilize their potential and link it with global events. It is their historical responsibility to do so.

After the momentous political events in Eastern and Central Europe in the late 1980s that led to the collapse of the Soviet Union, civil society was reenergized and became the engine for liberal democracy, inspite of the latter's limitations when applied to Africa. Bujra (2005) argues that liberal democracy was institutionalized in Europe and USA after they had achieved growth and economic development and that 'Economic growth and democracy did not go hand in hand.' (See also Sunny Bindra in this collection). In the words of Bujra (2005:7):

> Africa is being asked to develop liberal democracy and economic growth simultaneously and without the benefit of an industrialization process and wealth extracted from colonies, but with the disadvantage of a high level of its resources being continuously extracted by an unequal global economic system...

Significantly, liberal democracy to which Africa is being asked to turn has protected economic, political and social inequalities and excluded the masses from participation in public affairs in the USA and Europe. And African intellectuals and youth are not given the spaces and the presence of mind to think about viable models and alternatives for the continent.

We can see that the youth and intellectuals in Kenya are contributing to the democratization of the country, albeit at a slow pace and with, at times, prompting from donor agencies. There is indeed sufficient evidence that if well directed, the youth in civil society can contribute significantly in bringing about social change in Africa. We are witnesses to the collapse of dictatorships and the emergence of more open societies made possible by internal and external forces. In Kenya, since the 2003, there has been an aura of economic revival, despite the difficulties of the present moment whose foundation may be located in the misrule of the last forty years and the endemic nature of corruption among the political and economic elite.

We are beginning to see changes that can be accelerated if given proper institutional frameworks. Within the context of family and household, we have witnessed changes in gender roles and responsibility, as well as the interrogation and the reconstruction of femininity and masculinity. Spaces and responsibilities that were exclusively female dominated are being occupied by males and vice versa. Ancient assumptions have been questioned and at times subverted. The distinction between the private and public spheres has been blurred and boundaries of desires and expectations have been enlarged. Money lending institutions such as the World Bank and International Monetary Fund (IMF) are using the carrot and the stick to demand that governments liberalize their operations, embrace the free market economy, reduce public sector workforce and become more open in the conduct of national financial affairs. At the level of the state, consolidation of institutional and political processes, including the review of national constitutions and multi-party elections has been emphasized. The youth have come to be viewed as key players capable of bringing sustainable change in Africa and hip-hop is being used to speak back at authority. Youth dominated political parties are emerging through the identity of 'youthfulness.' There is a growing interest in youth in the economic and political spheres, even if this interest does not translate into real, tangible and deliberate involvement of younger people in national politics.

This growing interest in youth is propelled by a number of factors. First, they constitute the majority in most African countries and are affecting and shaping political, economic, social and cultural processes in fundamental ways. Second, they are situated between the local and the global. On the one hand, the majority are brought up by parents who have a base in the rural areas and who would like to impart age old values that have held their communities together. To do so, they invoke memory and occasional trips to their rural homes. On the other hand, though, globalization is challenging local knowledge and memory and bringing into play, through a range of aggressive media outlets, a culture significantly associated with the West. The 'new' culture is presented as 'non-local' and 'non-national,' despite leaning towards a value system that is significantly American.

This tension has had huge implications for the youth: their belief systems, aesthetics, social relations, economic activities and political engagements. The youth, especially from the urban areas, are seen as the possible instruments of change in Africa because they are linked to universal discourses of human rights while still connected to their cultures, even if superficially. But this new position which is being claimed by the youth is also seen as threatening. Among other things, a discomfort exists in the way they use their bodies and languages to express feelings, pleasures and sexuality as well as to respond to authority. The youth in Africa are redefining identity through a flattening of style that traverses ethno-linguistic borders and are refashioning identity and group membership. Indeed, through movement, dress and language they are setting conditions for inclusion and exclusion. These changes have implications on the way we do leadership related work in Africa.

Is Ethnographic Culture Relevant to Youth Leadership?

Let me state here that, first, there are many manifestations of culture in our lives and that ethnographic culture is only one such. Secondly, culture is not static but dynamic – always subjected to modifications due to changes in the larger society. According to Mensah (2006: 65):

> Like globalization, culture is a nested, heterogeneous, phenomenon, characterized by change and instability. Indeed, the notion of a pure, stable or static culture is theoretically unsustainable especially in this era of globalization.

Culture is essentially dialogic, if not 'plurilogic' (Njogu, 2004), heterogeneous, and hybrid. It is not singular or geographically bounded -given its process of coming into being as a product of internal and external forces. Youth leadership cannot take culture, of whatever form, for granted. They can learn from it and also use it as a process to bring about social change. We know that when the missionaries came to Africa they found a large body of knowledge. Among the Luo of Kenya, for example, there existed knowledge systems (*rieko*), which were metaphysical (*Jok*) and epistemological (*piny*) with a developmental trajectory (*dongruok*). Again, the pursuit of freedom (*wiyathi*) among the Gikuyu people was rooted the fundamental right to be fully human by being free; to be 'oneself'. In Southern Africa the concept of *ubuntu* (collective humanity) propelled the liberation struggle against foreign domination. It is no wonder that the youth in Africa played a key role in questioning the colonial project and agitating for independence. The urge to be free was integral to their cultural heritage.

At the onset of independence, the youth seemed to play two key roles: first, as bridges between the past and the present and secondly, as instruments of political and economic change. If the colonial experience had led to a state of alienation and loss, independence was seen as an opportunity to revive and restore lost identities. The youth were expected to play a major role in this restoration. But the old guard did not give way when they were supposed to do so due to constitutional weaknesses or the sheer love for power and privilege. Could the transition have been anticipated by culture?

In *Facing Mount Kenya* ([1938] 1978), Kenyatta shows that nations can put in place constitutional mechanism to ensure that one generation hands over power to another; and that the youth can, on behalf of the people, wrest power from unwilling dictatorships. He narrates how Gikuyu, the tyrannical ruler of Gikuyuland and grandchild of the elder daughter of the founder of the ethnic group, mobilized all young people to join his army and did not allow dissenting views on his style of leadership. Efforts by the people to change his approach to governance were thwarted and in desperation the *iregi* (revolutionary) generation revolted against him. This action by the *iregi* generation facilitated the shift by the Gikuyu people from being nomads to being agriculturalists. The generation that started cultivation was referred to as *ndemi* (cutters). The replacement of Gikuyu government, through the *ituika* (disconnecting) revolution paved the way for a democratic rule and broad public participation. The *Ituika* revolution transferred Gikuyuland from a dictatorship to a democracy and power was constitutionally expected to rotate between the *Mwangi* and *Maina* (or *Irungu*) age groups.

It was decided quite possibly in a cultural 'circle' that one generation would hold power for a limited period of time at the end of which the ceremony of *Ituika* would be held to declare that the old generation had completed its term of governing. The *Ituika* was a generational and ideological rupture with the past and an ushering in of newness through ritual and ceremony. This constitution, which paved the way for collective leadership, was drafted by the *Njama ya Ituika* (the Revolutionary Council) and presented to the general population for approval and endorsement. The last great *ituika* was held about 1890-98 and the Mwangi generation was given power by the people to govern according to the constitution and transitional mechanism. In 1925 the Maina (Irungu) generation started preparing themselves to take over from the Mwangi generation but their songs and dances were declared illegal by the British government. According to Kenyatta:

> From the *ndemi* generation onwards the principles of democratic government, as laid down by the first *ituika*, continued to function favourably until it was smashed by the British government, who introduced a system of government very similar to the autocratic government which the Gikuyu people had discarded many centuries ago (1978: 195-6).

In most of Africa, the pre-Independence generation has held on to power for over four decades, giving no room to the youth to bring in innovations. It is quite possible that the inability of the older generation to hand over power to the younger generation is a consequence of the colonial experience which was dictatorial in nature. A solution for the current dilemma of governance in Africa may be resolved through a deliberate and rigorous examination of the past. Equally, the past may offer a solution to the collapse of values. We say this despite our recognition of the limitations of that past well as some of its institutions and practices. The reexamination should not be viewed as an uncritical endorsement of the past but, rather, as an attempt to pick the best from yesteryears and to modify it and inject it with the content and rhythm of the present. History can be used to understand and restructure the present.

There have been cultural explanations to underdevelopment in Africa with constant comparisons between Africa countries and South East Asia. The causal explanations are misleading on a number of grounds and I would like to briefly mention a few. One, the class structures between the newly independent African countries and Asian nations were different – Asia has had a larger business community for ages. The business class was able to mobilize resources and to cross borders in the generation of capital. It was familiar with the process and discipline of investment and production. Two, the politics were different with political leaders in South East Asia playing a leading role in supporting business-centered economic initiatives. The political class was distinct from the commercial bourgeoisie, unlike in most of Africa where the political class is *also* the economic elite. The integration of political interests in economic pursuits by the ruling clique in Africa did not augur well to the growth of business. Three, the relationship between countries such as Korea and Japan as well as the United States made a big difference. Africa was a playground of global politics but was never a beneficiary of the tensions wrought by the Cold war. Four, the levels of literacy in South East Asia were much higher than in African countries where higher education system at independence was negligible. We know that with literacy comes better planning and management of resources. But, the whole of East Africa had one university at independence, namely Makerere University established belatedly in 1949. This meant that intellectual community that would generate ideas and engage the rest of the world was very small. Five, the cultural onslaught by colonialism in Africa removed the critical base around which discipline, productivity and knowledge generation could be grounded. These matters are important because without understanding the historicity of our current situation we may lose the confidence we need to move forward. I believe that culture does play a role in development within the context of social, political, and economic influences. Indeed:

> "If cultural issues are taken into account, among others, in a fuller accounting of societal change, they can greatly help to broaden our understanding of the world, including the process of development and the nature of identity...Once we dissociate culture from the illusion of destiny, it can help to provide a better understanding of social change when placed together with other influences and interactive social processes." (Amartya Sen 2006, 108).

Thus, without adopting a romantic view of the past, it may be important to reexamine it so that we can learn from it. Admittedly, there have been cultural practices that have curtailed our abilities to move forward in reaching our human potential but it is not true that our cultures are necessarily a hindrance to development. They are, in fact, a resource that, properly utilized, can provide opportunities available for all to enjoy the rights to health, education, shelter and food.

What else can youth leadership do?

The political culture inherited from the colonial experience needs to be purged. The colonial state redistributed resources, such as land, and determined relations and modes of production that would prevail in their spheres of influence. The development of infrastructure was guided by the interests of the state other than those of the people. It survived on cheap labour, at times forced, proletarizing and atomizing Africa societies. Through its instruments of violence and coercion, it accumulated resources and demanded unquestioning loyalty. At the dawn of independence, national leaders inherited these instruments and institutions without concomitant normative, institutional or ideological mechanisms which could sufficiently constrain them against abuse of power. They became alienated from the broad masses of the people and used their newly acquired positions for the appropriation of personal wealth. In many countries, there were no deliberate efforts to involve the people in the development agenda. Instead, ethnicity and sectarianism were invoked to protect and perpetuate class interests and to keep a hold on power. The ethnicization of politics, coupled with the phenomenon of patronage, led to unequal access of basic needs and the enjoyment of fundamental rights of the masses. On occasion, exercising political dissent and showing solidarity with ordinary people was interpreted as being 'anti-development.' Within the context of the Cold War, it was viewed as an effort to inscribe socialist ideology in Africa and this needed to be contained by all means possible. Creativity and the pursuit of political knowledge were criminalized.

There was no attention to the democratization of institutions of governance, management of the environment, rapid urbanization, decentralization of decision making, integrity in the performance of public duty, and the cultural integrity of each community, even as practices detrimental to the realization of human potential are interrogated, eradicated and revised. The spirit and dream of Pan-Africanism was set aside as national leaders sought to consolidate their power within their borders (Njogu 2006b). If the youth in Africa are to redeem themselves, a new paradigm for the continent would need to pay particular attention to these matters. There is an urgent need for African countries to focus on growth, productivity, and discipline in public service and to look for ways to engage communities in determining the preferred direction of development. Leaders must regain the trust of communities, engage in dialogue with them, learn new ways of doing things and believe in our ability to bring social transformation. They ought to cooperate with each other on matters of trade, commerce, the sharing of information and technology and the provision of health care, safe water and food. This development paradigm calls for 'people-centeredness' in perspective and action. It is a call for a re-definition of what really matters in the lives of people so that they can live fully and share in the benefits of science and technology. This integrated and comprehensive view of development will, of necessity, draw from indigenous knowledge systems and contextualize them within the contemporary world. Given the adaptive capacity of cultures, this redeeming experience need not be too difficult to fathom. There is a lot that the creativity of the youth, now and in the past, can teach us.

Maybe by looking deeply into our cultures and listening to the voices of the past, we may start opening up opportunities for the youth to take leadership roles and responsibilities because cultures provide the ground on which a nation can stand. Cultures that are receptive to other voices can open possibilities for people-centred development because they encourage consultation and consensus building. The circle around which the Council of Elders sat to deliberate epitomised a unity of purpose and vision; a continuity of cooperative engagement. To be a member of the circle was to accept that one's ideas were not the only possible ones and that they found completion through dialogue and consultation. The Circle needs to be brought back into contemporary leadership.

Conclusion

We have seen that the youth have a major role to play in shaping the political, economic and social direction of Africa. In the case of Kenya, that role is taking shape especially within civil society. But as argued in most of the chapters in this book, much still remains especially at the level of governance. It has become critical that we examine how the various strands of cultures shape the type of leadership we espouse and experience, including the ways in which leaders located outside of conventional politics are transforming lives through committed and selfless service to the people. The shared and distributed leadership, as well as the transitional mechanisms and systems of transferring authority from one generation to another practiced by communities may, in fact, be the basis on which to build a new governance and leadership ethos in Africa. A deliberate and systematic engagement with communities, where we are keen learners, may offer a way out of the uninspiring national leadership styles and the politics of patronage that dominate the continent and perpetuated by the colonial experience. The youth can take this as one of their tasks.

In addition, the youth can play a role in bringing peace in war torn areas by refusing to be manipulated by the political class. Peace and security allow for citizens to exercise their various freedoms, unfettered. Unfortunately, in many parts of our continent a sense of the emergence of violence always lurks in the background. People are never quite sure if clan and ethnic tensions will break at the seams and degenerate into violence. The accentuation of ethnic tensions is, in most cases, motivated by politicians bent on safeguarding their personal interests under the guise of protecting the well being of their communities. On occasion, they encourage their communities to 'restock' their animals by attacking neighbouring communities. Idle youth are constantly manipulated in the perpetuation of this violence. Youth leadership in civil society can resist this.

Also, the youth should address environmental issues diligently and urgently. And it is not just about protecting trees. Issues of environmental degradation (contaminated water, air pollution, unfavourable mining and logging practices) have a direct bearing on our lives and are too important to ignore. The choices and decisions we make today must champion the cause of a balanced ecology so as to safeguard future generations. As we treat the earth, so we treat each other. A peaceful physical environment is a metaphor about our lives with each other. Equally, an imbalance in the environment marks our own imbalance. As the integrity of our natural systems erodes, resources necessary for survival become scarce; land, water, minerals and fossil fuels are turned into battlegrounds. In many African countries, we can clearly see the interconnectedness of nature as one web of life. It cannot hold together if one part is broken. Without peace, the earth ceases being a space of solace and becomes one of pain and anguish.

How should youth leadership deal with issues of ethnicity that occasionally lead to violence? Does it mean that we suppress the competing identities and craft a unitary identity? Not really. Identity can be a source of vibrancy and richness as well as of violence. Amartya Sen (2006: 4) suggests that 'we have to draw on the understanding that the force of a bellicose identity can be challenged by the power of *competing* identities."These would include our shared humanity and other ways in which people are classified – Kenyans, gender, class, sports interests, politics, workers, taste in music, profession and so on. These collectivities to which we belong give us a certain identity. Thus to accept the singularity of ethnicity, as the only identity to which we belong, is to miss our complex natures. The youth have the ability to arrive at reasoned choice in resisting ascription of singular identity so constantly invoked by politicians. They will need to do two things: first decide on the identities to which they belong and second determine the relative importance of the identities they choose. Only by doing this can the youth in Africa make meaningful contributions to national development.

We know that politically motivated violence in Kenya flares around election time and is orchestrated by ethnically bound politicians. Why does this happen? According to Human Rights Watch (2002: 116):

> Electoral politics in Kenya are split along ethnic lines, pitting ethnic groups against each other in a competition for power and resources. Kenya's history of politically motivated violence targeting particular groups clearly suggests tactics political opportunists can emulate to achieve similar results, which they are all the more likely to pursue since the masterminds of past attacks have enjoyed impunity for their actions. Violence has been used so often for political ends and without accountability that it is at risk of being seen as a legitimate means of political discourse. The reliance on violence and the targeting of victims along ethnic lines, when combined with the increased availability of small arms, makes for an ever more dangerous mix. Those who have been the targets of past attacks have resented the suffering of their community and have reacted to fears about the future by increasingly seeking self-protection through the acquisition of more sophisticated weapons. This growing militarization and fear of other groups raises the possibility that

ethnic violence in Kenya might be triggered easily and spread rapidly, with devastating results.

A focused youth leadership can say 'No' to this manipulation.

There is also an urgent need to 'grow' youth leadership through focused reflection and networking. Let me share one example: In the course of 2003 - 2005, Twaweza Communications undertook a project on leadership in East Africa, with support from the Ford Foundation. Over 150 young leaders received trainings in leadership for social change. This was an exploratory endeavor into issues of leadership in East Africa and the organization sought to discover why leadership discussions tended to focus too much on political leadership, as if that is the only sphere in which change takes place. In implementing the initiative, Twaweza Communications targeted the youth and examined with them core boundary-crossing values that are blind to gender, age, ethnicity, nationalities and economies. There was intense sharing of experiences across spaces formerly seen as fixed, but which were shaking as they were being contested and challenged. The leadership values such as integrity and trust, elicited in discussions, were simultaneously universal and local. The organization believed that by empowering sectors of civil society such as community based organizations, business groupings, professional associations, women, youth and students, farmers' cooperatives and non- governmental organizations it is possible to facilitate the release of their creative and productive energies in the creation of a new leadership cadre. The overall goal was to change leadership in public perception and in fact. The initiative sought to expand public definitions of good leadership; to enlarge the range of people whose opinions are widely valued and respected; and to increase the cadre of influential young new leaders and to contribute in their development. This leadership activity is now being followed by a cultural leadership initiative linking younger leaders with universities in Kenya. By creating spaces for serious dialogue, it is possible to help the youth 'grow' into becoming better leaders at the national level and to bridge the gap between the political class and ordinary people.

References

Ake, Claude. *Democracy and Development in Africa*. Washington: The Bookings Institution, 1996.

Amutabi, Maurice. "Crisis and Student Protest in Universities in Kenya: Examining the role of students in National Leadership and the Democratization Process," In *African Studies Review*. Vol. 45, No. 2, September 2002.

Bujra, Abdalla. "Liberal Democracy and the Emergence of a Constitutionally Failed State in Kenya," In *Democratic Transition in Kenya: The Struggle from Liberal to Social Democracy*, (ed.) Abdalla Bujra. Nairobi: Africa Centre for Economic Growth, 2005.

Davidson, Basil. *The Blackman's Burden: Africa and the Curse of the Nation-State*. New York: Random House, 1992.

Davis, Susanna & Naomi Hossain. 'Livelihood Adaptation, Public Action and Civil Society: A Review of Literature." IDS Working Paper 57.

Diouf, Mamadou. "Engaging Postcolonial Cultures: African Youth and Public Space." African Studies Review, Vol. 46. No. 2, September 2003.

Gerzon, Mark. *Leading Through Conflicts: How Successful Leaders Transform Differences into Opportunities*. Boston: Harvard Business School Press, 2006.

Gramsci, Antonio. *Selections from the Prison Notes*. (Ed.) Q. Hoare and G. Nowell Smith. London" Lawrence and Wishart, 1971.

Human Rights Watch. *Playing with Fire: Weapons Proliferation, Political Violence and Human Rights in Kenya*. New York, 2002.

Kagwanja, Peter. "Post Industrialism and Knowledge Production: African Intellectuals in the New International Division of Labour," In *Africa at the Beginning of the 21ˢᵗ Century*. (ed.) Godfrey Okoth. Nairobi: Nairobi University Press, 2002.

Kenyatta, Jomo. *Facing Mount Kenya*. Nairobi: Kenway Publications, 1978.[

Mamdani, Mahmood. "The Makarere Massacre," In *University of Dar-es-Salaam Debate on Class, State and Imperialism*. Ed. Yash Tandon. Dar-es-salaam: TPH, 1982.

Mandela, Nelson. 'Statement by H.E Nelson Mandela at the Opening of the Sixth Ordinary Session of the Pan-African Parliament 13-24 November 2006.' Gallangher Estate, Midrand, 2006.

Mensah, Joseph. "Cultural Dimensions of Globalization in Africa: A Dialectical Interpenetration of the Local and Global." Studies in Political Economy, 77 Spring, 2006.

Mkandawire, Thandika (ed.) *African Intellectuals: Rethinking Politics, Language, Gender and Development*. Dakar: Codesria Books, 2005.

Njogu, Kimani. *Reading Poetry as Dialogue: An East African Literary Tradition*. Nairobi: Jomo Kenyatta Foundation, 2004.

_____. "Harnessing the Power of Language: Understanding How Language shapes Leadership," In *Leadership is Global: Co-creating a More Humane and Sustainable World* (Ed.) Walter Link, Thais Corral, and Mark Gerzon, 2006(a).

_____."The Hour is Late, the Hippos are Leaving the Lake," In *Cultures, Leadership and Development*. Nairobi: the British Council, Kenya, 2006(b).

Omolo, Ken. "Political Ethnicity in the Democratization Process in Kenya." *African Studies*, 61,2, 2002.

Rodney, Walter. *How Europe Underdeveloped Africa*. Dar es Salaam: Tanzania Publishing House, 1976.

Sen, Amartya. *Identity and Violence: The Illusion of Destiny*. New York: W. W. Norton & Co., 2006.

Southhall, Roger & Henning Melber (eds.) *Legacies of Power: Leadership Change and Former Presidents in African Politics*.

Zajonc, Arthur. (ed.) *We Speak as One: Twelve Novel Laureates Share Their Vision for Peace*. Peacejam Foundation, 2006.

2

Constitutions and Leadership in East Africa: The Crisis

PLO Lumumba

Introduction

In his book Chinua Achebe says, **"the trouble with Nigeria is simply and squarely a failure of leadership."**[1] The same is true for most of Africa. The history of Africa since attainment of political independence has been characterized by destruction of institutions, oppression of the citizenry and sacrifice of good governance to the Machiavellian gods of expediency.

Africa has been diagnosed as suffering from what has been described as the African crises.[2] In the African political lexicon this term refers to any of the problems faced by the African continent. In both the popular and academic press, the problems are usually defined in economic terms. One of the reasons to which contemporary difficult living conditions are attributed is the instability of the socio-political structures which are inimical to the growth of common politico- economic objectives.

Political leadership belongs to the realm of public administration, which primarily concerns itself with the organization of politico-economic, social and cultural lives of peoples. A proper understanding of leadership must therefore begin with the examination of the bureaucratic symbols which impact directly on the existence of social order. The Greek philosopher Plato in articulating his anthropological principle, holds that the political ordering of every society, be it in terms of a theory of the state or a theory of bureaucracy, reflects models of man found in the society under examination. By parity of reasoning it can be said that the African environment informs the African situation.

In 1976, S. A. Akintonye argued that the various problems faced by African countries have been determined by three factors, namely; *the heritage of colonial rule, the mode of acquisition of independence and lastly the problems of the independence era.*[3]

Regarding the colonial heritage Akintonye observes that the colonial governments were composed of a clique of elitist white officials in whom reposed immense privileges and draconian powers which they were not loathe to use with abject abandon to sustain their rule. The colonial governments were overly averse to criticism.[4]

Regarding the mode of acquisition of political independence, Akintonye argues that political freedom in Africa was usually not a revolution in the sense of a change of values but merely a change of rulers. The European colonialists simply left, surrendering the machinery of state power to their former auxiliaries in the civil service, the police force and the army and/or to the nationalists who made up the African elite.[5]

After the attainment of political independence the majority of new African rulers faced enormous problems. For instance, they had to observe and enhance national unity to prevent the new countries from being torn asunder by ethnic rivalry, engendered by multi-ethnicity which was conflictual when manipulated and activated by political forces. The combined impact of the numerous problems that confronted the new African leaders legitimised the application of styles of leadership which were designed to serve as antidotes to the monumental African problems, whether real or imagined, and in the process created leaders who arrogated to themselves the monopoly of knowledge and wisdom.

In this chapter, I examine the issue of leadership in East Africa as seen through constitutional amendments. It examines the constitutional and political evolution in each of the East African countries from independence to the present, and the post-colonial destruction of institutions and concentration of state power on the Executive by the first- generation leaders who had negotiated for the independence of their respective countries. The chapter shows how disregard for constitutional principles led to the emergence of dictatorship and 'monster leaders' like Idi Amin Dada of Uganda and the entrance of *de jure* single party statehood in Tanzania and Kenya. The latter marked the emergence of Imperial Presidents who are elevated to the level of 'demigods' each armed with a political philosophy like **Ujamaa** in Tanzania, **Harambee** and later **Nyayoism** in Kenya. It is argued that the culture of hero-worship, which characterized these regimes, was inimical to the growth of institutions and responsible leadership.

The era of pluralism came into being in the 1990s after the collapse of the Soviet Union in 1989, and the subsequent rise of American ideology of plural democracy and free market. This is the emergence of 'unwilling democrats' compelled by internal and external pressure to embrace plural politics. The experience of Kenya receives special mention owing to its protracted nature. Against this background the chapter examines how constitutions have been used to give a veneer of legality to political leadership even when such leadership is inimical to the principles of constitutionalism. A sampling of constitutional amendments in Uganda, Tanzania and Kenya demonstrate deliberate trend to concentrate power on the executive arm of Government by emasculation of the legislature and the judiciary.

Uganda

Uganda adopted the Westminster system of government as encapsulated in its 1962 Constitution. The constitution came into being after negotiations between the departing colonial power and other parties representing various ethnic and interest groups in Uganda. In its final form, the constitution had a quasi-federal arrangement. It recognized four kingdoms, but only Buganda enjoyed significant federal powers allowing it to raise its own tax revenues, pass laws on specified subjects, enjoy entrenched protection of land tenure and its local courts, and even control through its legislature the election of the Kingdom's representatives to the national parliament. Ankole, Toro, and Bunyoro and the district of Busoga became Federal States with fewer powers. The remaining districts retained sufficient autonomy to elect their own Councils and pass laws on specific topics but were otherwise governed directly by the National Authorities.[6] Non- federal districts were allowed to elect their constitutional heads, who occupied a position equivalent to that of the Kings in Buganda, Bunyoro, Toro, and Ankole. The Central Government held no power to alter the constitutions or form of government in Buganda or the Federal States. Thus, the 1962 Constitution stipulated complex distribution of powers that ensured equality within the regions and safeguarded the regions from being dominated by the central government.

On the political front, Uganda People's Congress and Kabaka Yekka united upon independence to form a government. The Late Milton Obote became the Prime Minister. He was responsible for keeping a loose coalition together[7] and even acceded to the demands for special treatment by Buganda. This set a precedent and Busoga chiefdoms banded together to claim recognition under their newly defined monarch, the Kyabasinga. Iteso people claimed *Kingoo* (title) though they had no history of pre- colonial King.

Though Milton Obote accommodated various demands, his goal was always to build a strong central government at the expense of entrenched regional interests. He set out to strengthen his political party by 'thinning' opposition party ranks, as members crossed the floor to join the government benches. This was achieved through combination of patronage offers and the promise of future rewards within the ruling coalition.[8]

Despite Obote's patronage, his United People Congress' MPs passed a vote of 'no confidence' in him[9]. Instead of resigning or engaging in political negotiations, Obote's response was to carry out a '*coup de tat*' against his own government. He suspended the Constitution, arrested UPC Ministers and assumed control of the state. At the same time he ordered MPs to pass the 1966 Constitution without debate. Though it was sounded as an interim Constitution, it removed all federal provisions in favour of a centralized government. Buganda and the three federal states lost their autonomy and the King of Buganda (Kabaka) lost his privileged status while Buganda was divided into four districts and ruled through martial law, a forerunner of the military domination over the civilian population. At the national level, the Prime Minister became an Executive President, in place of the preceding ceremonial President. He, Milton Obote, became the President. These constitutional arrangements strengthened Obote's position while at the same time appearing to respect the rule of law.

President Obote placed the 1967 Draft Constitution in Parliament, which debated and passed it three months later. It completed the process of centralization of power. It confirmed the President's position as an executive though it theoretically sanctioned multiparty political competition. Parliament was defined to include members of the National Assembly and the President making it impossible for Parliament to pass law without presidential assent. The president could also dismiss the National Assembly and legislate by decree in its absence. It abolished the kings, the kingdoms, and the constitutional heads of the district, thus removing official recognition of its cultural unity. Parliament now had the authority to change the form of district councils and to allow council members to be appointed rather than elected. It also empowered the government to employ preventive detention during states of emergency, or as the government deemed necessary. On citizenship, it deliberately deprived Indians, whose applications for Ugandan citizenship had not been approved by 1967, of citizenship when it stated that any Ugandan national holding dual citizenship who failed to renounce their other citizenship would lose Ugandan citizenship. The government could in effect treat Indians as non- nationals. In addition, while he was consolidating state power, Obote rapidly promoted Idi Amin Dada within the military as a personal protégé. He was thus able to use the threat of military power to coerce Parliament and consolidate power within the Presidency.

Obote was overthrown by Idi Amin[10] through a military coup. Amin's rule did not even pretend to be constitutional. He organized his government in military fashion. State House was renamed 'Command Post' and military tribunals were placed above the system of civil law. Amin's rulership is largely noted for its brutality against his real and imagined opponents. It was a murderous regime which lasted for about eight long years. Later, Idi Amin was overthrown by Tanzanian troops after he invaded and annexed part of Tanzania territory. Tanzania's invasion did little to calm political turbulence in Uganda.[11] Obote made a comeback in 1981 at the period that Yoweri Museveni and others declared themselves as National Resistance Army (NRA) and vowed to remove Obote from power by means of popular rebellion. In the next four years, Obote concentrated his efforts on destroying the NRA to the detriment of all else.

Museveni headed National Resistance Movement (NRM), which upon assuming power issued a Proclamation accepting the authority of 1967 Constitution but suspending portions that granted executive and legislative powers to the President and Parliament respectively. The NRM government declared that the National Resistance Council (NRC) "shall have the supreme authority of the government" including the powers to pass laws and choose the national President. Members of NRC included the Chair, the NRM and NRA representatives. NRC was enjoined to seek the views of National Resistance Army Council on all matters that NRC considered important. The 1989 amendments to the 1986 Proclamation expanded this principle by declaring that both NRC and NRAC "shall participate in the discussion, adoption, and promulgation of the Constitution,"[12]

The President became the head of the executive branch with power to appoint a Prime Minister and a cabinet of ministers with the approval of the NRC. He also appointed Inspector- General of Police, an Auditor- General and a Director of Public Prosecutions. The 1967 Constitution stipulating a five year term limit for the president was suspended. It was not clear how long the President would serve. Presumably he served until dismissed by the NRC, which was the appointing body, or until the end of the Interim Period.[13] NRM followed the principle of broad based government by appointing non- NRM members to cabinet posts.[14] The effect of bringing in non-NRM members into the government was to dilute the potency of NRM's Ten Point Program.

In 1988 the NRC passed the Constitutional Commission Act which established a Commission to hear public testimony and draft a new constitution. The government set minimum guidelines for the Commission, which included: guarantee of fundamental individual rights, separation of the three arms of government with checks and balances between them, an independent judiciary, popular accountability and a democratic free and fair electoral system.[15]

The Commission travelled across Uganda collecting citizens' views on the new constitution. The Commission handed its report to the Government towards the end of 1992[16] and recommended that the new constitution be adopted by a Constituent Assembly composed of an elected National Resistance Council and other interests groups.[17] The recommendations for a Constituent Assembly were informed by the peoples' view as collected by the Commission. Paragraph 48 of the Interim Report states that "the majority of the submissions to the Commission which have explicitly addressed the issue of the adoption processes support the Constituent Assembly option. It is also consistent with the overwhelming emphasis on participatory democracy in the submissions from the people and their emphasis on the need to adopt the new constitution in a way that differs from the non-participatory methods used for adoption of all past Ugandan constitutions." The Interim Report went on to state that "in the light of all these considerations, the recommendation of the Commission is that the majority view on this issue should be given effect through the establishment of a Constituent Assembly to debate the Draft Constitution prepared by the Uganda Constitutional Commission."[18] The NRM Government adopted most of the Commissions' recommendations by constituting a Constituent Assembly to adopt the new constitution.

The 1995 Constitution gave the NRM government the mandate to organize and manage the transition process. According to Benjamin Odoki the "government managed to discharge this mandate honourably by conducting free and fair election in accordance with the New Constitution at the risk of losing power. This was the litmus test for the viability and legitimacy of the Constitution and the commitment of the government to democracy and constitutionalism"[19]

The Preamble to the Constitution recalled Uganda's history, which had been characterized by political and constitutional instability. It declared Ugandan's determination to build a better future by establishing socio- economic and political order through a popular and durable constitution based on the principles of unity, peace, equality, democracy, freedom, social justice and progress. The 1995 constitution set out directives and principles of state policy designed to promote democracy such as; popular participation by the people in their governance; equal access to all positions of leadership, decentralization and devolution of functions and powers to the people, and political and civic organizations that conform to democratic principles in their internal organization. Leadership Code and the positions of Inspector General of Government and the Auditor General were set up by the Constitution to promote transparency and good governance in public affairs. It promoted social justice by catering for gender balance, fundamental rights, representation of marginalized groups, the right to development, balanced and equitable development, social and economic rights, food security and nutrition.

The Constitution had a Bill of Rights that was liberal and comprehensive and incorporated all the rights and freedoms enshrined in the International Bill of Rights. It included specific rights for women, children and persons with disability. A Human Rights Commission was set up to promote and protect human rights.

The 1995 Constitution provided for the recognition of both the 'Movement political system' and the multiparty systems. It defines the Movement system as "broad based, inclusive and non- partisan' and must conform to participatory democracy, democracy, accountability and transparency, accessibility to all positions of leadership by all citizens and individual merit as a basis for elections.[20] Under Article 69 the people of Uganda have the right to choose and adopt a political system of their choice through free and fair elections or referenda, which can be held under Article 74.[21] Transition provisions under Article 271 stated that the first presidential, parliamentary and local government elections after the promulgation of the constitution would be held under the Movement political system. A referendum would be held in the last month of the fourth year of the term of parliament to determine the political system. Such a referendum was held in 2000 and the Movement system was overwhelmingly retained. Another referendum was held on July 2005, which reinstated multiparty political system.

The new Constitution adopted the presidential system of government. In its Final Report, the Commission stated as follows;

> From the people's submission there is overwhelming support for the concept of a democratically elected President who should be the head of State of Uganda. This concern for a directly elected head of Executive emanated from the people's experience of both colonial and independent Uganda. Many lamented the fact the President of Uganda did not have a mandate supported by a popular vote of the people. Our own observation is that the people want direct participation in the election of their leader and also prefer to have a President who commands a national following and not one whose support is based on a particular region, group or force."[22]

The Commission outlined its rationale for a Presidential system to the Constituent Assembly as follows;

> The main argument that were advanced for a system similar to a Presidential one are that it ensures greater separation of power between the executive and the legislature, and an effective system of checks and balances. According to the people, it would help in removing what they perceived to be pressure exerted on the legislature to approve the position of the executive. While we have not recommended a purely presidential system, we tend to agree that some separation of power should improve the function of the executive as well as the legislature[23].

The size of the Cabinet is limited by the Constitution to 21 cabinet ministers and 21 ministers of state and can only be increased by a resolution of Parliament. The President appoints a Vice- President with the approval of the Parliament. The Executive also needs approval of Parliament to enter into international agreements, securing loans and declaration of war or State of Emergency. Article 107 lays down elaborate procedures for impeaching a President. Article 105 limited the term of office for a President to two five- year terms. However, the Ugandan Parliament amended the Article in 2005. The President can now serve as long as he wins Presidential elections.

The 2005 amendment to the Uganda Constitution to remove limitation of Presidential terms and the open bribery and intimidation which preceded it demonstrates how constitutions can be manipulated to give a veneer of democracy to benign dictatorship. Indeed, the manner in which Yoweri Museveni used the Law and Courts in 2005/2006 to harass the opposition leader Dr. Kizza Besigye is illustrative of how constitutions without constitutionalism undermine the growth of leadership.

Tanzania

Tanzania has had a less violent and tumultuous political history in the region. However, its history of constitutional changes is similar to that of Kenya and Uganda as they were designed to consolidate power. Tanzania did not set out to abrogate or fundamentally change its independent constitution of 1961. The tactics involved were to ensure that Tanzania became a one party state. Professor Pratt states that "in Tanzania the several parties, which appeared in 1962, were harassed out of existence, their leadership deported or detained and their rights to register and hold meetings severely restricted".[24]

In 1963, the President of the ruling party, TANU, argued at the TANU National Conference that "where there is one party, and that party is identified with the nation as a whole the foundation of democracy are firmer than they can ever be where you have two or more parties, each representing only a section of the community." On the strength of its own convictions, TANU decided to turn Tanganyika into a one party state. This decision was given legal backing in the Interim Constitution of 1965.

Nevertheless, a Commission on One-Party rule was set up to collect views on what kind of one party state Tanganyika should be. President Nyerere succinctly stated the mandate of the Commission thus;

> "... I think I should emphasize that it is not the task of this Commission to consider whether Tanganyika should be a one-party state. The decision has already been taken. Their task is to say what kind of one-party state we should have in the context of our own national ethic and in accordance with the principles I have instructed the Commission to observe."

Nyerere went on to articulate his reasoning thus;

> For the truth is that it is not the Party which is the instrument of government. It is the government which is the instrument through which the Party tries to implement the wishes of the people and serve their interests.[25]

The Party leadership controlled the government thus giving them power over both ideological and coercive state apparatus.[26] The Interim Constitution of 1965 rejected the Bill of Rights and attempts to place fundamental rights and freedoms in the Preamble. The TANU constitution was made part of the Constitution by being appended as a schedule to the country's Constitution. Though it was supposed to be 'Interim', the 1965 Constitution lasted for 12 years.

On 5th February, 1977 TANU and Afro Shiraz Party (ASP) merged to form *Chama Cha Mapinduzi* (CCM). The National Executive Council (NEC) of CCM adopted the Constitution Commission proposal which was published in the form of a Bill and within seven days submitted to the Constituent Assembly, which passed the new Constitution within 3 hours.[27]

People were extremely eager to participate in the 1983 Constitutional Debate. The Law Society of Tanzania took an active role in presenting well-considered memoranda. Nevertheless, the ruling party decided on contentious areas which were the scope of Presidential powers; consolidation of the authority of Parliament;

strengthening the representative character of National Assembly; consolidation of the Union; and consolidation of the people's power.

The Nyalali Commission[28] made recommendations that the constitutions of both the Union and Zanzibar be amended to make the whole of Tanzania a multi-party state. In 1992 a constitutional amendment was effected to make Tanzania a multi-party political system.

The fundamentally increamental growth of the Tanzanian Constitution and political fidelity to the Constitution which has seen Presidential transitions from Mwalimu Julius Nyerere to Ali Hassan Mwinyi to Benjamin Mkapa and Jakaya Kikwete after the 14th December, 2005 elections. This is demonstrative of how a good Constitution can be used to ensure political stability and predictability. This is to be contrasted with the Ugandan experience where the 2005 Constitutional amendment was introduced to serve the interests of an individual who has arrogated to himself a '*demi god*' status.

Kenya

Kenya's independent constitution was a highly complex document as it reflected the diverse positions taken by parties who negotiated it at the Lancaster House Conference. It was also a doomed document, as the protagonists did not believe in it because their version of Government was not included.[29] Nevertheless, it provided the parameters for all latter discourse on the political future of the country and its people.[30] The Constitution sought to instill values such as constitutionalism; limitations of the power of Government and the assurance of the rights of the citizenry; and liberal democracy. Patrick McAuslan argued that the importance of the Independent Constitution was "introducing certain values, rather than either reflecting already existing values or imposing certain values."[31]

The independent Constitution had two overriding principles; parliamentary government and the protection of the minorities. The American system of Executive President had been debated at the Lancaster House Conference and rejected.[32] The legislature had a very central role in the total political process; special majorities were required to alter the Constitution or to introduce a state of emergency and Parliament could pass a vote of no confidence in the Government. The Judiciary was the final arbiter in the interpretation of the Constitution and judges had security of tenure. The Civil Service and the police were insulated from political pressures as the Public Service Commission controlled them. Moreover, the Constitution assumed that there would always be an opposition party in Parliament which would be consulted whenever changes to the Constitution were proposed.[33]

The Executive power lay with the Queen who was the head of state, but in practice the Governor-General exercised those powers. The Governor-General had extensive powers relating to defense, external affairs and internal security and could even veto legislation. The Prime Minister was appointed by the Governor-General from amongst the members of the House of Representatives with a majority support.[34] The National Assembly was bi- cameral with the House of Representative as the Lower House and the Senate as the Upper House. The Senate acted as a political safeguard for *Majimbo* (regionalism); it had an important role in the procedure for constitutional amendment and declaration of state of emergency. There was direct election to the Senate from the forty districts, which included Nairobi. It was modeled on the American system, as it was a continuous body; one third of its members were to resign every two years. The longest term that a Senator could serve was six years.[35]

The Independence Constitution provided for regionalism. The country was divided into seven regions each having its own legislative and executive powers. Each region had elected and specially elected members.[36] It had restrictions on who should vote in a region. For example, in order to vote in a region, one had to show a 'genuine connection' with that region, such as having being born there or it being his/her permanent residence. Section 239 stated that the Central Government could not change boundaries of regions without their consent. The President of the region was elected by the elected members either from among themselves or from those qualified to be elected as such. The Executive functions of the region were exercised by the Finance and Establishment Committee of the Assembly. The Chief Executive Officer of the region was the civil secretary who was appointed by the Public Service Commission after consultation with the regional President. Each Region had its own police force under a Regional Commissioner, which was under the overall control of the Inspector General; an officer of the Central Government.[37] The relationship between the Central Government and the regions was complex and as McAuslan states, "powers were so divided between Central Government, the Regional Government and other authorities that the effective exercise, let alone the abuse of power on the part of the KANU Government was rendered extremely difficult if the Constitution was to be adhered to."[38]

Section 186-188 of the Independent Constitution established an independent Civil Service. Public Service Commission was responsible for recruitment and promotion of civil servants. Members of the Public Service commission were appointed on the advice of the Judicial Service Commission. The Commission also had jurisdiction over public servants employed in the regions. Officers could only be removed from office after judicial enquiry.

Amendments to the independent Constitution fell under two categories; ordinary amendments and amendments to specially entrenched provisions. The latter could not be altered except by a bill secured through 75% of the vote of all members on the second and third reading in the House of Representatives and nine-tenths of the members in the Senate. These provisions related to fundamental rights, citizenship, elections, the senate, structure of regions, the judiciary and the amendment itself. Non-entrenched provisions required 75% of all members in both Houses on the second and third readings. If a Bill failed to get enough votes, it could be presented to the electorate in a Referendum and if supported by 2/3 of the votes, it would be reintroduced into the House and passed by a simple majority.[39]

According to Ghai[40], the need to settle claims from various tribes and races to political power gave rise to entrenchment of minority rights in the independent constitution. The Asians and the Europeans were concerned with their own specific interests instead of political power.[41] Europeans wanted to be assured of their property and land rights. They wanted to be compensated in case of compulsory acquisition of their land and properties. The Asians were particularly concerned with the security of their investments and the right to continue working and residing in Kenya. Smaller African ethnic groups were worried that the bigger and more politically active communities would dominate them. They therefore wanted greater control of their own regions and less dependency on the Central Government. The Arabs wanted to secede to Zanzibar while Somalis wanted to join Somalia. Thus, The Independence Constitution entrenched minority rights enforceable by the judiciary.[42]

The complexity of the Independence Constitution was as a result of catering for innumerable fears and accommodating innumerable demands of the various groups.[43] Ghai argued that the Independence Constitution had been 'tailored to address subsisting problems without much regard for its long-term institutional viability.'[44] It was therefore primarily concerned with accommodating existing problems at the expense of the likely future developments. Githu Muigai states that the "Constitution sought to establish an entirely new form of governance that neither the new Governors nor the governed had any experience with. Because it showed an amazing distrust for power, it provided for a weak form of government by diffusing power into numerous institutions. This was in sharp contrast to the colonial state, which was one monolithic and unaccountable edifice of power."[45] Regionalism was one of the most contentious issues in negotiating the Independence Constitution, and according to Ghai, "the powers and functions of the state among the Central and various Regional Governments were so meticulously ... allocated between them that if the intention was to prevent a planned economic and social development of the country success could not have been more complete."[46]

So why did the main negotiating parties KANU and KADU accept the Independence Constitution? According to some authorities, the acceptance of the Independence Constitution was nothing more than a guarantee to 'quicken' the independence date. Munene states that "the acceptance was meant to enable KANU leaders to assume power as soon as possible without believing in the document they had accepted. Kenyatta told KANU delegates to reach a settlement if they did not want to have a government 'snatched from our hands.... But once we had the government we could change the constitution."[47] KADU accepted the Independence Constitution as a guarantee against domination and oppression of the communities they represented. The Colonial Office saw the Constitution as a discharge of its historical colonial responsibility of trusteeship of the underdeveloped and to protect the minorities.[48] Therefore, Kenya's Independence Constitution was doomed even before it was promulgated.

African political leaders of the time viewed amendments to centralized power as inevitable. Oginga Odinga stated, "we knew that the period for the regional constitution was short lived, ... we honoured the undertaking to hand over schedules but we improvised as new way of keeping as much centralized control as possible, ready for the new day when strong central administration would be reinstated."[49] Tom Mboya viewed the Constitution as an "experiment and it is obvious that it contains a number of unworkable and unfair provisions."[50] Charles Njonjo explained why amendments to the Independence Constitution had to be made as "First of all it militates against effective government at the center. Secondly, it prevented the co-ordination of the national efforts at a time when it was most important that development should be planned on a nation- wide scale. Thirdly, the system of regional government was both costly and cumbersome and made heavy demands on the country's inadequate resources of trained manpower. Fourthly, the independence constitution made provision for a monarchical form of government, a form which is alien to the Kenya people."[51]

Amendments to the Independence Constitution started in 1964.[52] The amendments established Kenya as an independent Republic. The position of a Prime Minister was abolished and replaced with an Executive President. The President became the head of state, head of government and the commander-in-chief of the armed forces of Kenya. The President was empowered to appoint and dismiss cabinet ministers including the vice president and all the civil servants without consulting anyone, as previously practiced by the governor. The net effect of these amendments was to concentrate power within the presidency.

Jomo Kenyatta defended the amendments as demanded by the people. He said, "During the campaign last year, KANU told the country that we would seek to establish in Kenya an independent republic. It was the wish of the voters of this country that we should have a republic on the very day of independence. The majority of the voters agree with KANU that the original nature of the constitution itself is rigid and unworkable. We have discussed with the people the modifications we need"[53]

In 1965,[54] the executive powers of the regions were abolished. The regions and their assemblies were designated as provinces or Councils and their functions reduced to the promotion and translation of government programmes. The then Minister for Justice and Constitutional Affairs said, "I see the position of Regional Assemblies as one which includes the translation of government policy and promotion of Government programmes at the regional level, as well as giving of guidance and assistance to county councils in their efforts to serve the day to day needs of our people at home. The Regional authorities are not government in themselves."[55] Constitutional changes were also effected on entrenched provisions. The amendments to the Constitution were now to be effected through a majority vote of 65% in both chambers instead of the original stipulation, which required a majority of 90% in the Senate, and 75% in the Lower House.

In 1966 amendments were effected that required MPs sentenced to an imprisonment of six months or more to vacate their seats and empowered the speaker to declare vacant the seat of an MP who failed to attend eight consecutive parliamentary sittings without Speaker's permission. The President was empowered to waive the effect of this provision.[56] Further amendments required an MP who resigned from the party that had supported him in the elections and defected to another party, to vacate his seat at the expiration of the session and face a by-election.[57] These amendments were designed to tame errant KANU members who challenged or failed to support the party position. It was a political problem that the KANU Government saw fit to resolve through constitutional amendments.[58] The President had had more powers to control the MPs and therefore Parliament itself. Githu Muigai considers these amendments ill-advised and states,

"This apparent inability of the Government Legal Advisors to distinguish between matters that could easily be regulated by ordinary legislation and those requiring constitutional amendment, was obviously the basis of most of the ill-advised amendments of this nature."[59]

By Act No. 18 of 1966[60], the President assumed immense powers whenever he considered the security of the state threatened. He could now abrogate the Bill of Rights by placing persons into detention without trial. Immediately this Act was passed, President Kenyatta detained nearly all trade unionists in Kenya People's Union[61], thereby almost crippling the party.

The Senate was abolished and amalgamated with the House of Representatives to establish a single National Assembly.[62] Senators were incorporated into the Lower House without as much as an election. Through Act No. 16 of 1968, the last vestiges of regionalism were removed. It eliminated the Provincial Councils which had been Regional Assemblies. It repealed pass laws of the Regional Assemblies. KANU finally had the unitary state it had always wanted. Act No. 45 of 1968 stipulated that the Vice President is to succeed the President in the event of incapacity or death, on an acting capacity for 90 days, after which the Vice President was to be subjected to elections. The Act also altered the composition of the National Assembly by empowering the President to nominate 12 members at his sole discretion. This was meant to give the President extra powers to bring into the House sympathetic MPs.

In 1969 a revised Constitution was published. Previously the constitution was contained in twelve different documents and the amendments brought all these documents together. The constitution was now more streamlined and compact though it was 'entirely coherent' and the philosophy behind various amendments discernible than when the amendments began. The Constitution came to be what the President wanted.[63] The President was now all-powerful and imperial.

An amendment was effected in 1975 that extended the President's prerogative of mercy to the removal of a disqualification imposed by an election court on a person against whom an election offence had been proved in an election petition. This amendment was passed by Parliament within one afternoon. The Bill was published 10 December 1975 and received Presidential assent on 11th December 1975. It was given retroactive effect and deemed to have come into force on 10th December 1975. The amendment was designed to save Paul Ngei, personal friend of President Kenyatta, from political oblivion after he was convicted of an election offence. The amendment is a clear testimony as to how the President regarded the

Constitution. He used the constitutional amendments to advance personal interests and was aided by Parliament.

Ill-advised constitution amendments designed to settle political issues continued under President Moi. Among them was an amendment to the effect that certain public officers had to resign in order to qualify to contest parliamentary elections.[64] The official reason of the amendment was that it was meant to eliminate abuse of office by persons employed in the public service who wanted to enter politics. In reality, it was designed to scare away "would be opponent of sitting MPs."[65] In 1982, Kenya was turned into a *de jure* one party state[66]. Opposition parties were outlawed and KANU came to enjoy monopoly of power. The amendment meant that anyone interested in contesting a seat must do so through KANU. At the same time if one was suspended or expelled from the ruling party, he lost his office. This amendment was in response to Oginga Odinga and George Anyona who had voiced their intention of forming a new political party, Kenya Socialist Party. KANU responded by expelling Oginga Odinga and placing Anyona under detention without trial. Thereafter, KANU ordered the Attorney General to prepare legislation making Kenya a one party state.

Other significant amendments included removal of security of tenure of constitutional office holders like the Attorney General and the Auditor General.[67] This was a clear attempt by the Executive to dominate all aspects of public life in Kenya without any legal impediments. The Auditor General as the custodian of the Consolidated Fund needs security of tenure to insulate the office from political pressures. Similarly, the Attorney General as the Chief Prosecutor needs security of tenure in order to exercise his discretion without undue pressures. Ironically, the Attorney General whose tenure was being removed supported the Bill in parliament. He said, "I would like to make it quite clear that the impression which the press and the Chairman of the LSK, in particular, portrayed to the effect that the amendment was intended to remove the protection of tenure of the office of the Attorney General and the Auditor General is completely misconceived.[68] The Attorney General was in his own world! In 1988, the security of tenure of judges was removed.[69] It gave authority to the executive powers to interfere with the judiciary by dismissing judges without elaborate procedures. These amendments were reversed in 1990.[70]

The New Democrats: Kenyan Context

The fall of the Soviet Union in 1989 as a geo-political power unleashed what has been called 'winds of change' across the African continent and other developing countries. Kenya had been a close ally of the United States of America and other

Western countries in their struggle for dominance with the spectre of communism and socialism as propagated by the Soviets. These Western countries, therefore, seemed to be in tacit agreement with the Kenyan government in its effort to eradicate what it continuously referred to as 'dissidents and malcontents.' They could loan money without conditionalities of good governance or plural democracy as long as Kenya did not let the communist ideology take root within its borders.

All this changed with the 'collapse of the Union of Soviet Socialist Republics and its satellite states and the consequent reorganization and realignment of geopolitical relationships in Europe, the Americas and Asia.'[71] The Government could henceforth not secure international financing unless it undertook democratization and free market reforms.

Locally, various groups composed of politicians, civil society, and the religious groups were making demands for a systematic review of the Constitution. The ruling party, KANU, formed a Committee in which demands were made for constitutional amendments to allow multi- partyism, to abolish detention without trial, to restore security of tenure for judges, the Attorney- General and the Auditor General, and to restore the principle of separation of powers. Sadly, the ruling party failed to heed this demands as the Committee argued that these matters went beyond its jurisdiction.[72]

Civil society organizations including the Law Society of Kenya, FORD (Forum for the Restoration of Democracy), local media among others continued to pile pressure by criticizing the Government as being dictatorial; for failing to respect the rule of law; of grand corruption and looting of public resources; the Police Force being at the whims of the Executive; and failure to respect the doctrine of separation of powers. Street protests came to be the norm in Nairobi and other urban centers. Finally, the international community composed of donors, bilateral partners, financial institutions like the IMF and the World Bank demanded certain economic and political reforms, and when the reforms failed to materialize, they imposed economic sanctions and Kenya could no longer access international loans.[73] It must be stated that at this time the focus was mainly on reviewing the current Constitution rather than writing a new Constitution.[74]

The KANU Government gave in to these demands by repealing section 2A of the Constitution and thereby returned the country to multi-party politics.[75] This expansion of political activity gave rise to clamour for the so-called 'minimum constitutional reforms' especially after the Opposition was trounced in the 1992 General Election. The Opposition accused the ruling party of rigging the elections especially through the Provincial Administration and control of the Electoral Commission. However, Opposition parties were hopelessly divided and could not offer a well-organized and vocal demand for comprehensive review. This was instead left to the non- governmental organizations.[76]

In response, the KANU government hijacked the process from the non-governmental organizations and channelled it through Parliament.[77] Both KANU and Opposition MPs formed the Inter-Parties Parliamentary Group (IPPG) to formulate both constitutional and administrative reforms before the 1997 General Election.[78] The IPPG managed to negotiate amendments. These included Section 7 of the Constitution, amended to remove the requirement that the president could only form a government from members of his own party; Section 33 which stated that parliamentary parties would nominate members to the National Assembly and not the President; Section 42A was amended to give Electoral Commission two other functions of promoting voter education and ensuring free and fair elections while Section 84 was amended to expand the right of appeal on constitutional matters to the Court of Appeal. Githu Muigai argues that these amendments lacked an underlying philosophy and ended up being 'a patchwork that did not address the problem of constitutions' serious internal inconsistencies.[79] The truth could be that both KANU and the Opposition had no intention of overhauling the current Constitution so long as they agreed on how to compete for and share power.

The civil society, religious groups and other stakeholders dismissed the IPPG agreement as self-serving and inadequate. Consequently negotiations with a large group of stakeholders were held culminating in the 1998 amendments to the 1997 Constitution of Kenya Review Act. The amendments contained provisions for a Review Commission made up of twenty five members nominated proportionately by stakeholders and not the President; a time bound procedure for nominations; appointment of nominated Commission members by the President; implementation of the one third policy for women representation; and structures of the review process to reflect a people driven constitution making process.[80]

Numerous disputes arose and the Review Act was amended several times. Nevertheless, the Constitution of Kenya Review Commission managed to collect people's views on how the country should be governed. It should be emphasized that as mandated by the Review Act, the Commission went around the country collecting Kenyans' views on what should be included in the Constitution. The Commission analyzed and collated these views and, based on them, produced a Draft Constitution.

The Draft Constitution was subjected to discussions and analysis at the National Constitutional Conferences (NCC) and finally adopted on the 15ᵗʰ March 2004.

As discussions at the NCC were going on, some delegates, who included Cabinet Ministers, walked out in protest when majority of delegates rejected a motion on political compromise reached between various political groups in the government. From that point on, the road to a new Constitution became less clear. As is well documented, the dispute is largely between those who want a centralized system with a strong Executive and those who want power devolved. To appreciate this dispute, it is imperative to note what the Draft Constitution said on Executive and on devolvement of power.

On Devolution of Power, the Draft Constitution provided for a four- tier devolution structure based on the province, district, location and village. It called for abolition of the existing Provincial Administration upon coming into effect. More importantly, it entrenched devolution of power. On Executive, it provided for an Executive branch consisting of a President and a Cabinet headed by a Prime Minister. The Prime Minister was given distinct and elaborate functions. The President's functions were exclusively defined and the circumstances under which he or she could be removed from office and procedure for impeachment.

It is interesting to note that the power wielders after the 2002 General Elections totally backed the Draft Constitution in regard to the devolution of power and Executive as faithfully reflecting Kenyans views, and yet they later castigated the same as not a true reflection of what Kenyans told the Commission.   Indeed, it is instructive that after the National Constitutional Conference, Parliament enacted the Constitution of Kenya Review (Amendments) Act 2004 No. 9 of 2004[81] which gave it the authority to amend whatever it deemed 'contentious' out of the Bomas Draft Constitution.

In exercise of the power, a segment of the Parliamentary Select Committee on the Constitution introduced fundamental amendments to the chapters on the Executive, Legislature and Devolution and when the 22ⁿᵈ day of August, 2005 the Attorney General published a Draft to be presented to the Referendum, the spirit of people participation had been fundamentally compromised in the critical area of the architecture of power. Ultimately, when the Draft was subjected to a Referendum on the 21ˢᵗ day of November, 2005 it was rejected.

The Lessons of History

The foregoing discussion provides important historical lessons for East Africans. These lessons should guide the region in institutionalizing constitutionalism, the basis for good governance and political stability.

Since independence, leaders from East Africa believed that a centralized system of government was the best, and that devolving power to the various regions and groups in each country was detrimental to statehood. This was, and still is, an arrogant worldview whereby the political elite decides what is best for the people. Local people demanding control over their own lives and resources are dismissed as a bunch of dangerous illiterates who will plunge the country into chaos and disintegration. The irony is that it is the political elite who have always without fail, plunged East African countries into violent chaos or constitutional crises. It is the desire of the political elite to tighten control of the country in order to enjoy power and resources of their respective countries. It has been shown clearly that centralization of state power within the Executive does not produce positive results, be they economic or political. The converse is true; centralization of power within the Executive muzzles divergent views that eventually coalesce into a potent force that ultimately overwhelms the Executive. Once this happens, the Executive becomes paranoid and violent. The most serious of this is, of course Uganda, which experienced a long period of military intervention in politics. In retrospect, if Milton Obote had not hijacked the Constitution with the help of the Army, Uganda may not have had to go through a destructive phase in its history. In Kenya, there has never been an attempt to operationalize the Independence Constitution as the ruling elite had declared it unworkable. In Tanzania, the ruling party, TANU, concluded that the one-party state is the best. All these countries never consulted the people on what they thought or what they liked. The presumptuous attitude has cost the region untold losses in terms of economic, political and social development. Despite claims by leaders such as Tom Mboya and Charles Njonjo, who advocated for a centralized system to accelerate economic development, it has actually retarded development in the region. In Kenya, a centralized Government created and widened the gap between the more developed areas and less developed ones. At the individual level, the political elite doubles as economic elite giving personal interpretation to Kwame Nkurumah's cry of 'seek yet the political kingdom and all shall be added unto you!" The gap between the rich and poor is widening and so are insecurity, crime and corruption. In Tanzania, the centralized system managed to unite disparate groups into a socialist type economy, which did not generate much wealth for the country.

In Uganda, centralized political power led to the brutal Idi Amin regime and stunted Uganda's growth shortly after independence.

Closely connected to the above is the failure of leaders to appreciate the benefits of unity in diversity. It was never going to be easy after independence to contain ethnic nationalism among diverse ethnic groups. For example, the Independence Constitutions of Uganda and Kenya acknowledged the need to protect ethnic and cultural identities of various groups. These Constitutions also gave various ethnic groups control of resources within their own regions. As have been discussed elsewhere on this chapter, protection of minority groups had been reached after protracted negotiation of the Independence Constitutions, yet the political elite decided to trash those efforts once they ascended to power. It is notable that several decades later, the people of Kenya and Uganda are clamouring for an opportunity to control their local resources. This is evident from views collected by Commissions to review their respective countries' Constitution.[82] In Kenya, the political elite normally dismisses Devolution of Power as unworkable, expensive and burdensome even when it is so obvious that most of them do not understand what devolution is all about and have never bothered to do a cost-benefit analysis. In reality, the cost of forced oneness has not shown any benefits.

It is clear that political developments in East Africa mirror constitutional development. One reason for this is that the constitution and constitutional making is all about politics. However, political leaders have gone out of their way to mischievously amend Constitutions to either consolidate state power within the executive or to use the Constitution as a weapon to crush political opponents, real or imagined. Milton Obote suspended the Constitution to resolve an essentially political dispute. His reaction to a vote of no confidence was by any account overboard and ill advised. Was it so hard to negotiate with the political opponent? Was it hard for him to resign and let the Constitution prevail? It was paranoia for Jomo Kenyatta to push for constitutional amendments in order to crush the Kenya People's Union. It is debatable whether KPU presented any overwhelming threat at the time for Kenyatta to amend the Constitution to protect KANU. Was he protecting KANU or himself? These two examples show that the leaders were insecure and did not differentiate between personal ambition and national good. For the Kenyatta government to push for a constitutional amendment in order to protect his close friend Paul Ngei from political oblivion cheapens and trivializes the Constitution. Actually, the Kenyatta Government could have had the same result had it amended the Electoral laws, but this process would not have cheapened constitutional amendments. For TANU to annex its constitution as a schedule to the Tanzania Constitution shows lack of understanding and appreciation of the country's Constitution as the basic law.

Parliaments in East Africa have played a conspiratorial role in strengthening the Executive at the expense of other arms of Government, including the Legislature itself. As argued above, the Executive bought off MPs to vote for their own emasculation. Sometimes MPs, when faced with military force or the threat of being detained decided to support the Executive. The impact of such conduct was to institutionalize Legislative weakness. For example, there are reports that the Ugandan President Yoweri Museveni paid off MPs to vote for the amendment of the provisions of the 1995 Constitution that placed a limit on how long a President can serve. The intention of this amendment was to let President Museveni go for a third five-year term. So much has changed in Uganda and so much remains the same; like manipulating the Constitution to empower the Presidency.

It is imperative that MPs realize their role in safeguarding the Constitution and constitutionalism. This can only be achieved by electing persons of integrity to the legislature. Kenya's Ninth Parliament has proved that even if MPs are well remunerated, they will always sacrifice principles.

Notes

[1]   Chinua Achebe *The Trouble with Nigeria.* Nairobi, Heinemann P. 1

[2]   Moyo J. N. The Politics of Administration understanding Bureacracy in African History, 1992, P. xvii

[3]   Akintoye, S. A. Emergent African State: Topics in the Twentieth Century African History, P 79

[4]   Ibid.

[5]   Ibid.

[6]   Karamoja became a special district under central government as it was the least developed.

[7]   Among coalition members were George Magezi who had the support of the Bunyoro compatriot; Grace S. K. Ibingira whose strength lay in Ankole and Felix Onama the northerner leader of West Nile District. Milton Obote's strength lay among his Langi kin.

[8]   By 1966 Uganda People's Congress was the most dominate political party in Uganda. It had 74 MPs while the rest had a combined number of 18MPs.

[9]   It was passed on February 4th 1966 and was organized by UPC Secretary General Grace S. K. Ibingira.

[10] Amin took power on January 25 1971

[11] Between April 1979 and January 1986, Uganda had four Presidents. Tanzania had sent its soldiers to overthrow the regime of Idi Amin. Lule was installed as president but held the position for three

months. Binaisa took over but was overthrown in May 10, 1980. Milton Obote made a comeback between 1981- 1985.

[12] Legal Notice No. 1 of 1986. The thinking behind this move can be traced to the Ten- Point Program launched by NRA when it was waging a guerilla war. The First Point argued that real democracy had to be organized from the village up to the people's Committees' on the basis of a decent standard of living to preclude bribing for votes. The Second Point stated that the insecurity was state sponsored and could therefore be eliminated by "a politicized army and police and absence of corruption at the top." The Third Point advocated for promotion of national unity through elimination of sectarianism. This could be achieved by eradicating politics based on religious, linguistic and ethnic lines. The Fourth Point argued that Ugandan could stop foreign interference in Uganda's domestic affairs by developing independent priorities based on Uganda interests. The Fifth Point envisioned a construction of an independent, integrated, and self-sustaining national economy that would stop leakages of Uganda's wealth abroad. The Sixth Point stated that basic social services like clean water, health, literacy, and housing should be restored as a matter of priority. The Seventh Point undertook to eliminate corruption from the public service. The Eight Point set out to resolve problems of victims of past governments and to return land to thousands of people displaced by mistaken development and land seizures. The Ninth Point advocated for closer cooperation with other African governments especially the neighbouring countries in creating a bigger market for all. The Tenth Point declared that Uganda should have a mixed economy combining both capitalists and socialists methods.

[13] Interim Period was originally four years long, but was extended in 1989 to another period of five years in order to allow time to draft, debate, and adopt a permanent constitution. In 1989, The Power to dismiss the President was made explicit in February 1989 through amendments to the original proclamation.

[14] For example; DP leader Ssemogerere was appointed minister of internal affairs; Kisseka, associate of former President Lule became the PM; Moses Ali, leader of Uganda Rescue Front was appointed the Minister of Tourism and wildlife.

[15] Uganda's Constitutional Commission Act of 1988

[16] Odoki, Benjamin, The Search for a National Consensus: The making of the 1995 Uganda Constitution.

[17] Ibid pg. 258.

[18] Interim Report Paragraph 54

[19] Supra note 12

[20] Articles 69 and 70 of the 1995 Constitution.

[21] Request for a referendum under Article 74 can be by resolution supported by more than half of the number of MPs, or if requested by a resolution supported by the majority of the total membership of each of at least one half of all district councils; or if requested through a petition to the Electoral Commission by at least one tenth of the registered voters from at least two-thirds of the constituencies for which there are directly elected representatives.

[22] Final Report P319

[23] Supra note 12

[24] Pratt, C. "The Critical Phase in Tanzania 1945- 1968: Nyerere and the Emergence of a Socialist Strategy, 1976

[25] He was speaking on the Uganda People's Congress Conference on 7th June 1968.

[26] Chris Maina Peter, Constitutional making Process in Tanzania: The Role of the People in the Process; Dept of International Law, University of Dar es Salaam August 2000.

[27] Supra Note 26

[28] Nyalali Commission was inaugurated in March 1991 to collect people's views on whether Tanzania should continue with the single party system or adopt a multi- party system.

[29] Githu Muigai, Constitutional Amendments and the Constitutional Amendment Process in Kenya (1964- 1997): A study in the Politics of the Constitution Ph.D 2001.

[30] Ghai, "The Government and the Constitution in Kenya Politics", P 74

[31] McAuslan, "The Evolution of Public Law in East Africa in the 1960s" P.7

[32] Singh, "The Republican Constitution of Kenya" P. 76

[33] Cherry Gertzel, "The Constitutional Position in Kenya: The Appeal for Efficiency." *East African Journal* 4, 6 (1967)

[34] Supra Note 24

[35] Supra Note 24

[36] Section 92 of the Independent Constitution

[37] Chapter Six of the Independent Constitution.

[38] McAuslan, "The Evolution of Public Law in East Africa in the 1960s" P.20

[39] Section 71- 71 (3) of the Independent Constitution.

[40] Ghai, "Independence and Safeguards in Kenya" 1967 P. 27

[41] Ghai, "Constitutions and the Political order in East Africa" P. 407

[42] Ibid No. 35

[43] McAuslan, "The Evolution of Public Law in East Africa in the 1960s." P. 1

[44] Ghai, "Constitutions and the Political Order in East Africa." P. 403

[45] Githu Muigai, Constitutional Amedments and the Constitutional Amendment Process in Kenya (1964- 1997): A Study in the Politics of the Constitution; Ph.D Thesis 2001, University of Nairobi

[46] Ghai, "The Government and the Constitution in Kenya politics". P. 10

[47] Munene, "Constitutional Development in Kenya: A Historical Perspective," PP.51 – 63. Macharia Munene was then a Professor of History at the University of Nairobi.

[48] Ibid No. 40 P. 103

[49] Oginga Odinga, *Not Yet Uhuru* , P. 242. He was then the Minister for Home Affairs

[50] *The East African Standard*, 15 May 1963

[51] Njonjo, "Recent Constitutional Changes in Kenya", P. 98. Charles Njonjo became the first African Attorney General and played a crucial in amending the independent constitution.

[52] The Constitution of Kenya (Amendment) Act No. 28 of 1964

[53] *Sunday Nation August* 15, 1964

[54] This was effected through The Constutition of Kenya (Amendment) (No. 2) Act No. 38 and (Amendment) Act No.14 of 1965

55 *The East African Standard*, 20th March 1964

56 The Constitution of Kenya (Amendment) Act No. 16 of 1966

57 The Constitution of Kenya (Amendment) Act No. 17 of 1966

58 Ogendo, "The Politics of Constitutional Change in Kenya since Independence" P. 23

59 Ibid No. 40 P. 123

60 The Constitution Of Kenya (Amendment) (No. 3) Act /no. 18 of 1966

61 KPU was formed by Oginga Odinga among others after idelogical differences on the organization of state power, economic development strategies and land among other things. Henceforth, the ruling KANU clique would amend constitution to consolidate power.

62 The Constitution of Kenya (Amendment) (No. 4) Act No. 40 of 1966

63 Ibid No. 40 P. 135

64 The Constitution of Kenya (Amendment) Act. No. 5 of 1979.

65 *The Weekly Review,* 16th February 1979

66 The Constitutional Amendment Act No. 7 of 1982

67 The Constitution of Kenya (Amendment) Act No. 14 of 1986

68 Hansard Report 26th November 1986. Column 1765

69 The Constitution of Kenya (Amendment) Act No. 4 of 1988

70 The Constitution of Kenya (amendment) Act No. 2 of 1990

71 CKRC Final Report P. 39

72 Republic of Kenya, *Report of the KANU Review Committee.* The Commitee was headed by the then Vice President Professor George Saitoti.

73 This is well chronicled in the popular press and other sources including the Final Report by the Constitution of Kenya Review Commission.

74 CKRC Final Report P. 41 states that only a few groups demanded a new constitution before 1992 elections

75 The Constitution of Kenya (Amendment) Act No. 12 of 1991

76 Ibid note 43

77 President Moi was extensively quoted in the media telling the Opposition politicians to support KANU's government effort of channeling the reforms through Parliament.

78 Statute Law (Repeal and Miscellaneous Amendments) Bill 1997

79 Ibid no.43

80 CKRC Final Report P. 42

81 It commenced on 22nd April 2005

82 Constitution of Kenya Review Commission Final Report and the Constitutional Commission of Uganda Final Report

3

The Law and Leadership: The Post-Colonial Experience in Kenya

Kibe Mungai

Introduction

There are many definitions of leadership all dependent on the ends that the men and women privileged to lead their fellow countrymen set out to achieve. On the one hand, *The Blackwell Encyclopaedia of Political Science*[1] defines leadership as the "power of one or a few individuals to induce a group to adopt a particular line of policy leadership".

On the second hand, "leadership," wrote Arthur M. Schlesinger Jr., "is really what makes the world go round." Love no doubt smothers the passage, but love is a private transaction between consenting adults. Leadership is a public transaction with history. The idea of leadership affirms the capacity of individuals to move, inspire and mobilize masses of people so that they act together in pursuit of an end. Sometimes leadership serves good purposes, sometimes bad; but whether the end is benign or evil, great leaders are those men and women who leave their personal stamp on history."[2]

For purposes of this chapter we shall view leadership from the two extremes of the democratic leadership and the totalitarian leadership. Using the United States as an example of a democratic nation endowed with successive generations of democratic leadership Schlesinger Jr. argues that a society based on equality of all men in which rights are given to every citizen and the sovereignty of all is established, requires a government based on reflection and choice. In his words:[3]

> Government by reflection and choice called for a new style of leadership and a new quality of followership. It required leaders to be responsive to popular concerns, and it required followers to be active and informed participants in

the process. Democracy does not eliminate emotion from politics; sometimes it fosters demagogy; but it is confident that, as the greatest of democratic leaders put it, you cannot fool all of the people all of the time. It measures leadership by results and retires those who overreach or falter or fail.

When leaders have as their goal the supremacy of a master race or the promotion of totalitarian revolution or the acquisition and exploitation of colonies or the protection of greed and privilege or the preservation of personal power, it is likely that their leadership will do little to advance the cause of humanity. When their goal is the abolition of slavery, the liberation of women, the enlargement of opportunity for minorities, the defence of the freedoms of expression and opposition, it is likely that their leadership will increase the sum of human liberty and welfare.

On the other extreme the totalitarian leadership is based on force or coerced consent in which the duty of followers is to defer and to obey. Indeed the one fundamental element in all totalitarian regimes is the claim to exclusive leadership on the part of autocrat, one party and ideology. Rival political parties or groups are precluded, and fundamental claims to individual liberty and civil rights are denied. Adoration of and subservience to the leadership are two key characteristics of the totalitarian leadership. Thus:[4]

> The total monopoly of the party, the leading elite and the leader, of power and control over state and society, is sanctioned and elevated not only pseudo-democratically but also pseudo-religiously, with ideology becoming political religion. Equipped with the attitude of infallibility these highest echelons of totalitarian systems demand glorifying veneration on the part of the masses which are being organized, indoctrinated and mobilized to this end and led, in gigantic parades and public spectacles minutely ritualized and theatrically staged, to deafening orgies of mass adulation. The aim is total consensus, manipulated in terms of social psychology to the point of exalted submission. This dogma of total consensus, formulated in the motto 'the leader the party is always right', aspires to solve definitively the perennial and basic problem of all government by insisting on the full identity of leadership and people.

In truth the leader is only but "the privileged few in society who happen to occupy particular positions in the institutional framework set up for the good or bad government of men like the rest of us. Like us they have high and low moments that make them laugh with joy or tremble in tears and trepidation. They put on their trousers one leg after another just like ordinary mortals"[5].

Indeed the leader so often embodies the qualities, sensibilities and outlook of his countrymen and the very diversity of leadership is a testament that leadership cannot be divorced from the environment within which it occurs. All too often the leader exhibits the habits of and projects the prejudices his society. Thus Fredrick Douglas, the great anti-slavery crusader, in his "Oration in Memory of Abraham Lincoln", commented on this great leader in the democratic world as follows:[6]

> I have said that President Lincoln was a white man, and shared the prejudices common to his countrymen towards the colored race. Looking back to his times and to the condition of his country, we are compelled to admit that this unfriendly feeling on his part may be safely set down as one element of his wonderful success in organizing the loyal American people for the tremendous conflict before them, and bringing them safely through that conflict. His great mission was to accomplish two things: first, to save his country from dismemberment and ruin; and, second, to free his country from the great crime of slavery. To do one or the other, or both, he must have the earnest sympathy and the powerful cooperation of his loyal fellow-countrymen. Without this primary and essential condition to success his efforts must have been vain and utterly fruitless. Had he put the abolition of slavery before the salvation of the Union, he would have inevitably driven from him a powerful class of the American people and rendered resistance to rebellion impossible. Viewed from the genuine abolition ground, Mr. Lincoln seemed tardy, cold, dull, and indifferent; but measuring him by the sentiment of his country, a sentiment he was bound as a statesman to consult, he was swift, zealous, radical, and determined.
>
> Though Mr. Lincoln shared the prejudices of his white fellow-countrymen against the Negro, it is hardly necessary to say that in his heart of hearts he loathed and hated slavery...

Now the reason why Abraham Lincoln is one of the greatest leaders is precisely because despite the great odds facing him, he seized the rare opportunities that came his way to advance the cause of freedom and equality. Whatever the motive for his great accomplishments, history records that his rule was on the whole beneficial to his country and possibly the whole of mankind. It is important to note that law is one of the most effective tools of great leaders. The law established all the despicable dictatorships of the ancient and the modern world in as much as it set free millions of people living in racial or colonial bondage. In a word, law is the sharpest of the swords in the armoury of the great leader. Indeed Napoleon Bonaparte's summed-up this well in his famous reminisce to the effect that among the many great things and conquests he accomplished in his epic lifespan, the drafting of the Civil Code was the greatest and enduring legacy to his countrymen.

The extent to which a leader may deploy the instrumentalities of the law to achieve his ends vary from one country to another and from one era to another. Leaders do play a major part in influencing and determining political actions but the opportunity is greater in some circumstances than in others and especially greater at times of crisis or when a new country is created.

Generally speaking, in the established democracies the scope for leaders to accomplish major achievements or shifts in policy and ideology is limited during peacetime. The reason is that a developed legal order in the modern Western liberal society is both general and autonomous as well as public and positive. The generality of the law establishes the formal equality of the citizens and thereby shields them from the arbitrary tutelage of government. There is a formal and constitutionalised separation of powers whose effect is to limit the powers of government. Administration must be separated from legislation to ensure generality; adjudication must be distinguished from administration to safeguard uniformity. These two contrasts represent the core of the rule of law ideal and through them the legal system is supposed to become the balance wheel of social organization. Thus in the modern Western liberal society the distinction between politics or administration, on one side, and adjudication, on the other, became the cornerstone of constitutional and a guiding principle of political thought.[7] It is not surprising indeed that in such established nation states, charismatic and strong leadership has occurred during and between two world wars and during times of serious social or political crises. Winston Churchill, Charles de Gaulle, – Roosevelt and Harry Truman fits this categorization.

In the less developed nations that became independent in the 20th Century there is greater scope for charismatic leadership to emerge. Considering that the state is largely an imposition from above not having developed organically from the society itself, there is larger scope for experimentation, revolutions and counter-revolutions that for better or worse lead to emergence of great leaders. The Kenyan experience falls under this category as shortly demonstrated below.

The primary focus of this chapter is to examine the role and impact of the law in shaping the public affairs and governance in post-independent Kenya. However, a lucid appreciation of this subject requires a critical understanding of the circumstances, limitations, challenges and opportunities in which that leadership has evolved and made its impact.

The Colonial Legal Heritage

The liberal legal order is probably the most enduring of colonial legacies in Kenya. The colonial state was primarily an instrument of primitive accumulation and economic exploitation for the benefit of the minority settler community. Colonial laws were instrumental in the recruitment of indigenous labour, alienation and appropriation of African land, confiscation of livestock and destruction of obstructive indigenous structures. The government was necessarily oppressive, brutal and despotic in order to control the majority of the people in the interest of the dominant minority. In his paper entitled *Law, Modernization and Mystification*, P. Fitzpatrick argues that law has two other functions in the colonial situation:[8]

> Law has two other functions in the colonial situation that have something of a distinct significance. One function involves providing a system of law that is personal to the colonist and serves the metropolitan bourgeoisie – one more in accord with liberal legality and operating apart from the authoritarian legal administration that regulates the colonized. This function as we will see later, takes on a further significance in the post-colonial setting when indigenous class elements make use of this system of law in their own advance. The other function of law is ideological: on the one hand, the colonist presents "the gift of law" as an important part of the civilizing mission (Huttenback, 1976: 13-21), thus justifying legal intervention in disruption of the traditional mode where needed; on the other hand, law is closely identified with ideologies of "trusteeship" and "protection," thus justifying legal action in conservation of the traditional mode.

> The period following the second world war marked a somewhat more intense involvement of capitalism in the third World, particularly in the greater part played by industrial capital and the expansion of the so-called multination enterprise. These changes can be associated with the growth then in the scale and complexity of production world-wide and the consequent need for "planning" and "stability" (Murray, 1972). At the same time, indigenous class demands for greater self-determination emerge, often taking nationalist and populist forms. These demands usually originated in the economic crisis of the inter-war years when metropolitan dominance was weakened and

recession heightened discontent. Thus, as the third World was being more closely integrated into the capitalist world-system, indigenous class elements were becoming more self-assertive. This led to long-enduring conflicts, but the predominant response of capitalism in this situation involved the more or less peaceful co-optation and containment of indigenous class elements. In this process, potentially disruptive class elements are controlled and compliant class elements are promoted by the colonists through new political and economic structures that bound and shape their advance.

Thus the advent of independence brought to power political elites that had been socialized to accept the values of, Western capitalism. Capitalist law, whilst continuing to serve the metropolitan bourgeoisie, now also provides a supportive system that is conformable to and in advance of the indigenous emergence of compliant class elements in two ways. First, it creates and protects disposable private property and provides for and enforces contracts of impersonal exchange necessary for indigenous capital accumulation and class advancement of the elite class. Secondly, it also provides ideological support for the new political elite in its emphasis on individual freedom, on formal equality and universal justice.

Kenya's Independence Constitution is the fulcrum upon which the new legal order was anchored. The Constitution was written to abolish formal inequality, remove colour bar and to uproot the oppressive monolithic colonial system which had denied Kenyans their fundamental rights and freedoms. The following checks and balances were incorporated in the Independence Constitution to ensure that the independent government did not have totalitarian powers.[9]

a) *Majimboism:* Governmental power was to be shared between a federal government and regional governments *(majimbo)*.

b) Governmental power was divided between three organs of government: the legislature, the executive and the judiciary, which would act as checks against each other.

c) The Legislature was made up of two houses, the House of Representatives and the Senate. The Senate had to approve legislation passed by the House of Representatives.

d) There was a Bill of rights specifying areas of an individual citizen's life in which the government could not interfere.

e) The Bill of Rights was to be enforced by an independent judiciary which was insulated from political influence by guaranteeing it a high degree of security of tenure.

f) The civil service was insulated from political influence by the establishment of an independent public service commission, with a high degree of security of tenure.

g) Senior civil servants such as the Attorney-General and the Auditor-General were given security of tenure to ensure governmental accountability and independence of action.

h) A multi-party system was established to guarantee democracy and the voice of minorities against the tyranny of a majority.

In the same way that the colonial state was imposed on African societies, constitutionalism too had no organic roots in these new policies. Constitutions were supposed to settle the problems of the new nations but soon they proved inadequate or restrictive for the ambitions of the new power elites with the result that constitutionalism was undermined, neglected and in many cases the constitutional order was overthrown in *coup d'etats* that became the bane of good governance in many African countries soon after independence. In countries such as Kenya where constitutional order survived military intervention the political settlements made at independence did not endure owing to a combination of factors that will shortly emerge. At this stage it should suffice to say that like the English oak, Western concepts of constitutionalism could not do well in Kenya, as elsewhere in Africa, without careful tendering.[10]

The tragedy turned out to be that the leaders had either not been socialised in notions of limited government that constitutionalism betokens or the socio-political climate was simply too harsh for it to flower. In their seminal study titled *Public Law and Political Change in Kenya*[11], Professor Y. P. Ghai and J. P. W. B. McAuslan explain that the shallow roots of constitutionalism in Kenya was partly due to the fact that decolonisation in Kenya occurred relatively rapidly through a series of major constitutional changes that between 1954 and 1963 would convert Kenya from colonial despotism to a parliamentary democracy headed by Jomo Kenyatta who had been jailed by the British authorities for organizing the Mau Mau armed rebellion. It was certainly hoping for too much to expect the African nationalists to change so suddenly from accomplices of colonial rule to the vanguard of parliamentary democracy. The two professors add:[12]

> In older countries, a constitution and its values emerge from the values of the society at large so that its values reflect those of society or a large part of it. In Kenya, however, the Constitution was designed to introduce liberal democratic values, of which constitutionalism (the limitation of the powers of government, the assurance of the rights of the citizens) and representation (the government must be regularly elected by, and responsive to, the people) are among the most important, and these were values which, while they may have existed in traditional societies in Kenya, did not exist in the society established by colonial rule. For the vast majority of the population, the values of colonial society were autocratic, and took the form of an authoritarian administrative structure. Thus this structure and its values were at variance with the Constitution and its values, and it is the Constitution which has been adjusted to the administrative structure, and not, as was clearly envisaged, the other way round.

The Character of the New Power Elites

It bears noting that decolonization itself did not result in a direct transfer of power from the British sponsored settler government to the legitimate representatives of the Africa people. In this regard it is important to recognize that whereas the Mau Mau were instrumental in termination of minority rule in Kenya, the levers of the state at independence were handed over to a cabal of moderate and conservative politicians that had either been co-opted in the colonial system or had co-operated at various levels with colonial authorities. It is from the ranks of this class that the British selected representatives of the African people for the Lancaster constitutional talks. By their socialization and ideological persuasion this class was anti-democratic in mindset and outlook. The late Prof. Katama Mkangi once described it as follows:[13]

> Colonialism created a warped personality in the colonised African. Detached from its cultural and historical roots, this personality bases its "authenticity" more on nostalgia and accident of geography, than on historical praxis. The

nationalist aspirations in the struggle for *uhuru* were more on the need for being accepted in the "whiteman's world", than on the need of regaining the true democratic culture of the pre-colonial era. It is this personality of the colonised African which Frantz Fanon has described in *Black Faces White Masks;* and it is to this African that the colonial state handed state power when it granted flag independence to the new states. This African had had no initiation in democratic governance. He lacked a cohesive, indigenously rooted cultural background of self-worth; all he had been exposed to was deculturizing European education and military knowledge. He had not contributed to the creation of the political entity which was being handed over to him to govern. It was these people who collectively constituted a social stratum, which was itself a creation of colonialism, who moved into state houses and constituted governments in the 1960s. This class was expected to oversee the reinstitution of a democratic culture of which it had no concrete experience itself. Its immediate role model was the sheer use of naked power by the state as practised by its European colonial functionaries.

In concrete terms the ascendancy of the new elites to power placed in their hands considerable national resources, control of the legal order and the tools to dispense patronage, and all that pertains to the power of making and unmaking economic fortunes of individuals and entire communities. In the first three years of independence various constitutional changes necessary to consolidate power in the African government were passed by Parliament and at the same time the roots of authoritarian government were sown.

In a real sense the socio-political settlement that paved way to the 1963 Constitution and independence contained the peace terms negotiated during the Lancaster House Conferences of the 1960s, on which the Mau Mau war was settled between Britain as the colonizing power and the representatives of Kenya's colonized people. The fact that the legitimacy of these representatives of the African people was open to serious doubt particularly in Central Kenya where the divide between radicals (or political rebels) and conservatives (the loyalist brigade) was most pronounced is worthy of note in order to understand the political fears and insecurities that motivated the rapid constitutional changes of the 1960s. Political scientist Mutahi Ngunyi observes:

> The African ruling elite that emerged after independence was as a result largely constituted by the "loyalist crowd" as its political core and its most important explanatory feature. According to Ogot (1971), unlike "…the

loyalists in the American revolution who lost their war and their place in American society, the Kenyan loyalists won the military war, lost their argument but still dominate the Kenyan society in several significant aspects" (1971:72). To Kipkorir, the post-independence ruling elite "... was overwhelmingly composed of those who either denounced Mau Mau or were passive to it, or (were) conveniently absent from the country for much of the time..." (1969:378). Demonstrating this assertion with evidence, he notes that of the seven Kikuyus in Kenyatta's cabinet, five were in this category: Kenyatta himself was cold towards the Mau Mau, James Gichuru had signed a pledge of loyalty to the colonial administration, while Charles Njonjo, Njoroge Mungai and Peter Mbiyu Koinange were all conveniently abroad during the entire period of the struggle (Ibid., 378). Kipkorir further distinguishes the core of this elite from their main supporting stratum. This was the so-called "loyalists" who actively collaborated with the colonial regime. The latter generally acquired middle-level education in the colonial period and were then co-opted by the state as provincial administrators. This group of collaborators was later to be "recycled" by the new African regime, grafted into the ruling elite and assigned the job of running the provincial administration in politically sensitive areas like the Rift Valley and the Coast Province.

Thus as early as 1962 Novelist Ngugi wa Thiong'o observed in a paper titled *Kenya: The Two Rifts*[14], that even as Kenya moved towards independence the concept of nationhood was very fragile and characterised by two rifts, one vertical the other horizontal. In his own words:[15]

In Kenya then, there is really no concept of a nation. One is always a Kikuyu, a Luo, a Nandi, an Asian or a European. I think this diminishes our strength and creative power. To live on the level of race or tribe is to be less than whole. In order to live, a chick has to break the shell shutting it out from the light. Man too must break the shell and be free. Political freedom from foreign rule, essential as it is, is not the freedom. One freedom is essential. This is the freedom for man to develop into his full potential. He cannot do this as long as he is enslaved by certain shackles...

In the past, the virtues and energies to be found in different peoples have been used for the political struggle in a society vertically divided into tribal and racial pillars. These good qualities should now be harmonized to work for a national ideal. In the long run, however, tribalism and even racialism will die. Tribalism cannot withstand for long the rising tide of African nationalism and commercial individualism. And so one looks hopefully to a time in the near future when this vertical rift will vanish. There will then be no conflicting pillars in the same society. But Kenya, like many other countries in Africa, is faced with another rift: a horizontal rift dividing the elite from the mass of the people. In a sense this rift in society dividing the upper from the lower is a universal one, not solely confined to the emerging nations of Africa. It divides the rich from the poor, the educated from the uneducated. Disraeli saw this rift in nineteenth-century Britain and wrote about it in his novel *The Two Nations*.

Leadership Report Card of the Neo-Colonial African Elite

Since it became a republic in 1964, Kenya has been ruled by three presidents – Kenyatta ruled until his demise in 1978 and Moi until 2002. The current President Kibaki is serving his fourth year in power at the time of this writing. It is convenient therefore to delve into the discourse of law and leadership in Kenya by analysing the major legal milestones during the reigns of Moi and Kenyatta, who between them have been in power for 40 years out of 43 years that Kenya has been an independent nation.

The Jomo Kenyatta Elite: The Challenges of Nation-Making and Rise of Constitutional Authoritarianism

Throughout the colonial period despotism, massive violation of human rights and institutionalized social inequality were the dominant themes of Kenya's socio political order. However, at independence the British handed down to the African nationalist elites a limited state whose powers were circumscribed by a written constitution and economic dependency on the departing colonial power. Thus, the newly independent states were expected to be managed democratically and their economies would run along capitalistic lines. In Kenya these political expectations were repudiated within the first year of Uhuru but to date the unjust capitalist economic system is yet to be questioned. The explanation is that the capitalist economic system promised definite benefits to the ruling elite but democracy places limits on the authority and discretion of state officials to govern. No wonder the objective of the first assault on democracy in Kenya in post-independence Kenya was to monopolize political power in the hands of KANU. In calling for the establishment of the one party political system in Kenya the late Mzee Jomo Kenyatta said[16]:

> We reject a blueprint of the western model of a two-party system of government because we do not subscribe to the notion of the government and the governed in opposition to one another, one clamouring for duties and the other crying for rights. The westernized model of government has evolved from the traditions of the people of Britain over many hundreds of years ... constructive opposition from within is not an alien thing in so far as the traditional African society is concerned. Did we have to create leaders of opposition, maintain them from public funds and tolerate their insatiable desire for agitation merely because they wanted to oppose for opposition's sake? Certainly not.

Barely four months after Kenyatta made this statement the official opposition party, KADU dissolved itself upon the defection of all its members to KANU. Thus Kenya became a *de facto* one party state before it celebrated its first anniversary as a democratic multiparty state! The significance of this political development was that institutionalized competition for political power and adversarial system of political accountability was effectively weeded out of Kenyan politics before it was really experimented.

It is therefore difficult to disagree with Harry Goulbourne's argument that the "first generation of post-colonial leaders in Africa has failed in one of the most important and far reaching tasks of this era in the history of Africa – development of democratic institutions and modes of conducting public affairs"[17]. The argument that single-party political system accorded with African tradition is hollow when viewed against the fact that similar arguments were not made against the economic system which was equally alien and indeed atrocious to the well-being of the majority. Moreover, the haste with which African elites moved to suppress or eliminate political competition is a pointer to the selfishness of the ruling elite to safeguard their position. Moreover the far-reaching constitutional amendments in the first three years of *Uhuru* in Kenya leave no doubt that the ultimate aim of the ruling elite was to concentrate power in the hands of the President. The cynicism with which this process was accomplished was breathtaking.

As a case in point Kenyatta became President of Kenya courtesy of the first constitution amendment[18] which inter-alia declared Kenya a sovereign Republic and stated that the first President of Kenya was to be "the person who, immediately before December 12th, 1964, holds the office of Prime Minister under the Constitution". Subsequent to his installation as President by the Constitution Kenyatta remained Kenya's President for 14 years without having to defend his position in an election courtesy of political and legal actions against potential competitors.

The fifth constitutional amendment[19] is a case in point. This amendment was passed to stifle the political threat posed by formation of the Kenya People's Union (KPU) by Jaramogi Oginga Odinga and his allies. This amendment – which is embodied in section 40 of the current Constitution – required any MP who had been supported in his election by a political party during his election but later resigned from that party while it was a parliamentary party to vacate his seat in Parliament at the expiration of the period. In two respects this amendment cuts the most draconian of the myriad machiavellian schemes that the law has been deployed in Kenya to promote or secure the political ambitions of the governing class. First the amendment was backdated to cover the resignation of Odinga and his allies and as a result 30 MPs had to seek fresh support from the electorate in by-elections held in June 1966 that are popularly known as the Little General Election.

Secondly the fifth constitutional amendment was tailor-made to check the growing political challenge of KPU. Specifically the amendment consciously excluded the defection of KADU MPs in 1964 a move that turned Kenya into a *de facto* one party state under KANU. Thus to KANU the Constitution was a tool for partisan political wars for supremacy and this contributed a lot to delegitimation of the Constitution as the embodiment of the ground rules for democratic contest for power. A Kenyan legal scholar has commented on this amendment thus:-[20]

> The political motivations of the fifth constitutional amendment were glaringly obvious. The amendment was aimed at promoting one section of the government by removing opposition MPs from office. The opposition pointed out the real politics of the moment when they argued that the amendment was an intimidating measure designed to prevent further resignations that might endanger the Government itself. In the June 1966 Elections, KANU won most of the seats: 8 in the Senate and 12 in the Lower House; KPU won 2 Senate and 7 Lower House seats. The poll was low, but KPU polled most of the votes, thus making it clear that it had controlled Nyanza, and could have a substantial following among the public. The preparation for the Election and the day itself showed the Government's total intolerance of opposition. Administrative harassment was a constant attendant of KPU's efforts at electioneering. Its leaders were refused permits to hold public meetings on 'security grounds'. The Government openly used the administrative machinery to campaign for the KANU candidates. The administration's supervision of the electioneering and the election procedures was anything

but impartial. Both the Government and KANU openly challenged the very
legitimacy of opposition *per se* and portrayed KPU as having betrayed Kenyan
Unity. This line quickly developed into public questioning of KPU's loyalty
to the State.

This illegal deployment of the law in politics took a savage turn in 1969 when KPU,
the only opposition party, was banned and some of its key leaders detained without
trial. Kenya thus once again became a *de facto* one-party state, and the Government
announced its intention to hold a general election towards the end of the year (1969),
though under the Constitution election were not due until 1970. It bears noting in
passing that though in the 1963 general election MPs acquired a five year term of
office they ended up serving more than six years because a constitutional amendment
passed in 1966 to dissolve the Senate[21] – the upper house of Parliament – had
prolonged the life of Parliament by two years ostensibly because it would be unfair
to end it sooner for those former Senators whose terms would not have expired
until 1970. The real reason, however was that this was a bargain struck between the
KANU Government and the Senators for the abolition of their house.

> Much of the democratization discourse in Kenya has taken place at the
> wholesale level, outside the "organic environment" of the majority rural
> Kenyans. It has not paid sufficient attention to the social constraints which
> determine political behavior at the local level. Peasant politics does not pre-
> occupy itself with abstract concepts such as the state, human rights and
> democracy. It revolves around people, their social relations, and tangible
> local benefits.

In Kenya's rural areas, kinship ties, the family, clan and tribe are still powerful political
forces. The late Okot p'Bitek argued that the African "is not born free, he cannot be
free and he is incapable of being free". He is "everywhere in chains" of his family and
blood relations. This social imprisonment extends to Kenya's political and intellectual
elite who unconsciously carry with them an incredible amount of invisible tribal
baggage. They are each locked in their own "ethnic universes" which, in a significant
way, determine their political behaviour. Peasant politics is predominantly local
interests. The peasant universe is limited to the immediate social and geographical
locality. It is difficult to mobilise rural people around broad issues related to the
overall development of society. They have to be mobilised around concrete local
demands such as land, roads, schools and hospitals which have immediate tangible

benefits for them. The peasants have an instrumentalist theory of politics. They have no problem with corruption, nepotism, looting the treasury, undermining national interest singing false praises, and short-changing other ethnic groups, if to do so will bring tangible material benefits to their families and their immediate local community. Thus, Kenyans have no ideological attachment to political parties. They will support politicians, parties and their leaders on the basis of potential satisfaction and protection of their local interests. The inability of political parties to develop an alternative political agenda has left politicians to express local grievances and frustrations in a highly competitive ethnic political market. Political parties provide an inadequate institutional political framework and operate through informal personal networks and inward-looking strategies of their electorate which exacerbate ethnic machinations and conflict.

The banning of KPU took place barely a year after the assassination of the influential Minister for Planning Tom Mboya, who like Odinga, was a prominent politician from the Luo community. Indeed in many ways the political fall-out occasioned by Mboya's assassination in July 1969 set the stage for the vicious power struggles that culminated in the proscription of KPU on 30th October, 1969. A month later, President Kenyatta dissolved Parliament and the stage was set for the first post uhuru general election. The significance of these series of rapid events was three-fold. First, in banning KPU Kenya joined the ignominious club of single party states for which competition for power was anathema. Put differently, Kenya discarded multipartyism before holding its first general election in the post-independence era. Secondly, KANU was thereby saved from burden of gauging its popularity but that would not dissuade Speaker, then KANU MP, Francis ole Kaparo[22] - about three decades later (1988) – from making the grandiloquent claim that the "most important development of our time is the mass party which is to be found in both one-party and multi-party states."[23]

Finally, the events leading to the proscription of KPU left a permanent mark in the evolution of ethnicity as a dominant feature of Kenyan politics. At independence the ethnic factor took the dimension of big versus small tribes and the adoption of the majimbo constitution at independence is a lasting testament of that struggle. The Gikuyu and the Luo – the two most numerous communities supported KANU whilst the rest largely supported KADU. However after KADU MPs defected to KANU and subsequently KADU dissolved itself, the battle for political supremacy pitted the Luo and Kikuyu politicians. By accident or design the bulk of constitutional amendments upto 1969 were either aimed at stifling Luo political power or resulted in strengthening the position of Kenyatta (read the Kikuyu) vis-à-vis Odinga and Mboya (read the Luo). Thus by the close of 1969 the Constitution had also become the most potent weapon in inter-communal or ethnicised struggle for political power in Kenya. After the 1969 general election KANU's political dominance was so gripping that in most of the 1970s the Kenyatta court steadily turned into a parochial affair of a close coterie of politicians mainly from Kiambu District. And the caution of Franz Fanon – issued in 1961 – turned prophetic for Kenya:[24]

> This party which of its own will proclaims that it is a national party, and which claims to speak in the name of the totality of the people, secretly, sometimes even openly organizes an authentic ethnical dictatorship. We no longer see the rise of a bourgeois dictatorship, but a tribal dictatorship. The ministers, the members of the cabinet, the ambassadors and local commissioners are chosen from the same ethnological group as the leader, sometimes directly from his own family. Such regimes of the family sort seem to go back to the old laws of inbreeding, and not anger but shame is felt when we are faced with such stupidity, such an imposture, such intellectual and spiritual poverty. These heads of the government are the true traitors in Africa, for they sell their country to the most terrifying of all its enemies: stupidity. This tribalizing of the central authority, it is certain, encourages regionalist ideas and separatism. All the decentralizing tendencies spring up again and triumph, and the nation falls to pieces, broken in bits. The leader, who once used to call for 'African unity' and who thought of his own little family wakes up one day to find himself saddled with five tribes, who also want to have their own ambassadors and ministers; and irresponsible as ever, still unaware and still despicable, he denounces their 'treason'.

The prospect of losing power is one of the most critical moderators of political behaviour in a functioning democracy which Kenya had ceased to be after the banning of KPU at the end of October, 1969. Stripped of the fear of losing power, Kenyatta's courtiers literally took a tumble into the sea of political stupidity and parochialism that Fanon had so poignantly pointed in his epochal book. A governing elite does not quite deserve the label of dictatorship unless and until it closes all the legitimate channels for its competitors to oust it from power. This is achieved either through manipulation of the electoral system and the physical elimination of real and potential political opponents. Put differently, political dictatorship represents that phase of a country's history when the privilege of rulership and the right to choose the rulers vests in the rulers themselves. The assassination of Mboya and the proscription of

KPU could be viewed as the earliest manifestation of this phenomenon but it was in the 1970s that all illusions about democracy in Kenya were finally shattered though the leadership occasionally indulged in populist stunts that projected a false veneer of a people's government.

In 1974 a populist move was made to change section 53 of the Constitution and make Kiswahili the language of the National Assembly[25] supposedly because certain MPs had difficulty expressing themselves in the English language. Indeed as soon as President Kenyatta issued that decree debates were immediately conducted in Kiswahili pending the formal amendment of the Constitution. Unfortunately this populist stunt backfired as it created such a farce in parliamentary debates, that by 1975, another amendment was effected to make Kiswahili and English the official languages of Parliament[26].

In March, 1975, J. M. Kariuki, a former freedom fighter and MP for Nyandarua North, who after 1969 spearheaded critical opposition in Parliament and within KANU, was brutally murdered by State security officers, according to the findings of a subsequent Parliamentary Select Committee of Inquiry. The assassination of J.M. Kariuki took place at a time when the question of Kenyatta succession had became urgent given the advanced age of Mzee Kenyatta and the fear of contenders that the populist MP would be hard to beat in a presidential contest occasioned by Kenyatta's imminent demise. Thus J. M.'s death was directly connected to political succession and its apparent objective was to keep power within the safe hands of Kenyatta's hand picked clique of courtiers.

In December 1975 Parliament passed yet another significant constitutional amendment that underscores our contention about the tendency of dictatorship to engage in the systematic subversion of the electoral system and specifically the sovereign power of the people to freely elect holders of political offices. By this amendment[27] Parliament extended the presidential prerogative of mercy to include election offences. The necessity for this amendment was clearly to enable President Kenyatta to pardon Ngei who had been found guilty by Court of having committed an election offence. This amendment is popularly known as the Ngei amendment in respect of which Prof. Kimani Njogu observes:[28]

> This amendment was enacted in order to solve a special problem involving Paul Ngei, a Minister in the government of Jomo Kenyatta. Ngei had been found guilty of an election offence and Kenyatta wanted to extend the Presidential prerogative of mercy to his friend, with whom he had been

detained by the colonial government. The amendment was made in record time and Ngei was forgiven under it of his election malpractice and consequently reelected in a by-election.

Thus by the end of 1975 Kenyatta was virtually a Republican Monarch. He was above Parliament and even the Constitution itself. Though in theory Kenyatta derived his power from the Constitution, in reality he was its master – indeed its ultimate grundnorm – because the Constitution could be changed at his will to give him whatever power he deemed expedient. Hence a country that had started off in 1963 as a promising liberal democracy had within a decade transformed into an elective dictatorship. At the peak of this elective dictatorship in the mid – 1970s, the powers of the government revolved exclusively around Kenyatta as Colin Leys graphically captures the scenario:[29]

> Kenyatta's court was based primarily at his country home at Gatundu about 25 miles from Nairobi in Kiambu District; but like the courts of old it moved with him, to State House in Nairobi, to his coastal lodge near Mombasa, and his lodge at Nakuru in Rift Valley. This corresponded to his actual roles of Kikuyu paramount chief and national leader of the comprador alliance. To the court came delegations of all kinds; district, regional, tribal and also factional. Most of them came from particular districts often in huge numbers, accompanied by teams of traditional dancers and choirs of school children, organized and led by the MPs and local councillors and provincial and district officers from the area. They gave displays of dancing and singing; the leaders presented cheques for various causes sponsored by the president and expressed their sentiments of loyalty and respect; and would finally outline various needs and grievances. In return, the president would thank them, commend the dancers and songs, exhort them to unity and hard work and discuss their requests, explaining why some could not be met and undertaking to attend to others.

The massive concentration of power around Kenyatta bred arrogance and complacency among the Kiambu elite that it seemingly overlooked the fact that excepting Kenyatta's deleterious impact upon the political system, Kenyatta had not completely repudiated democracy and constitutionalism. The Constitution still envisaged that in the event of Kenyatta's demise elections would have to be held to determine his successor. Therefore any would-be pretender or successor to Kenyatta's throne needed to cultivate public goodwill but none of the Kiambu political mafia –

as they were derogatorily referred by critics – had time for that. To his credit, then Vice President Moi understood this and so when Kenyatta died in 1978 he was the candidate to beat. Indeed, within two months of Kenyatta's demise he became Kenya's second president without breaking a real sweat!

The Moi Era – The Rise and Fall of Political Terrorism in Kenya

Typical of a leader who "inherits" political office, Moi ascended to power without an independent power base though the political networks he had carefully cultivated in the late 1970s constituted a considerable counterweight to the dominant Kenyatta elite that still controlled key levers of state power. Indeed, Moi's biographer Andrew Morton notes that "in the early days as President he was dismissed by the ruling Kikuyu elite as "the passing cloud", a man unfitted to the highest office"[30]. Sooner than later Moi would prove that he was equal to the challenges foisted upon him by the protracted and complex politics that surrounded the Kenyatta succession.

Populism was Moi's first recourse in his deft schemes to upstage the remnants of Kenyatta's power men still in Cabinet and other important public offices. Whilst Jomo Kenyatta usually addressed Kenyans through the radio, Moi preferred direct contact with the people. The new President was literally everywhere and he was so notorious in making important policy pronouncements at public rallies and by the roadsides that his successor Mwai Kibaki declared in his inauguration speech that the era of "anything goes" is gone forever: "Government will no longer be run on the whims of individuals. The era of roadside policy declarations is gone"[31]. Andrew Morton comments on this unusual public visibility as follows:[32]

> In his presidential progress he would regularly swap his official Mercedes limousine for an old Volkswagen Kombi so that he could reach the more inhospitable regions of Kenya. He travelled from sunrise to sunset, spending nights under canvas, washing from a small basin and eating under the shade of a tree. In the first year of his presidency he visited more places and received more people than had Kenyatta during his fifteen years as President.

At the height of the Kenyatta succession attempts to hold KANU national elections had been thwarted after it emerged that the group that was campaigning for constitutional change to block a serving vice-president from assuming presidential office upon death or resignation of the president were bound to lose. Thus KANU had been significantly neglected since mid 1960s and so upon Kenyatta's demise, Moi saw in it a political vehicle that he could easily take over to build an independent base for himself. Thus at the KANU conference in October 1979, "the election of Mwai Kibaki as KANU Vice-President together with a slate of candidates virtually hand-picked by Moi to represent the eight provinces of Kenya, was the first move in establishing a loyal power base, independent of Parliament and the executive."[33]

At this stage it bears noting that hitherto constitutional and legal changes in Kenya tended to occur in the prelude or aftermath of elections. This indeed was the case in 1966 and 1974. The Moi era soon proved to be no exception and, just like during his predecessor's era, the one significant constitutional amendment in 1979 was passed with the general election in mind. This amendment[34] added a new subsection (6) to section 35 of the Constitution which relates to disqualification for election to the National assembly. The subsection provided that the Minister for the time being responsible for elections to the National Assembly may, by order published in the *Kenya Gazette*, provide that a person shall not be qualified to be elected by virtue of holding any office specified in paragraph (f) of subsection (1), or specified for the purposes of that paragraph under subsection (5), which is prescribed in the order, which date shall not be more than six months prior to the date of nomination for the preliminary elections prescribed under an Act of Parliament. Andrew Morton explains the motive and impact of these changes thus:[35]

> It was the parliamentary elections of November 1979 that truly marked Moi's emergence as a national leader in his own right, a President making a conscious effort to stamp his own style on government. In spite of his immense popularity – candidates vied with one another in voicing their loyalty to the Nyayo philosophy – Moi was uncertain that the complexion of Parliament would reflect his aims. Before the elections he used his countrywide tours to endorse favoured candidates, donating huge sums to their *harambees*. These gatherings thus proved an effective method of demonstrating to the *wananchi* that their local MP was able to deliver economic benefits to their communities. At the same time the ruling party's decision in the run-up to the election to ban Odinga and other former KPU politicians from standing for election on obscure technical grounds indicated that here was a populist president not entirely confident of his political support.

The significance of the 1979 general election was two-fold. First, almost half of incumbent MPs, as had been the case in the previous two elections, lost their seats, including Mbiyu Koinange, Jackson Angaine and Kihika Kimani, all prominent members of the change the Constitution group. Thus the electoral result gave Moi enormous room for political manouvre. Secondly, the results of the elections enabled Moi to consolidate his power. Thus Moi "appointed his former private secretary Nicholas Biwott and G. G. Kariuki, who had masterminded the recent KANU elections as Ministers of State while his political mentor Moses Mudavadi, who entered Parliament in 1976, became an education minister, with two of his most stalwart supporters, Shariff Nassir and Stanley Oloitiptip, being appointed to front bench posts."[36] Thus at the opening of the epochal 1980s Moi had achieved considerable control of the party, and the Executive Parliament though all the three levers of power comprised several Kenyatta-era political supremos and Moi's own mentor Attorney General Charles Njonjo remained an influential factor in politics especially given his control of State Law Office and leverage over the Judiciary.

In early 1980s Njonjo was "convinced" to resign as Attorney General and stand for Parliament at a by-election in Kikuyu having agreed with Moi that a post of Minister of Home and Constitutional Affairs would be created for him once he was elected. Njonjo was indeed elected and appointed to the Cabinet but the real victor was Moi because now he had a freehand to "take over and deploy the justice system to achieve his political objectives. Interestingly, Njonjo was one of the earliest victims, though indirectly, of the Nyayo Judiciary in the post Njonjo (1980) era. Thus in 1980 an unsuccessful legal attempt to oust Njonjo by discrediting him through the *Muthemba* treason case[37] was made. Muthemba was acquitted and though Njonjo survived the politically motivated trial of his first cousin the die had been cast against him.

In 1982 the attempt by Jaramogi Oginga Odinga and George Anyona to form a socialist-oriented political party led KANU and the government to use Parliament to enact a constitutional amendment, as well as an amendment in the election laws, to declare Kenya a *de jure* one party state[38]. By this constitutional amendment a new Section 2A was introduced to provide that. "There shall be in Kenya only one political party, the Kenya African National Union".

When Kenya was a *de facto* one party state the President had great but not absolute control over Parliament because the tenure of MPs was not legally dependent on being a member of KANU. However, upon Kenya becoming a *de jure* one-party state the tenure of MPs was first and foremost dependent on continuance of membership of KANU and this in turn was a matter of discretion of the President and party leadership.

As early as 1976 when Kenya was still a *de facto* one party state, Professor J. B. Ojwang – now a High Court judge – observed that "by virtue of certain constitutional norms, the National Executive, which is also the party executive is so placed as to demand and rely on receiving the loyalty of Parliament." Upon Kenya turning into a *de jure* one party state, loyalty to KANU was a condition precedent to a parliamentary career and so Parliament – through its members –was legally obligated to be loyal to KANU and so for all practical purposes Parliament was subordinate to KANU. As Prof. Shadrack Gutto puts it:[39]

> Also following the unconstitutional banning of KPU in 1969, KANU became increasingly terroristic and authoritarian. It started using "clearance" of all those wishing to contest any elections, civic and parliamentary, as a method for screening and excluding, not only former KPU members and sympathizers from participation in elections, but also its own members and even officials … sometimes those holding party 'life-membership cards' … who are viewed to be critical of the growing fascism of the state and party. elections in Kenya increasingly became farcical… a process of allowing specially KANU appointed cronies to challenge each other for leadership seats. KANU also started asserting, contrary to the constitutional structure of the country, that it is "above" parliament and government. This became particularly dangerous in the 1987-88 period, when the party machinery demanded that even remarks made by members of Parliament *in Parliament* could be censured by the Party. The Party, which was suffocating parliamentary freedom in the 1970s, had by the 1980s, strangled parliamentary sovereignty. Thus, we see a process where the Party in power "overthrows" its own Parliament by making it less than a rubber-stamp while retaining it for public relations exercises.

Kenya became a one-party state on 17th June, 1982 upon publication of President Moi's assent. Barely two months later some officers of the Kenya Air Force unsuccessfully staged a *coup d'etat* on 1st August, 1982. This coup attempt was a turning point in Kenyan politics because it set the stage for large scale purge of public officials on account of loyalty and ethnicity. Veteran politician G. G. Kariuki, one of the most powerful cabinet ministers in the Nyayo era observes in his autobiography[40] that although Major General P.M. Kariuki, the then commander of the Kenya Air Force was not involved in the coup, he was nevertheless court-martialled and jailed for four years on 18th January, 1983. The same fate befell Ben Gethi, the Commissioner of Police, who was detained despite the fact that he had worked hard to suppress the coup. Kariuki concludes:[41]

In addition, scores of people were arrested and detained. The soldiers among them were tried in courts martial and at least nine of them were hanged. Among those hanged were the two key coup leaders: Senr. 10 privates Ezekiah Ochuka and Pancras Oteyo Okumu. Little did we know, however, that the aftermath of the attempted coup would be used against the Gikuyu community in politics as well as in public service, although no one in the community was either crucially involved or implicated. The inclusion of Major General P. M. Kariuki and Police Commissioner Ben Gethi appeared to have been a political move with the intention of giving the coup a national outlook.

The aftermath of the August 1982 coup attempt witnessed the systematic intimidation of lawyers who took up cases to defend progressive politicians, scholars and government critics or to represent them in civil cases. As example veteran lawyer Dr. John Khaminwa was detained in 1982 for having been counsel for George Anyona and Jaramogi Oginga Odinga.[42] Indeed in October 1982 David Fredrick Onyango Oloo, a Nairobi University student charged with sedition said the two lawyers who had withdrawn from his case had violated natural justice. A newspaper report by Edward Rihnaa captures the incident graphically:[43]

> David Fredrick Onyango Oloo has denied writing, publishing and possessing a seditious publication, *A Plea to Comrades*. On Monday, defence lawyer R. O. Kwach withdrew from the case saying he was surprised that Oloo had pleaded "not guilty". On October 15, Mr. C. P. Onono had withdrawn from the case. Oloo also blamed the prosecution of using the lawyers, a police officer and other people to convince him to plead "guilty" to a lesser charge of sedition. Oloo, now unrepresented, made the claim during the hearing of his case before senior resident magistrate, Joyce Aluoch. Oloo, a social science student, said in an unsworn statement that he did not see why the prosecution should take a short-cut by inducing him to plead guilty. "Apart from pleading guilty to the charges, I have been threatened that if I don't plead guilty, I will be sentenced to a maximum jail term,' Oloo said, adding he wanted his case to be heard and that he be given a fair trial.

The political witch-hunting triggered by the 1982 coup reached a crescendo in April 1983 when several ministers issued statements accusing one of their unnamed colleagues of wishing that the Government would fail. After nearly a month of political manoeuvring, on May 8, 1983, President Moi threw the nation into total confusion when he announced that some foreign countries were grooming a certain person they wanted as President. The hitherto unnamed minister was Charles Njonjo who was then in Britain. The following day, the British High Commission to Kenya issued a statement denying that Britain was grooming someone to take over Kenya's leadership. For Njonjo the end had come. He subsequently resigned as Cabinet Minister and MP for Kikuyu. A Commission of Inquiry was appointed to inquire into his conduct. It reported in 1983 that indeed Njonjo had engaged in treasonous conduct but Moi pardoned him immediately thereafter. Save for Vice President Mwai Kibaki, Moi had finally wriggled himself from the political orbit of Kenyatta. A premature general election was held in 1983 that was used to weed out all the unwanted politicians. G. G. Kariuki recalls the hilarious *modus operandu* of KANU in expelling "disloyal" MPs of which he himself was a victim for obstructing their political careers:[44]

> My persecution was not yet over. On September 11, 1984, I attended a KANU National Executive Committee meeting in the Old Chambers (Uhuru Chambers) at Parliament Buildings under the chairmanship of Moi as the party president. In that meeting, the issue of discipline came up. It was decided that Said Hemed should not be allowed to contest the by-election in his former constituency, where the post MP had fallen vacant as a result of a petition. The reason for this decision was that he had been mentioned in the Njonjo Commission and had not defended himself. The resolution was passed without voting, which, at least in theory, meant that every committee member agreed with the verdict. Before the discussion of Hemed came to an end, I stood up with the permission of the chairman to seek clarification of his case. I particularly wondered what machinery the committee had in place with which to scrutinise the genuineness of Hemed's denial, assuming he had chosen to deny. Everyone in the meeting knew that I also had been mentioned in the Njonjo inquiry and had not bothered to comment since the allegations were based on hearsay. As I faced a similar predicament, it was important for me to know how such cases would be treated within KANU.

G. G. Kariuki did not have to wait for long for three days later he, too, was expelled from KANU. What is amazing about these expulsions and political persecution is the submissive and resignatory attitude with which victims accepted their fate and even hoped worse calamities would not befall them. Thus on September 19, 1984 G. G. Kariuki wrote a letter to President Moi pleading as follows:[45]

Following the recent decision by the KANU Governing Council to expel me from the active involvement and membership of the ruling party, KANU, I am writing to convey my compliance with that verdict without reservation. In mitigation, my family and I take it that Your Excellency's fatherly nature has acceded to our continued engagement in other spheres of life, especially farming, business and travel. We believe at some time you will, with God's guided wisdom, consider my readmission into the party and full participation in the development of this beloved country. Lastly, may I assure you of our sincere loyalty to you personally.

Thus by the end of 1984 Moi was governing the country through a combination of legal control, political witch-hunting and fear. Thus after the 1982 constitutional amendment declaring Kenya a single party state, Moi was constitutionally freed of legal restraints to achieve his political goals. Between 1982 and 1992 these constitutional powers at Moi's disposal were deployed with a viciousness that continues to shock Kenyans to date. It was during this period that torture became routine in police cells and *Mwakenya* political trials were enacted. In July 1987 a report[46] of Amnesty International decried the serious attack of human rights in Kenya in which the government appeared to have adopted a deliberate program to silence or intimidate its political opponents. The report added:[47]

Human rights have come under serious attack in Kenya in the past year as the government appears to have adopted a deliberate program to silence or intimidate its political opponents. Prisoners of conscience have been tortured and detained indefinitely by administrative order. Other political prisoners have been secretly and illegally detained, tortured into making false confessions and then jailed for years after unfair trials. Most victims of human rights abuse have been arrested on suspicion of having links with a clandestine opposition group but many appear to have done no more than criticise the way the country is run. At least two political prisoners have died in custody. The body of one was found to be bruised, wounded and emaciated with skin blistering and peeling off – just 21 days after he had been seized by Kenya Special Branch officers. Similar effects have been reported after the "swimming pool" torture used by the special Branch, in which prisoners have been held naked for long periods in waterlogged underground cells, in some cases until their feet began to rot. Other tortures have included starvation and brutal beatings with truncheons, chair legs and lengths of rubber hose.

Complaints about torture and prolonged "disappearance" of prisoners during interrogation have been ignored or dismissed by the courts.

The *Mwakenya* political trials were preceded by a far-reaching constitutional amendment[48] in 1986 that inter-alia removed security of tenure from the holders of the offices of the Attorney General and the Controller and Auditor-General. By 1988 numerous appeals from the *Mwakenya* trials had reacted to the High Court and Court of Appeal and some convictions had been reversed. The Government reached by instigating a further amendment to the Constitution in which the security of tenure of the Judges and the Public Service Commission was removed[49]. This amendment also empowered the Police to hold suspects of capital offences for as long as 14 days thereby eroding the constitutional safeguard to personal liberty and presumption of innocence besides creating further loopholes for repressive conduct by security forces.

Equally worrying is the procedural short-cuts deployed in passing this constitutional amendment of far-reaching consequences. Before the Bill was moved in Parliament, the then Minister for Health Mwai Kibaki, moved a procedural motion requesting that the requirement for its notice of publication be reduced from the usual fourteen days to five days. The then Attorney General Justice Guy Muli introduced it at 3.00 p.m. and by 6.00 p.m. it had gone through its third reading without even token opposition! Even the *Weekly Review* – a fairly conservative weekly newspaper – was appalled by the cavalier manner Parliament passed this earth-shaking amendment:[50]

> Whatever the government's reasons and objects in proposing the constitutional amendments and rushing them through Parliament, the amendments raise some disturbing questions about the government's and parliament's perception of the sanctity of the Constitution and the guarantees pertaining to freedom and independence of the judiciary as well as the rights of freedoms of the individual enshrined in it. Even more disturbing in the long-term, are questions likely to arise regarding the role of the country's Parliament, both as supreme guardian of the Constitution and as an estate of government separate and independent from the executive. Kenyans will have to examine these issues more closely after the dust and mistrust raised by the manner in which the whole affair has been handled has settled.

Why was Parliament so quick to pass this amendment that was almost universally viewed as outrageous by most Kenyans. Part of the answer lies in the fact that this was the first and the last retrogressive constitutional amendment that the sycophantic Fifth Parliament which had been elected through the queue-voting system or *mlolongo* voting. By this amendment the *mlolongo* Parliament completed the transformation of Kenya from a liberal parliamentary democracy to an autocratic one-party state. As author P. O. Agweli Onalo concludes:[51]

> By 1988, the amendments had rendered the doctrine of the separation of powers meaningless, unfunctional and merely theoretical. The amendments to the Constitution made from 1964 to 1988, taken as a whole, successfully produced a repressive and autocratic system of government firmly backed by rigid one-party structures. This period was characterised by a tough crackdown on dissenters, through the use of repressive criminal laws, especially sedition and detention without trial. Security of tenure for judges, the Attorney-General, the Controller and Auditor-General and officers of he Public Service Commission had been removed, leaving no credible checks on the Executive.

The *mlolongo* voting system deserves some commentary because it effectively overthrew the fundamental norms of the democratic electoral systems without any formal amendment of he Constitution text. Briefly, the queue voting system which replaced the secret ballot method in the 1988 general Elections, was outrightly primitive and intimidatory method in which voters lined up behind candidates. Koigi wa Wamwere postulates why this method was favoured by the *Nyayoists*:[52]

> Unchallenged in his rigging of elections before 1988, Moi became bolder and bolder and no longer saw why he should not adopt the easiest and the surest method of selecting his cronies into Parliament and local councils. That method was queuing. Because queuing is done under the full glare of the police, government and party officers, no returning officer, always a government employee, would dare fail to carry out instructions by his political bosses to rig elections. Because results of queuing elections cannot be petitioned against in a court of law due to party rules, rigging under queuing is safest since it cannot be used later to embarrass the government in courts of law.

Despite intense opposition to *mlolongo* system by Kenyans, KANU stuck to its guns and the consequence was massive rigging of the 1988 General Elections results. The NCCK magazine **Beyond** was proscribed in March 1988 when it published a special issue on the *mlolongo* elections in which it concluded in its editorial that "It must be concluded that elections by queuing were not fair. Consequently democracy in Kenya has slipped a step downward, putting the country on the path of self-destruction which many African countries have followed…"[53]

Unperturbed by the controversy generated by the *mlolongo,* KANU announced that its party elections would also be held by the same method. Political logic was finally stood on its head. Even the dovish Mwai Kibaki, until then the party's Vice-President was subjected to primitive rigging schemes that he uncharacteristically commented that rigging was no longer done with intelligence:[54]

> Rigging has some intelligence. This scheme (rigging by queuing) is by people who have no sense of intelligence. It is not rigging but direct robbery.

In constitutional terms the *mlolongo* system deprived many people the right to vote either because they could not openly take sides or for fear of victimisation after elections by powerful winners and losers who can easily identify those who opposed them in queues. In the result the absolute majority of voters did not turn up for both the General Elections and the KANU elections thereby leading to minority government. The credibility of *Nyayoism* reached its lowest ebb in 1988 and it never recovered its legitimacy. What is even chilling about *mlolongo* is that in many respects it was the first step in a twisted scheme to abolish elections in Kenya. In an interview with the *Weekly Review* magazine held after the 1988 General Election Shariff Nassir, then assistant Minister for National Guidance and Political Affairs and close confidante of President Moi, intimated that after getting rid of the secret ballot, the next "nuisance" to go would be the façade of queuing itself. Excerpts of the interview bear this observation:[55]

> **When saying that the secret ballot will be scrapped, you also said that Kenyans have no time to waste on all these elections because they want to concentrate on development?**
>
> The problem is that first we go through queuing, then the secret ballot and then others go to court. So much time is wasted in elections when people should be engaging in development.
>
> **Going by that argument, would you like to see a situation where there were no elections at all, so that people could concentrate on developments?**

Of course, when people have good leaders, they don't want to go for elections. That is why people are elected unopposed in various places because the people there do not want trouble. They want development.

Thus within a space of nine months in 1988 the *Nyayoists* succeeded in exposing their devious political schemes. All sectors of the society were alarmed and despite increasing crackdown on dissent more and more people began to speak against the imminent rise of totalitarianism in Kenya. Deep mistrust of government set in and its legitimacy was badly eroded. Professor B. A. Ogot captures the public mood then as follows:[56]

Unfortunately, the dust and mistrust never settled. Instead, more dust and mistrust, which had been generated by the 1988 party and general elections, which were characterized by an unprecedented wave of rigging and other malpractices, spread to the whole country. The image of the government, the party and Parliament was marred, the trust in those institutions eroded and their legitimacy challenged. A strong civil society with a public voice was beginning to develop outside the state.

The fall of the Berlin Wall in 1989 and the dramatic collapse of the one-party communist regimes gave vital impetus to pro-democracy movements in Africa. In Kenya, these external developments coupled with economic decline and appalling human rights record triggered massive discontent with KANU thereby forcing it to take a defensive mode. KANU's season of reckoning had finally arrived. On New Year's 1990, Rev. Timothy Njoya proclaimed that Kenya was ripe for a multiparty system, arguing that events in Eastern Europe would inevitably occur in Kenya. This proclamation raised a lot of hue and cry among the KANU circles but it was welcome by ordinary citizens, radical politicians and lawyers. No sooner had the dust of Dr. Njoya's sermon settled than the Rev. Dr. Henry Okullu produced a programme for radical change in demanding, inter alia, the scrapping of section 2A of the Constitution which had made Kenya a single-party state, the dissolution of the Sixth Parliament, which he regarded as illegitimate, the limitation of presidential tenure to two terms of five year each, and the convening of a national convention to chart out Kenya's political future.[57]

By mid 1990 it was clear even to KANU itself that its preferred political system had become too discredited to survive the calls for reforms and so on 21st June, 1990 the KANU Review Committee was appointed under the chairmanship of Prof. George Saitoti, the Vice-President of the party, to look into three areas namely the party's nomination rules, the election rules and the KANU code of discipline. Those who appeared before the Review Committee demanded the abolition of the queue-voting system; dissolution of Parliament, removal of Section 2A of the Constitution to allow multipartyism, limitation of presidential tenure, restoration of the security of tenure of he Attorney-General, Judges, Controller and Auditor-General and Public Service Commissioners, immediate abolition of detention without trial, immediate release of all political detainees, and strict observance of human rights.

President Moi called a special KANU Delegates Conference on 4th December 1990 to discuss the 170-page Saitoti Report. The Conference adopted the report with only a few amendments but it shelved all the key recommendations for political reforms made by the people. However, during the Conference President Moi instructed the Attorney-General, Justice Mathew Guy Muli, to introduce a bill restoring the security of tenure for the Judges, the Attorney General and other public officers. These proposals themselves amounted to too little too late and so they ignited the clamour for even more changes particularly for the repeal of section 2A. In February, 1991, Oginga Odinga called a press conference at Nairobi's Press Centre at Chester House to launch a new political party, the National Democratic Party (NDP). He reminded the media that in his New Year Message to the people of Kenya, he had said that the year 1991 would be the year for the repeal of Section 2A in order to establish multiparty democracy in Kenya. On the same day Odinga released the NDP's Manifesto, whose preamble read:[58]

> A crisis has engulfed Africa. It is a crisis of governance. Everywhere established governments are being challenged from below to listen to the voices of the people. Everywhere they are being challenged to deliver the fruits of independence and to ensure development. Where military dictatorships have held sway for decades, the masses have risen up to overthrow them, and to demand representative government. Where one-party authoritarian regimes have survived on bankrupt ideologies, the multi-party democracy has demanded democracy. The one-party regime has been thoroughly discredited and only rearguard politicians with no new ideas to offer, and only their ill-gotten wealth to protect, can continue to defend the one-party system of misgovernment.

The NDP turned to be a still born because the Registrar of Societies refused to register it and a case challenging the said refusal was summarily dismissed by the High Court as unconstitutional in July, 1991. However by now the die had been cast against section 2A of the Constitution. In August, 1991 a pressure group known as the Forum for the Restoration of Democracy (FORD) was formed whose stated objective was to fight for the restoration of democracy and human rights in Kenya. On 16th November, 1991, the leaders of FORD attempted unsuccessfully to organize a pro-democracy rally in Nairobi in defiance of a government ban. Later that month the Donors Consultative Group deferred consideration of Kenya's request for financial assistance for the next six months pending the introduction of political and economic reforms.

On 3rd December, 1991, barely a week after the donors' decision to defer financial assistance KANU called a National Delegates Meeting at Kasarani Sports Centre in Nairobi. The 3600 delegates were informed that they were to make a choice between retaining KANU as the sole party or permitting the formation of more parties. By then the KANU Governing Council (NGC) had already recommended that KANU should ask Parliament to repeal Section 2A of the country's Constitution. The KANU hardliners used the same old argument that the country would be torn apart by ethnic animosities if pluralism were introduced. Kalonzo Musyoka, organizing secretary and one of the hardliners of the party characterized the big decision as follows: "The choice is between KANU and violence. It is for you to decide."[59]

Given the aforementioned recommendation of the party's NGC, President Moi was in favour of repealing Section 2A, which he did begrudgingly, as attested by his grumbling that the time had come to "choose between the good eggs and the bad eggs by putting them in the water."[60] Subsequently, on 10th December 1991, Parliament passed the constitutional amendment repealing Section 2A, thereby effectively ending KANU's legal monopoly of political power.[61] Thus the repeal of Section 2A resulted from the combined pressure from within and without calling for democratic return and economic liberalization. At this stage we need to note five lessons from KANU's decade of legal monopoly of political power.

First the extent of KANU's authoritarian control of the political life in Kenya during this dark decade is borne by the fact that constitutional changes were effected to serve its self interest of consolidating and retaining political power. The constitutional amendments of 1990 and 1991, in particular, makes this contention abundantly clear. Dr. Karuti Kanyinga has explained why this control of the country's political processes was inevitable:[62]

> Moi reinvigorated KANU, giving it administrative and political powers matching those of Provincial Administration. This development resulted in a

blurred line of distinction between the party and the government. Party officials became increasingly powerful to a point where some could give instructions to Provincial Administration officials and, as were other organs of the government. The party established a party disciplinary committee designed along communist party models. The committee membership comprised some of the powerful cabinet ministers also known to be close to the President. The party disciplinary committee slowly assumed enormous powers. It could discipline MPs and cabinet ministers for what they said in parliament notwithstanding the parliamentary immunity they enjoyed.

Secondly, contrary to the hopes of many the repeal of section 2A did not lead to the transition from an essentially authoritarian regime to a basically democratic one. In Kenya, besides the reintroduction of multipartyism and the formation of new political parties nothing else really changed. The main leaders of these parties had been socialized politically on KANU's ranks and files, not to mention the fact that the repeal of section 2A did not in itself create a new constitutional order. All the demands made by the new opposition political parties such as immediate convocation of a National Constitutional Conference, the dissolution of Parliament, the resignation of President Moi and his government and the establishment of an interim Government of National Unity were not met. Instead, the parties rushed to an election within the framework of a one-party constitutional framework. Thus the 1991 multiparty transition failed to solve the problem of democratization and transformation of society but only succeeded in restoring the single party constitutional structures under a façade of *multipartyism.*

Thirdly, the 1991 multiparty transition did not remove the single major obstacle to democratization in Kenya namely the phenomenon of *presidentialism* which Dr. Smokin Wanjala has described as "a feature of African leadership that combines absolute power which African traditional rulers exercised over primitive society and the modern executive authority derived from deficient Lancaster House type constitutions. This combination has produced many an African president whose preoccupation has been to destroy democracy in its evolutionary stages... It is such presidents who instead of using their immense authority to further the development of democratic sentiments, practises and institutions throw their weight behind the construction of all sorts of oppressive systems and use their authority to justify the forms of repression engendered by those systems. The African presidency is an executive monarchy whose very features are undemocratic."[63]

Fourthly notwithstanding the repeal of Section 2A of the Constitution, the legacy of the one party system persisted both in terms of the legal infrastructure and political ethos. Thus democratic change has not served a deeper purpose such as fair distribution of crucial resources of power and authority. As Kenyan Constitutional Lawyers Prof. Kivutha Kibwana and Wachira Maina observe, the ruling elite have reacted to demands for change by adopting the forms rather than the substance of democracy. In their words:[64] ... the ruling party in Kenya has satisfied the formal criteria of democracy but that is itself not transformative if it does not embrace the ethical and substantive justifications that make democracy worth pursuing. This commitment to the democratic process as a form of distributive justice is yet to occur... notwithstanding democratic change people are still powerless to control government. The weight of public opinion is negligible. This leaves the government legally limited but structurally, omnicompetent. The result is that the ruling party monopolizes the distribution of crucial national resources. This in turn has only served to strengthen patron-client linkages that existed in the one-party era. Crucially, it has undermined the institutional effectiveness of the opposition as a countervailing power against government excess, first because the opposition is generally broke and second because *inter se* the opposition has also built its own patron-client networks."

Fifthly, the multipartyism transition has shown that constitutional and statutory change alone cannot lead to democratization especially when such changes do affect the socio-economic and political foundations of single party authoritarianism. For example, the 1988 constitutional amendment act that took away security of tenure for judges among others also empowered the police to detain suspects of capital offences for upto 14 days. This power can and has been previously used to detain suspects of sedition and public order offences for longer than 24 hours because the police can always pretend that the suspect was detained on account of a capital offence. In 1990 a constitutional amendment restored the security of tenure for Judges, but left intact these drastic powers of the police that the Moi regime in subsequent years often deployed to frustrate opposition parties and curtail critical civil society activities.

The year 1992 is unique in Kenya's politico-legal evolution because it was the first year of political pluralism yet the Parliament in place consisted exclusively of KANU MPs. This notwithstanding the discredited Sixth Parliament nonetheless passed or attempted to pass constitutional amendments of great significance. In March 1992 Attorney General Amos Wako drafted a Bill[65] seeking to alter the nature of the Kenyan executive by abolishing the position of vice-president and introducing the post of Prime Minister to be appointed by the President from the party which in the opinion or the "judgement" of the President was able to command "the support of the majority of the members of the national assembly"[66]. This Bill was widely criticised inter- alia on the grounds that it sought to prolong Moi's stay in power and that despite its preference to make the premier the head of government in reality the executive power would remain in the presidency. Due to the massive opposition against it, the Attorney General withdrew it before it could be tabled and debated[67].

In July, 1992, the Sixth Parliament amended[68] the Constitution in three major ways. First was to introduce the famous 25% rule by basically providing that the candidate for the presidency must not only get a majority of the votes cast but must also gather 25% of the votes cast in at least five of he eight provinces of Kenya. The ostensible reason for this amendment was to make the presidency more widely accepted by stipulating that a successful candidate had to garner support from a cross-section majority. The real intent of the amendment, however, was to prevent opposition candidates from the populous community – the Gikuyu in particular – from winning the presidency under the simple majority first – past the post rules because by now the leaders of opposition parties had emerged as spokesmen of their respective ethnic groups. In the political context of the 1992 general election only the KANU candidate – the incumbent President Moi – could win the presidency under the 25% rule without a run-off. Thus the 1992 constitutional amendment was a mechanism to manipulate political succession.

The second limb of this amendment was to introduce a limitation of tenure clause to provide that the President would hold office for a maximum period of ten years or two five year terms. In the last analysis it was this constitutional amendment that ushered Moi out of power in 2002 and arguably it is the single most important obstacle to emergence of authoritarianism along the 1980s mode. Thirdly, this amendment repealed section 127 of the Constitution which vested in the President the power to make regulations specifically for North Eastern Province and contiguous districts. Thus for close to 30 years residents of Northern Kenya had been legally deprived fundamental human rights and freedoms whose major effect was to stifle development of critical leadership. As a result, in the first decade of political pluralism in Kenya northern Kenya was a KANU political stronghold mainly because opposition to governing party in these areas had long been associated with state reprisals; a fact which indeed the KANU government reminded them after 1992 by intimidating or preventing opposition parties from operating and campaigning there. No wonder even in the 2002 general election when KANU was overwhelmingly rejected by voters elsewhere in Kenya, in North Eastern Province NARC got only one MP who went through with a slim majority.

Finally, in October 1992 the Sixth Parliament amended the Parliamentary Standing Orders ostensibly to facilitate the work of a multi-party Parliament but in reality "this was yet another survival strategy for the one-party government come the multi-party Parliament"[69]. In principle it is questionable whether a single-party parliament could legitimately amend these Standing Orders given KANU's historical aversion towards multipartyism. Subsequent events during he Seventh Parliament showed that the motive for amending the Standing Orders was to ensure that there would be no official opposition party in Parliament which it easily achieved by inducing Ford-Asili's MPs from Western Kenya to defect to KANU and win subsequent by-election as KANU candidates.

Multi-Partyism and the Crisis of Leadership in Kenya 1992-2006

As expected the 1992 multiparty general elections were so politically and legally skewed against the opposition parties that the victory of KANU – though achieved with considerable manipulation – did not come as a surprise. Moreover, the personal ambitions and ethnic suspicions conspired to work against unity of purpose that could have helped them to defeat KANU. Moreover, opposition leaders' campaigns were curtailed by the police and KANU youth wingers, opposition leaders were denied access to state-owned KBC radio and television, and they were also denied permits to hold rallies and also prevented from opening branch offices particularly in areas KANU had declared as its zones. Further, KANU sponsored militia and tribal thugs launched a wave of terror in Western Kenya in which more than 1000 people were killed and over 250,000 displaced from their homes in systematic scheme of ethnic cleansing. With all these, the odds against fledgling opposition proved insurmountable as attested by Smith Hempstone, then US Ambassador to Kenya:[70]

> Meanwhile, the money supply increased by 38 percent to fund KANU candidates and bribe voters. That the actual balloting was peaceful was almost irrelevant. Despite all this, the opposition has only itself to blame for losing… Moi was able to win with only 36 percent of the vote: he polled 1.9 million votes, Matiba had 1.4 million, Kibaki tallied 1 million and Odinga registered 944,000. Had any two of the opposition candidates been able to get together, their candidate would have out-polled Moi. The same inability to agree upon

common parliamentary candidates, gerrymandering and constituency-loading, cost the opposition control of the legislature. While the combined opposition polled 70 percent of the parliamentary vote, it won only 47 percent of the seats at stake. Despite all the chicanery, the election was a stunning rebuke to Moi. The opposition won 88 of 188 parliamentary seats, nearly half of his cabinet was defeated at the polls and little more than a quarter of the incumbent KANU parliamentarians were returned to office. The opposition swept the municipal elections.

In all fairness a multiparty system of government ameliorated socio-political life in Kenya in various ways. Kenyans could now enjoy greater civil and political liberties, the media became freer and government began to take public opinion more seriously. However state repression did not abate and so at the end of the aftermath of the 1992 general election multipartyism had truly succeeded in creating a squatting democratic space. The Editor of *The Kenya Jurist* captured the crisis of leadership in the first year of multiparty Kenya as follows:[71]

The shift to democracy in our country was really a measure to save the government's face. We are making some changes, especially economic reforms, to look good to the outside world. Politicians continue to make very irresponsible statements – most of it hot air – concerning the future of this country. Selective prosecution, where only opposition politicians are arrested and prosecuted for allegedly inciting people to violence, whilst powerful politicians in the good books of the government remain untouched even when the statements they make are more vitriolic and absurdly inflammatory. Our legal structures and the administrative machinery are such that they greatly inhibit any move to meaningful democracy. Mediocrity has replaced merit and the ability to think is a definite bar to a prominent position in the system. And what's more, the populace continues to waste chances by failing to choose the right leadership whenever they have the chance. To invoke the words of Macbeth, albeit in a different context, "we have eaten on the insane root that takes the reason prisoner". The Catholic Bishops recently warned in their open letter to President Daniel arap Moi, that the country was falling apart and that something must be done now if we are to prevent rivers of blood, a concern which we share. The Bishops also pointed an accusing finger at the Government as the cause of the insecurity which has engulfed some areas of the country. The charge has never been convincingly challenged, a situation which no doubt greatly undermines the credibility of the Government and its suitability to be entrusted with the governance of this Nation.

Thus in the aftermath of the 1992 general election the credibility of Kenya's political leadership in government as well as in the opposition was questionable. None of the political protagonists appeared genuinely interested in addressing the real problems facing the nation particularly the vast majority of impoverished Kenyans eking out a living on less the one dollar a day. The manifestos of all the mainstream political parties – then as now – are so strikingly similar that one wonders whether the victory of candidate X or Y makes any difference to the lives of the people. On the economy all the parties proclaim their commitment to a free market economy supposedly one in which government plays the role of a facilitator for the domestic and foreign investors but also remains the referee to ensure fair play.

In principle multiparty system of government is supposed to create or expand political choices but in reality this is yet to happen in many African countries especially in Kenya. Apart from the fact that all the leading presidential candidates in the last three general elections since the reintroduction of multipartyism were former cabinet ministers of successive governments of KANU, in the possible exception of the late Oginga Odinga, there were no ideological differences among them. Thus democracy is, in many respects, still choiceless in Kenya and its capacity to advance to the welfare of the citizens is at best minimal. Thus in the wake of the 1992 multiparty general election in 1992 a political commentator rightly observed:[72]

> One of the remarkable characters of Kenya's opposition parties is that they are generally no different from each other in the usual matters like policy and ideology. All concede and mark up as a priority the liberalization of the economy in free market capitalism; the legal containment of the almost limitless presidential powers; the establishment of a truly democratic human rights respecting culture and all the politically correct positions that a modern liberal political party in Western Europe would love (and curiously not far from what the ruling party believes in). Better still, beyond the fact that the ruling party is in a position to effect the changes and therefore in a position to be judged by deeds as well as by words, the opposition parties are in no fundamental way different from the ruling party in matters of declared party philosophy and intentions. What they vehemently disagree on is how and whether the policies have been effected. The quarrel is simply over *the man*. In effect there is a more pronounced difference between the Republicans

and the Democrats in the United States than there is between the ruling party and the opposition in Kenya.

In order for democracy to become a means of offering solutions to the problems of dictatorship, poverty, corruption and social inequity, it must evolve beyond being a mechanism for the organization of elections. The problem of corruption is testimony to the fact that too often in Kenya, democracy gives scope for personal interests to take precedence over public good. Moreover, democratization in Kenya, as elsewhere in Africa, is occurring at a time when the economy is either shrinking or collapsing leading to budgetary crises. Thus democratization makes it easier to make greater political demands than a state can satisfy thereby posing a crisis of legitimacy to the government of the day and even the state itself. In political terms this crisis takes the form of leadership crisis which at worst can promote political instability and *coup d'etats*. In his acceptance speech after election as FORD-Kenya Chairman in January 1997, Michael Kijana Wamalwa described this crisis of leadership as follows:[73]

> Fellow citizens, if you reflect carefully upon our nation's fortunes, you will agree with me that what is at trial today is the entire political class. People are asking themselves: what do the politicians matter if all we hear is their corruption and their irrelevance. How do they matter when what matters to us never seems to concern them? Our challenge today is to return respect to leadership. It is a respect that will only return through purposeful action on a progressive front. Kenyans are angry. They are angry over corruption. Corruption that humiliates the poor who must bribe small officials for minimal services; corruption that bankrupts the small trader; corruption that empowers the unscrupulous captains of commerce and their partners in politics. Corruption that spreads like a cancer to kill all that is decent in society. Programmes of economic growth must be focused on the fight against poverty. They must address the reduction of powerlessness among the impoverished. They must in the final analysis seek to empower those who today are mere spectators of the power and wealth games. Ford-Kenya under my stewardship will aspire to mainstream the concerns of the voiceless as the rationale for popular leadership. To date the poor in our society have been treated like untouchables. We only remember them when our material comfort is threatened. Or when we want their votes. The current system is cruel to the little man and the small businessman.

Faced with a growing crisis of legitimacy Kenyan leaders have, as in previous eras, resorted to the law for solutions that have sometimes kept the country afloat or on fewer occasions failed spectacularly. The reason for this is that during the multiparty era the capacity of the ruling elite to manipulate the law to serve narrow or selfish political ends has diminished and whether this is good or bad depends on circumstances of the moment as we shall shortly demonstrate.

Political Paralysis and Legal Impasse in the Multiparty Era

The Constitution of Kenya provides that Parliament can only amend the Constitution if a bill to amend the Constitution receives support of 65 per cent on the second and third readings by votes of all members of the National Assembly.[74] Thus the relative ease with which the Constitution was amended between 1964 and 1992 masks the fact that the constitutional amendment procedure is fairly rigid. The conclusion is therefore irresistible that one of the radical effects of a single-party rule is the virtual emasculation of Parliament by the party in power so that it becomes a mere rubber stamp dramatized by the ineffectiveness of the constitutional amendment procedures. Conversely, the first major achievement of multipartyism is the strengthening of the constitutional amendment procedures which in Kenya has largely been caused by the inability of political parties to win parliamentary elections with the majority required to pass constitutional amendments. More than anything else, the amendment factor explains the paucity of constitutional amendments since 1993 when the Seventh Parliament – elected on multiparty basis – first convened. In a multiparty context without a dominant party in parliament amendments of the Kenya Constitution would require greater consensus between political parties than has been possible in the Seventh and Eighth Parliaments. This consensus was difficult to achieve due to political polarization along ethnic lines and KANU's predatory tactics against the opposition parties.

It was therefore not until the sunset of the Seventh Parliament that Civil Society led demands for constitutional reforms forced moderate party leaders to reach consensus to pass a slew of statutory and constitutional amendments popularly known as Inter-Parties Parliamentary Group (IPPG) reforms.[75]

The 1997 amendments changed the Constitution in four major ways. First it was amended to introduce a new Section 1A to formally declare that "The Republic of Kenya shall be a multiparty democratic state." The legal significance of this change was that the Constitution now expressly recognized Kenya is a multiparty democracy. Subsequently in the famous **Njoya Case**[76] the High Court partly relied on section

1A of the Constitution to declare that adoption of a new Constitution in Kenya requires ratification by the voters through a referendum. Secondly, Section 33 was repealed and replaced with a new section requiring, inter-alia that nominated MPs be nominated by parliamentary parties according to the proportion of each such party in the National Assembly, taking into account the principle of gender equity.

Thirdly, a new Section 84(7) was introduced to give the Court of Appeal power to hear appeals from the High Court in respect of the cases on enforcement of fundamental rights and freedoms under Section 84. Fourthly, and perhaps most importantly, section 16 was directly[77] and indirectly[78] amended to empower the President to choose cabinet Ministers from amongst members of the National Assembly. Effectively this amendment restored the mode of cabinet appointments that existed prior to reintroduction of political pluralism in 1991 and so it was now possible for MPs elected on opposition party tickets to be appointed to the Cabinet. The motivation of this amendments was to provide for a way in which opposition MPs could be appointed to the Cabinet without having to defect to KANU against the wish of their supporters. In other words, it was now possible for opposition MPs to urge their supporters to hate KANU but they themselves could serve in a KANU government now that it was obvious KANU was the runaway favourite to win the impending 1997 general elections.

Finally section 41 of the Constitution was amended to a) increase the membership of the Electoral Commission of Kenya (ECK) to a maximum of twenty one, with the President appointing ten more members from a nominal list proposed by the parliamentary opposition parties and b) introduce a new subsection 41(1A) providing that, "Every member of the Commission shall be a citizen of Kenya". It is significant to note that the presumed right of the parliamentary opposition parties to nominate some members of the ECK is not expressly or impliedly enshrined in the constitutional text. Part of the explanation for this serious omission lies in the peculiar political setting in which the IPPG reforms package was agreed.

At the height of the clamour for constitution and statutory reforms in July – August, 1997 moderate opposition and KANU MPs united under the aegis of the IPPG to ostensibly save the country from the brink of civil war and chaos engendered by NCEC/NCA uncompromising demands for comprehensive legal reforms. Dr. Willy Mutunga has contended that the possibility of a civil war has always been exaggerated by politicians in order to rationalise their bias towards retention of the status quo. In his words:[79]

The Moi-KANU regime by strokes of political genius had taken the political initiative from the NCA/NCEC on reforms. The regime isolated the religious organizations from the NCA/NCEC constitutional reform project and these organisations formed projects of their own on constitutional reforms. The NCCK and the Catholic Church had their own projects which they abandoned to take up the mediation initiative. The regime understood how the religious leaders would react to the suggestion of mediation. The religious leaders had always asked of the President, "Is there anything we can do?" The Moi-KANU regime had then turned on the politicians and Members of Parliament and asked them, "Why are you led by unelected people?" The regime understood the egos and the culture of status among the Kenyan Members of Parliament and how to massage these egos appropriately. The regime also understood that, ideologically, it was closer to many of these Members of Parliament, and that many did not support the radical programme of the NCA/NCEC. The regime also knew that through patronage and intimidation, it could keep many of them on board its policies.

The raft of statutory changes contained in the IPPG reforms package are worth mentioning albeit in passing. The bulk of these changes related to laws that either deal with conduct of elections and the general political climate especially with respect to concerns of political parties and individual politicians. These reforms can be categorized into two sets. The first set, which deals specifically with the conduct of elections, engendered repeal or amendment of the National Assembly and Presidential Elections Act (Cap 7), the Public Order Act (Cap 56), the Penal code (Cap. 63), the Administration Police Act (Cap 85) the Societies Act (Cap 108), the Chief's Authority Act (Cap 128) and the Election Offences Act (Cap 66).

The amendment of the Public Order Act removed the provision giving powers to the Provincial Administration to licence political and other public meeting and replaced it with one requiring the Police to be notified of such meeting 24 hours before. Further the police could only stop a public meeting or procession in the face of a clear or imminent danger of a breach of the peace or of public order. The Preservation of Public Security Act was amended by repeal of Section 4(2) (a) that allowed for detention on political grounds during peacetime. As regards the Penal Code the most significant amendment was the repeal of Sections 56-58 to repeal the laws of sedition that between 1982 and 1996 provided a lethal weapon against critics of KANU and the Nyayo government.

The second set of laws touched on the laws providing for matters dealing with freedoms of association and speech. These laws include the Films and Stage Plays Act (Cap 222), the Public Collections Act (Cap 106) and the Kenya Broadcasting Act (Cap 221) which was amended to require the Kenya Broadcasting Corporation (KBC) to be equitable in allocating airtime to political parties during elections. In the end these changes turned out to be superfluous, inadequate and rather misguided. As Makumi Mwagiru observes:[80]

> The opposition candidates were interested in wresting power from KANU and from Moi; power which both had had for two decades. However, these interests could not be met in the context of a constitutional and electoral law system that heavily favoured the incumbent. KANU did not favour constitutional and legal reforms which would have weakened its chances of electoral victory however fair the reforms would have been. The political conflict – and conflict of interest between the protagonists – was therefore highly polarized and difficult to resolve. In this context, the IPPG reforms were merely a palliative, as the re-opening of the constitutional debate in the period leading to the 2002 elections has demonstrated.

Since the return of multipartyism in 1991, IPPG reforms package – inadequate as it was – constitute the most comprehensive constitutional and legal reforms. It cannot be denied that KANU conceded to these changes reluctantly in order to solve a serious political crisis which was spearheaded by the civil society. Two things deserve to be mentioned. First, though IPPG reforms liberalized political space which helped the cause of democratization in subsequent years, its immediate effect was to legitimize the flawed electoral process that in 1997 general election would result in victory for the Moi-KANU regime. Thus Dr. Julius E. Nyang'oro observes:[81]

> If we go by the behaviour of the opposition in Kenya with regard to the extent of constitutional reform it would push for, any change would be minimalist indeed. Thus it would seem that the opposition time and again becomes vulnerable to manipulation by the regime which occasionally promises electoral reform. A most charitable characterisation of the Inter-Parties Parliamentary Group (1997), a coalition of ruling party and opposition parties parliamentarians dialoguing on changes to be made in electoral and related matters, would be that once any changes are accepted by the regime, then it would be a slippery slope for the regime in power. The assumption here would be a slippery slope for the regime in power. The assumption here would be that once initial reforms are underway, it would seem obvious why

more reforms have to be undertaken thus leading to the final analysis to the denied objectives of constitutional reform anyway. Evidence, however, suggests that the regime has again outmanoeuvred the opposition and is calling the shots in the direction of KANU's consolidation. A most cynical characterisation of the opposition leaders would be that they are simply authoritarian presidents in waiting. Most Kenyan would not dispute that view.

The second observation is that IPPG reforms and the subsequent electoral victory for the Moi-KANU regime could possibly have guaranteed the continuity of Kenya's constitutional order. This contention should be viewed against the charged political climate at the height of NCEC/NCA mass action whose success portended doom for the Moi-KANU regime. Thus there is reason to believe that contrary to the protestations of Dr. Mutunga the risk of a palace *coup d'etat* was real in the prelude to the 1997 election. This indeed is a view that Prof. Peter Anyang' Nyong'o has expressed thus:[82]

> Willy says that the danger of civil war was exaggerated. I do not think so. Especially noting the steps the regime eventually took to rig the elections. If they could not keep power through rigged elections, they would have maintained the same by keeping elections away through a regime coup. The NCEC was planning a civilian coup; what type of coup was the regime expected to plan? Of course both civilian and military. The IPPG became the civilian coup by the regime. Some of us who were in it realised this was the game – but too late. And without the NCEC within the IPPG we could not stem the tide.

The second and so far the last constitutional amendment since the 1992 multiparty elections was passed in 2000 and its limited objective was to establish the Parliamentary Service Commission (PSC)[83]. Whilst the PSC gives Parliament some limited autonomy its greater significance lies in its unstated role as the trade union of MPs which explains why it sailed through in Parliament with virtual consensus. Again the passage of this amendment during an era when constitutional changes have been conspicuous by their paucity is testimony to the politicians' solidarity on matters that affect them directly.

As I write this paper on the fourth year of NARC's rule, the Ninth Parliament is yet to amend the Constitution even once despite the compelling necessity to do so. Perhaps part of the reason why no amendments have been passed is in November

2005 Kenya was on the brink of getting a new Constitution. However at the time of this writing a Bill[84] seeking to amend section 59 of the Constitution to, inter-alia, empower the National Assembly to control its calendar has been tabled for debate in Parliament. In principle, there is no reason why other sections of the current Constitution cannot be amended even as Kenyans strategize on how best to replace it[85]. Thus the only explanation for this state of affairs is that Kenyan politicians have a penchant for trumping their interests virtually always but people of reflection must begin to wonder for how long Kenyans will tolerate this chicanery.

Indeed contrary to the expectations of many Kenyans the defeat of KANU in the 2002 general election is yet to result in realization of meaningful democracy and social justice for the disadvantaged. Apart from persistent infighting and intrigues the NARC government has been singularly distracted from its election agenda that public discontent is dangerously high on its fourth year in power. Unlike the Kenyatta and Moi eras when the problem of presidential succession emerged towards the end of the autocrat's rule during he NARC era succession wars literally began the very week that President Kibaki announced his first cabinet. On this sad development, Prof. Walter Oyugi comments:[86]

> The behaviour of some key members of the NARC government suggests that the road to consolidation of the little gains that have been achieved in the sphere of democratisation may be full of potholes. Public pronouncements by key ministers have been contradictory on the main, as the ministers continue to operate at cross purposes, creating the impression of the absence of a central coordinating mechanism that informs and guides the activities of the various ministries. On top of this, there is the uneasy co-existence within the NARC family parties. The fragile relationship that exists has the potential of creating instability in the body politic. The net effect may be democratic 'rollback', instead of consolidation, as factions begin to plot and counterplot against one another. It is these kinds of plots and counterplots that usually end up in some factions "knocking at the barracks" door. Indeed, the fear about the future lies in the fact that there is a lot of anti-democratic behaviour already that can be discerned in the NARC government so far. The manner in which some ministers have supposedly dismissed public servants in utter disregard of the established guidelines in the civil service leaves a lot to be desired. The autocratic manner in which some ministers carry out their business is equally a manifestation of the lingering authoritarian culture acquired during the one-party era.

As we conclude this section it bears noting that in 2002 the National Assembly and Presidential Elections Act was amended[87] to allow the counting of votes at the polling stations. This amendments helped a great deal to minimize rigging in the 2002 general election which ordinarily occurred during the transportation of ballot boxes to constituency polling centres.

At this stage the twin legacies of the law on evolution of leadership in Kenya during the multiparty era are easily discernible. These twin legacies are that first law can be manipulated to serve partisan objectives but, two, whilst that may be so law is not infinitely elastic and so at some point the legal order may simply lose its utility for its manipulative creators. Thus law is a double-edged sword that today may serve your ends but tomorrow it devours you. This indeed is the tragic story of KANU in multiparty Kenya. Commenting on this bizarre though fascinating feature of the Law, eminent constitutional scholars Kivutha Kibwana and Wachira Maina write:[88]

> At every turn, the constitutional agenda embraced by the government has been reactive and generally defensive. Whenever a crisis has developed or pressure built up, the government has moved in to effect the minimal change to defuse the crisis. In other words, the philosophy underlying the reform process right from the days of the Review Committee to the changes of the Constitution which we shall address shortly was not informed by a desire to democratise: it was informed by a desire to defuse a perceived crisis. So that the result of the reform has been *to ameliorate the more intolerable aspect of one party government* rather than *to create an enabling environment for democracy*. In other words, the government's constitutional preoccupation has been the desire to make itself more palatable to the people. It has not been striving to meet the demands for democracy that the people have been making.

The success and fairness of an election can be best determined from the holistic electoral process rather than the substance *per se* of the laws governing elections. In 1997, as in 1992, the constitutional and legal regime governing elections were so inadequate, unsatisfactory and skewed in favour of the incumbent party that the conduct and administration of the elections could not yield a legitimate verdict of "free and fair". Indeed the 1997 election results were proof of the common knowledge that the legal regime in place favoured KANU in any contest for political power. Thus Makumi Mwagiru is justified in concluding that the "1997 elections emphasized that it is not the laws, *per se* that matter in nurturing the democratic process but their spirit. Most importantly, it is not the legal framework but the spirit of fairness that eventually delivers free and fair elections."[89]

Thus by 2002 the contradictions and dialectics of the pro-KANU constitutional dispensation came to a head; the very constitution that had kept KANU in power for nearly four decades and helped it to solve political crises was now the single largest impediment and threat to its tenure in power. First, the 1992 constitutional amendment limiting presidential tenure to two five years' terms had automatically knocked out the incumbent President Moi from the contest. Thus for the first time in Kenya post-independence history KANU was contesting the presidency through a candidate other than the incumbent. Secondly, with the advent of multipartyism KANU lost the power to tinker with the Constitution at will in pursuit of its power ambitions and so it had to face the 2002 general elections under a constitutional system that was less than ideal.

The point here is that unlike diamonds law is not forever – today it serves your interest but tomorrow it savages you. Nothing bears better testimony to KANU's self-inflicted constitutional predicament than Moi's ultimate failure to manage his succession. After winning his re-election bid in 1997 President Moi did not appoint a vice-president for about 15 months out of the fear of losing control over the vicious wars among his allies to succeed him. Finally he re-appointed Prof. George Saitoti but, in a retrospect, without any intention of grooming Saitoti to succeed him. At the time, journalist turned politician Jackson Mwalulu captured Moi's succession dilemma as follows:[90]

> Moi's dilemma is that, although personally he may be likable and quite innocent of some of the shenanigans going on in his government, over the years he has surrendered himself to some of the most unsavory characters in Kenya. This has developed to the extent that as he seeks a successor today, he finds it difficult to find someone who can be acceptable to both him as well as the electorate. He might not feel at ease with anyone outside his inner circle but at the same time this inner circle is made up of the individuals who are most often blamed for Kenya's economic and political mess, Professor Saitoti for example. By far the most formidable challenge facing President Moi today is to hold KANU together in face of the divisions that could result from Professor Saitoti's reappointment. With regard to appointing a VP, keep in mind that he was last year reported to have said that, "If I appoint one, the rest will cry foul. This can divide Kanu." Still, no matter how one looks at it, it is clear that Moi has read the sign of the times and appears to be preparing for retirement.

There is yet another legal factor that complicated the Moi succession namely its slim parliamentary victory in the 1997 general election where it won 52 per cent against the combined opposition total of 48 per cent of the seats. Thus in the eighth Parliament KANU had 113 seats whilst the combined opposition had 109 seats.[91] With this slim majoriy KANU started to court the Raila Odinga led National Development Party (NDP), which had 22 MPs. Moi took advantage of the IPPG constitutional amendments to appoint NDP MPs to his Cabinet and in March, 2002 this political alliance culminated in the merger of KANU and NDP thereby complicating the vicious struggle for his successor. As Dr. Karuti Kanyinga observes:[92]

> The hurry in which NDP expected to join the Moi succession race was noted early on when NDP pushed for a motion of no confidence in the Vice President, George Saitoti, in Parliament. By virtue of his position, the Vice President stood a better chance than anyone else in the party to take over from Moi. NDP, however, filed a motion of no confidence in the Vice President citing his involvement in several corruption scams and therefore his inability to lead. The motion was defeated. The Vice President got support from a combined force of the opposition and KANU. The Vice President got support especially from the Democratic Party MPs. MPs from the Kikuyu ethnic community particularly argued that the Vice President was better placed to succeed President Moi and that NDP was behind the vote of no confidence so as to prepare ground for Raila Odinga to take over from Moi.

To accommodate NDP into KANU required the latter to conduct the long overdue national elections. As in the 1970s the party line-up was bound to reveal not only the President's biases but also have a bearing on the impending Moi succession. As it turned out the return of pluralism in 1991 had either failed to democratize KANU's *modus operandi* or the management of the Moi succession required adoption of its time tested opaque and authoritarian ways. In the end the party elections was a complete fiasco and a tragic political mistake. Dr. Kanyinga records KANU's elections sham of March 2002 as follows:[93]

> The Moi-Raila faction was as active as any other faction in ensuring that the delegates were not "interfered with" prior to the morning of the meeting. Having won the first round of the contest in ensuring that acclamation would be the preferred method of voting, they drew a list of party officials they preferred for different party positions. They distributed all the party positions on ethnic lines. On the eve of the meeting, some delegates were rehearsed

on how they would shout their acclamation and were informed about who would occupy which position. During the meeting, the Kamotho faction learnt of the party list and of the acclamation method that was to be used. They consulted among themselves and appreciated that they had no viable alternative but to withdraw their candidacies. The names of the candidates nominated by the Moi-Raila faction were read one by one for each of the positions that each was vying for. The delegates acclaimed in approval and in the support of these candidates. Although there were other candidates who had shown interest in all the party position, their names did not appear in the list that was read out. They were omitted. Those elected for the positions of the Vice Chairmen were: Uhuru Kenyatta from Central Kenya; Kalonzo Musyoka from Ukambani; Musalia Mudavadi from Western Kenya; and Katana Ngala from the Coast. The name of Vice President, George Saitoti was glaringly missing in the party line up despite his having been validly nominated to vie for the position. The President sharply rebuked Saitoti when the latter sought to know why his name was missing from the list. The President shouted him down and told him to 'shut up'. Other party leaders such as the Secretary General, Joseph Kamotho, took this to mean that they would not be allowed to vie for any position. They became aware that delegates had already rehearsed what to do and how to apportion positions in the party. They consequently withdrew their candidacies. The position of the party Secretary General was given to NDP leader, Raila Odinga. Others in the Kamotho-Saitoti faction did not vie for the positions they had identified. The delegates simply approved by acclamation the names in a list prepared by the KANU and NDP inner court cabal.

Thus a party that for nearly four decades had deployed every imaginable political scheme to keep power including unbridled constitutional and legal manipulation sowed the seeds of its own self-destruction. KANU had long been haunted by the prospect of being felled by opposition 'bullets' but in the end it demised from prolonged political suicide. Soon after the KANU-NDP merger, a group of young politicians led by William Ruto, Cyrus Jirongo and Julius Sunkuli, with implicit support of Moi, began to campaign for Uhuru Kenyatta to succeed Moi. By July, 2002 KANU's other three vice chairmen – Mudavadi, Ngala and Musyoka – and Secretary General Raila Odinga had become jittery about Moi's backing for Uhuru's presidential candidacy on KANU ticket. However, on Sunday July 28, 2002, whilst addressing a delegation from Jirongo's Lugari constituency, President Moi said:[94]

I have chosen Uhuru to take over leadership when I leave. This young man Uhuru has been consulting on leadership matters. I have seen that he is a person who can be guided. If there are others who are chosen then it will depend on the people.

With this declaration – and despite public indignation at his decision – Moi began a countrywide tour to popularize his candidate which culminated with Uhuru's endorsement as the Party's presidential candidate on October 14, 2002. The previous day four ministers belonging to the Rainbow Alliance front of KANU namely Raila Odinga, William Ole Ntimama (Office of the President), Adhu Awiti (National Planning), and Education Assistant Minister, Moody Awori, resigned from government. Then on 14th October, 2002, whilst KANU was formally endorsing Uhuru's candidature, the Rainbow Alliance members held a huge rally at which they unveiled their new party namely the Liberal Democratic Party (LDP). At the rally they were joined by the leaders of the National Alliance (Party) of Kenya (NAK) spearheaded by Mwai Kibaki of the Democratic Party (DP), Michael Wamalwa of FORD-Kenya and Charity Ngilu of the National Party of Kenya (NPK) and other lesser parties and civil society groups. At the meeting the leaders conceded to the demands of the crowds of approximately 100,000 people to unite which they did on Monday, October 22, 2002 when NAK and LDP formed the National Rainbow Coalition (NARC).

Subsequently, NARC chose Mwai Kibaki as its presidential flag bearer who proceeded to win the seat with 62.2 per cent of the valid votes cast against KANU's Uhuru Kenyatta's 31.3 per cent. NARC won 103 out of the 210 contested seats. Thus KANU's 39 years' uninterrupted reign came to a crushing end not only because of tragic errors of political judgement but as a result of a decade long paralysis and ossification of the constitutional dispensation and legal regime that prior to reintroduction of multipartyism in 1991 had served it so well. As early as 1995, prominent human rights activist Maina Kiai had argued that KANU stood to gain from serious constitutional changes at least to help it end the culture of sycophancy and management of political succession in a competitive political environment. As he pus it:[95]

> Constitutional reform would expand the political space within KANU, reduce sycophancy and allow differences of opinion. And this is vital for any dynamic party. Moreover it is hard to believe that a normal human being could actually enjoy being a sycophant. But I may be wrong. Power in Kenya and KANU is

wielded by a few men surrounding he President. Because of the enormous powers of the presidency, their access to the president makes their role bloated and dangerous. Crossing them has life consequences. Constitutional change would reduce their role and importance and lead to less sycophancy. The clamour for space within KANU has already begun even through only minimal changes have taken place in Kenya. The recent Uasin Gishu KANU branch elections are a good illustration. Top KANU barons wanted their own men but the locals had a different idea. The result prompted the President to express displeasure at the outcome. Such expression of independence would never have occurred in the pre-multi-party days. In a real democracy the President's attempt to bulldoze his own people would not be tolerated and people would not expect trouble for following their consciences. The there is the succession issue. Under the present Constitution, President Moi must vacate office by the year 2002. Even if this provision is dropped, as some in KANU would like, President Moi will remain mortal with a limited life span. Proper constitutional reform would also allow the best people to rise to the top within KANU. There are quite a few KANU and Government members who have been mentioned as either interested in, or capable of, being president. They have to hide their talent and conduct their manoeuvres in a covert manner for fear of alienating those who can derail their plans.

The obstinate refusal of KANU's top leadership to support constitutional reforms and internal democracy in KANU contributed immensely to NARC's victory over KANU in the 2002 general election.

Notes

1 Vernon Bogdanor *The Blackwell Encyclopaedia of Political Science, Cambridge, Blackwell Publishers, 1991, pg. 321-22.*

2 See Arthur M. Schlesinger Jr. *On Leadership*, a preface to *World Leaders Past and Present: Kenyatta*, London: Burke Publishing Company Limited, 1988, pg. 7.

3 Ibid pg. 9-10.

4 Supra note 1, pg. 615-616.

5 Supra note 2, pg. 10.

6 Lewis Copeland et al (ed), the World's Great Speeches New York: Dover Publications, Inc. (1999)pg. 811.

7 For detailed analysis see: R. M. Unger "Law in Modern Society" in Lloyd et al (ed) *Introduction to Jurisprudence*, London Stevens & Sons Ltd., 1985, pg. 639-6.

[8] P. Fitzpartrick "Law, Modernisation and Mystification" in Ibid pg. 948.

[9] Kivutha Kibwana (ed) *Law and Administration of Justice in Kenya,* ICJ-Kenya Section 1992 pg. 58-59.

[10] Nyali vs. Attorney General (1956) 1 QB1, where at pg. 16-17 Dennings L. J. (as he then was) said: "Just as an English Oak so with the English Common Law. You cannot transplant it to the African Continent and expect it to retain the tough character which it has in England. It will flourish indeed but it needs careful tending. So with the Common Law. It has many principles of manifest justice and good sense which can be applied with advantage to people of every race and colour all the world over; but it has many refinements, subtleties and technicalities which are not suited to other folk. These offshoots must be cut away."

[11] Y. P. Ghai and J. P. W. vs. Mcauslan *Public Law and Political Change in Kenya*, Nairobi: Oxford University Press, 1970.

[12] Ibid pg. 513.

[13] Katama Mkangi, "A critical Reappraisal of the Socio-Cultural Background to the Anti-Democratic Culture in East Africa," in Joseph Oloka – Onyango *et al* (ed) *Law and The Struggle for Democracy in East Africa* Nairobi: Claripress 1996 101 at 144.

[14] Ngugi wa Thiong'o's *Homecoming*, Nairobi: Heinemann, 1972, pg. 23.

[15] Ibid pg. 23, 24.

[16] *Daily Nation*, 14th August, 1984, Page1.

[17] Harry Goulbournne, "The State, Development and the Need for Participatory Democracy in Africa", in *Popular Struggles for Democracy in Africa,* pg. 30, edited by Peter Anyang' Nyong'o, London: Zed Books Ltd., 1987.

[18] Amendment Act No. 28 of 1964.

[19] Constitutional Amendment No. 3 Act No. 17 of 1966.

[20] P-L. Agweli Onalo, *Constitution-Making in Kenya*, Nairobi: Transafrica Press, 2003.

[21] Act No. 17 of 1966.

[22] Kaparo is the current Speaker of he Kenyan Parliament. He was then KANU MP for Laikipia East and Assistant Minister of Guidance and National Heritage.

[23] *Law and Society*, 1988, selected papers from a Seminar held 24-26 November, 1988 at the Green Hills Hotel, Nyeri, Kenya, a publication of ICJ Kenya Section, pg. 22.

[24] Franz Fanon, *The Wretched of the Earth* Penguin Books, Middlesex 1967 pg. 147-148.

[25] Constitution of Kenya (Amendment) No. 2 Act No. 10 of 1974.

[26] Constitution of Kenya (Amendment) Act No. 1 of 1975.

[27] Constitution of Kenya (Amendment) No. 2 Ac No. 14 of 1975.

[28] Kimani Njogu "Manipulating the Constitution" In The *Moi Succession Elections 2002* Herve Maupeu et al (eds) Nairobi: Transafrica Press, 2005.

[29] Walter O. Oyugi et al *The Politics of Transition in Kanu – From KANU to NARC*, Nairobi: Heinrich Boll Foundation 2003, pg. 65-65.

[30] Andrew Morton, *Moi The Making of an Africa Statesman*, London: Michael O'Mara Books Limited pg. 12.

[31] Speech published in *Ng'ang'a Mbugua, Mwai Kibaki: Economist for Kenya* Nairobi: Sasa Sema Publications, 2003 pg. 81.

[32] Supra note 30 pg. 170.

[33] Supra note 30 pg. 173.

[34] The Constitution of Kenya (Amendment) No. of 1979 Act No. 5.

[35] Supra note 30 pg. 173-4.

[36] Supra note 30 pg. 174.

[37] Republic vs. A. M. Muthemba and Kamau Muchiri, Criminal Case No. 25 of 1981, High Court, Nairobi (unreported).

[38] The Constitution of Kenya (Amendment) Act, No. 7 of 1982 and Election Laws (Amendment) Act No. 8 of 1982.

[39] Gutto, S. B. O. *Human and Peoples' Rights for the Oppressed* Lund, Lund University Press, 1993 pg. 313.

[40] G. G. Kariuki. *Illusions of Power: Fifty Years in Kenya Politics*, Nairobi: Kenway publications, 2001.

[41] Ibid pg. 91-92.

[42] Supra note 39 pg. 312.

[43] *Daily Nation* (Nairobi) of Wednesday, October 27, 1982.

[44] Supra note 40 pg. 108-109.

[45] Supra note 40 pg. 111.

[46] *Kenya: Torture Political Detention and Unfair Trials*, London: Amnesty International Publications, 1987.

[47] Ibid pg. 25.

[48] Constitution of Kenya (Amendment) Act No. 14 of 1986.

[49] Constitution of Kenya (Amendment) Act No. 20 of 1987.

[50] *Weekly Review*, Nairobi, 5 August, 1988, pg. 6.

[51] Supra note 20 pg. 189.

[52] Koigi wa Wamwere, *The People's Representative and the Tyrants*, Nairobi: New Concept Typesetters, 1992, pg. 109.

[53] *Beyond: The Christian Leadership Magazine*, Vol. 4, No. 4 March 1988 on Election Special.

[54] *Weekly Review*, September 23, 1988.

[55] *Weekly Review,* April 29 1988.

[56] B. A. Ogot & W. R. Ochieng' (e.d.) *Decolonization and Independence in Kenya 1940-93* Nairobi: EAEP, 1995 pg. 213.

[57] Ibid pg. 240-42.

[58] *Nairobi Law Monthly*, February 1991, pg. 30.

[59] *Weekly Review*, 6th December, 1991, pg. 7.

[60] Ibid pg. 9.

[61] The Constitution of Kenya (Amendment) Act (No. 2) Act No. 12 of 1991.

[62] Karuti Kanyinga "Limitations of Political Liberalization: Parties and Electoral Politics in Kenya, 1992-2002", Published in Supra Note 29 at pg. 103.

[63] Smokin Wanjala, "Presidentialism, Ethnicity, Militarism and Democracy in Africa: The Kenyan Example" in Joseph Oloka-Onyango et al *Law and Struggle for Democracy in East Africa,* Claripress, Nairobi, 1996, pg. 88.

[64] Kivutha Kibwana and Wachira Maina, *"State and Citizen: Visions of Constitutional and Legal Reforms in Kenya's Emergent Multi-Party Democracy*, published in Supra Note 13 420 at pg. 463-464.

[65] The Constitution of Kenya (Amendment/Bill, 1992 in Kenya Gazette Supplement No. 16 (Bill No. 2).

[66] Ibid Section 10.

[67] *The Nairobi Law Monthly*, No. 42, February/March 1992.

[68] The Constitution of Kenya Amendment Act No. 6 of 1992.

[69] Supra note 64 pg. 462.

[70] Smith Hempstone "Defiant Acts in Nairobi," *World News*, pg. 10.

[71] *The Kenya Jurist* pg. 3.

[72] Jonah Njonge "The Kenyan Supreme Chiefs" *The Kenya Jurist*, September/December, 1993, pg. 12

[73] Hon. Michael Kijana Wamalwa, "Our Nation Yearns for a Vision and a Commitment," *The Nairobi, Law Monthly* No. 67 February, 1997.

[74] Section 47.

[75] The Statute Law (Repeals and miscellaneous Amendments/ Act, 1997, The Constitution of Kenya (Amendment) Act, 1997 Special Issue of Kenya Gazette Supplement No. 76 Act No. 9 of 1997, 7th November, 1997.

[76] Njoya & Others vs. Attorney General and Others EALR (2004) 1 EA 194 (HCK).

[77] Section 5(2) of the Constitution provides: "The President shall, subject to the provisions of any written law, appoint the Ministers from among the members of the national Assembly."

[78] Section 17(5) of the National Assembly and Presidential Elections Acts (Cap 7) provides as follows: No person who is elected or nominated as a member of the National Assembly with the support of or as a supporter of a political party (other than the party whose candidate has Minister of the Government of Kenya under section 16 of the Constitution without the concurrence of the party which supported him for election or nominated him for appointment as a member of the National Assembly.

[79] Willy Mutunga, *Constitution-Making from The Middle: Civil Society and Transition Politics in Kenya, 1992-1997* Nairobi: SAREAT, 1999 pg. 211.

[80] Ludeki Chweya (ed) *Electoral Politics in Kenya,* Nairobi: Claripress, 2002 pg. 45

[81] Julius E. Nyang'oro "The Politics of Constitution-Making in Kenya, 1992-1997: A commentary" in Supra note 79 at pg. 277.

[82] Prof. Anyang' Nyong'o, "Civil Society and the Transition Politics in Kenya: A Commentary". In Supra note 79 at pg. 289.

[83] Sections 45A and 45B of the Constitution.

[84] *The Standard* Wednesday, April 19, 2006 pg. 17.

[85] President Mwai Kibaki vide Gazette Notice No. 1406 of 24th February, 2006 appointed a Committee of Eminent Persons Chaired by Ambassador Bethuel Kiplagat whose terms of reference included:

a) facilitate the airing of views by the people of Kenya on the Constitutional review process so far in terms of what Kenyans consider the weaknesses, strengths, successes or failures of the process, and make proposals on the way forward;

b) Identify any legal, political, social, economic, religious, governance or other issues or obstacles, whether past or present, which stood in the way and/or may stand in the way of achieving a successful conclusion of the constitutional review process;

c) Receive written memoranda and/or oral presentations by organized groups and individuals on all foregoing matters and matters incidental thereto;

d) Undertake consultations and receive advice from local, regional and international constitutional experts on the foregoing issues and in particular, on how to establish an effective legal framework for the completion of the review process;

e) Prepare and submit a report of its findings to H. E. the President on the committee's findings, on or before the 30th May 2006 recommending:

(i)   a process for national healing to facilitate reconciliation and fruitful dialogue;

(ii) a process that will facilitate the resolution of contentious issues;

(iii) Legislation that will underpin the review process and lead to a new Constitution of Kenya.

[86] Walter Oyugi "The Politics of Transition in Kenya, 1992-2003: Democratic Consolidation or Deconsolidation" in Supra note 29 pg. 374-75.

[87] The Presidential and Parliamentary Elections Regulation under Section 34 of the National Assembly and Presidential elections Regulations 35-36 as revised in 2002.

[88] Supra note 13 at pg. 459.

[89] Supra note 80 at pg. 51.

[90] Jackson Mwalulu, "Twilight of the Nyayo era?" *E.A. Alternatives* May June, 1994, Issue No. 4 pg. 14.

[91] Marcel Rutten et al (ed) *Out for the Count: the 1997 General Elections and Prospects for Democracy in Kenya,* Kampala: Fountain Publishers Ltd., 2001 pg. 629.

[92] Supra note 29 page 113.

[93] Supra Note 29 pg. 116-17.

[94] *Daily Nation*, Monday, July 29, 2002.

[95] Maina Kiai, "Why KANU Stands to Gain from Serious Constitutional Changes" in Kivutha Kibwana et al (ed) *In Search of Freedom and Prosperity — Constitutional Reform in East Africa.* Nairobi: Claripress Limited, 1996 pg. 288-289.

4

Leadership Challenges in the African Diaspora

Macharia Munene

Introduction

What is the African diaspora and who are diaspora Africans? There are black people in the Americas and in Europe who deny their African roots and prefer to be considered as nationals of the countries in which they reside. Not wanting to have any linkage with Africans, such people are not likely to have much value for the African continent. They deliberately develop amnesia on matters African and at times imbibe the language of the master when talking about Africa and Africans.

There is also the issue of making a distinction between recent African immigrants to the West and fourth and fifth generation Diaspora Africans. Recent migrants, or "contemporary migrants" are also divided between those who are there by right of their skills and intellectual abilities, those recruited to provide specific/special services, and those who are economic, social and political refugees. While the first group would be in a position to take pro-African positions as they enjoy the bounties of the West, the latter would most likely be hiding from an assortment of governmental officials and are not likely to raise issues. It is those who consider themselves migrant Africans and still have a lot of personal attachments to Africa that can offer some kind of leadership.

Despite this scenario, analysis of leadership challenges in the African Diaspora can be divided into three chronological segments. First, are those that had to deal with pre-independent Africa and what it is that the African in Diaspora had to do to meet the challenges. Pre-independence challenges tended to be based on emotional attachments and solidarity hinging on a sense of mutual suffering. Second, are the challenges associated with independent Africa during the Cold War, roughly from 1960 to 1990. Once colonialism in Africa ended and black elites became accepted in the various mainstreams, the attachments weakened as each concentrated on proving themselves to be good nationals or patriotic Africans with emphasis being on promotion of their respective national interests. Third are the contemporary challenges associated with the post-cold war period, after 1990, a period identified with 'globalisation' or *postmodern colonialism*.[1]

In each of these periods, there were a number of Africans in Diaspora who distinguished themselves in the way they drew attention to the African continent or sought to be identified with, or to distance themselves from, things African. And they all had to deal with different types of challenges ranging from social, intellectual, ideological, political, and economic ones. They also have had to face the dilemma of identity presented in 1903 by W.E.B. DuBois, whether one was primarily Negro and then American or primarily American and then Negro. This dilemma can be extended to other regions and the question would still be relevant is one primarily European or North American or South American or Australasian and then second an African or is one first an African and then a national of the place of residence and citizenship? In answering that question, Africans in Diaspora who identify with Africa have had to resort to a balancing act of ensuring that the national interests of the country of residence or citizenship are not detrimental to African interests.

And in each of these periods, the African political and economic elite in the Diaspora faced at least three types of challenges. First, were motivational challenges that had to do with the Africans in the Diaspora deriving inspiration from Africa or Africans in the continent deriving inspiration from the successes of those in the Diaspora. Second, were the educational challenges that called for Africans in the continent and the Diaspora to help each other acquire the necessary tools for liberating themselves from the miserable conditions that afflicted both. Third, were political challenges that officially relegated Africans to the bottom of the ladder in every aspect of life which in turn made political liberation a condition of other types of liberation. The interplay among the three challenges defined the type of leadership that Africans in Diaspora could offer.

The Colonial Days

In the colonial days, the three types of challenges were particularly pronounced and a symbiotic relationship between the African elite in the Diaspora and in the continent tended to exist. They inspired each other, offered each other a wide ranging education, and generally endorsed the political aspirations of each other or considered them to be inter-dependent. The combination of the three produced interesting results.

The inspirational aspect related to the comfort that each side drew from the other or the knowledge of what the other was going through. For instance, those who led the intellectual rebellion in the United States by emphasising the study of Black History drew inspiration from the achievements of continental Africans.[2] They were countering their own intellectual training that emphasized white superiority and elitism.[3] They, therefore, needed an alternative reference point which they found in the African past, subsequently founded the *Crisis* and *The Journal of Negro History*, and published articles about the successes of African states, empires, and kings. It was this search for past African glory that would inspire the production of some of the most interesting books on Africa.

A line was developing that emphasised the Africanness of ancient Egypt to counter white people's claim that Egypt was white. The main proponent of this line of thought was Cheikh Anta Diop of Senegal who, in his *African Origins of Civilisation: Myth or Reality*, drew attention to European distortions of Egyptian history in effort to justify colonisation in Africa. An American contemporary of Diop, George G.M. James, in his *The Stolen Legacy* in 1954, went a step further and accused Greek philosophers such as Plato and Aristotle of thievery. Most of what passed as Greek philosophy, he claimed, was nothing more than plagiarism of the Egyptian mystery system.[4] Another contemporary was John G. Jackson who studied Egyptian religions and argued that the idea of a virgin birth was not unique to Jesus since the Egyptian Horus had claimed it thousands of years before the birth of Jesus. One sees the same line of thought in Ivan Van Sertima's 1976 book, *They Came Before Columbus: The African Presence in Ancient America*, in which he detailed pre-Columbian African contacts with the Americas.

While the Diaspora elites drew inspiration from past African achievements, Africans in the continent tended to be inspired by their contemporaries. Political activist Harry Thuku in Kenya, for instance, drew inspiration from the educational and political activities of Booker T. Washington, W.E.B. DuBois, and Marcus Garvey and he tended to lump them together as black Americans who could help him in his political goals. He hoped that such leaders would help him to establish schools in Kenya which would become political tools for getting rid of colonial domination.[5]

Garvey's publication, *The Negro World*, inspired Jomo Kenyatta. While in England he teemed up with Paul Robeson, an American entertainer with whom he shared a room and acted in a film. In Europe, Kenyatta published a book in 1938, *Facing Mount Kenya* intellectually attacking the logic of colonialism in which people who masqueraded as agents of civilization destroyed other societies and made a living being "professional friends" of Africa who claimed to know what was in the best interest of the African.[6] In putting the final touches of the book, Kenyatta was helped by Mbiyu Koinange, son of a colonial chief.

While Kenyatta was in Europe, Koinange had been in the United States, being one of the Africans inspired by James Aggrey to seek American education. In the United States, he had imbibed American political values and also recruited black Americans into the cause of African liberation. He returned to Kenya in 1938 to start a college in which anti-colonial agitation occupied a large part of the curriculum.[7] He was in exile during the Mau Mau War in the 1950s and he too wrote a book, *The People of Kenya Speak for Themselves*, while he was in England contrasting Dedan Kimathi favourably with British atrocities. Another person inspired by Aggrey's success was Francis Kwame Nkrumah who went to the United States and Britain to study philosophy. Nkrumah would later team up with Kenyatta, DuBois, and George Padmore at the Fifth Pan-African Congress which, until 1945, had been run by black Americans, mainly DuBois.[8] Nkrumah went on to lead the Gold Coast into self-government and independence

The Mau Mau War, and self-government for the Gold Coast, took place in the 1950s, at the height of the Cold War and this forced general reassessment that favoured Africa. There had been Diaspora elites like DuBois and Robeson who had openly petitioned the United Nations, in the 1940s, against perceived US support for colonialism and continuing racism in the United States. Establishment and politically minded Diaspora elites such as Walter White of the NAACP and Trade Unionist A. Philip Randolph used such criticism to play up the Cold War card to support anti-colonialism and increased educational opportunities for Africans. In part, this was because the Mau Mau War had attracted a lot of interest and the Diaspora community was more than willing to listen to Gikonyo Kiano blaming the British for the violence against a people demanding their basic rights. Mau Mau violence, therefore, was a good reason for black elites to pressure the American government to distance itself from European colonialism. A reassessment was in the offing, especially after 1956.

The result of the reassessment was the increased interaction between the Diaspora and the continental African elites. As Ghana attained independence in 1957, which was a boost for civil rights in the United States, pressure to minimise official racism intensified and effort was made to appear to be more concerned with African interests. It was around this time that a lot of Black Colleges, partly at the urging of Julius Gikonyo Kiano and Tom Mboya opened their doors to African students with the climax being the students airlifts of 1959-1961. Through the airlift and related operations, thousands of students found educational opportunities on the eve of

Kenya's independence, which later helped to ease the transition from colonialism. The student airlift was a big show of support from the African leadership in America for African education. And among those in the forefront were Harry Belafonte, the musician, and Martin Luther King Jnr. who hosted an airlift student.

Not all black people in Diaspora who benefited from the growing reassessment were supportive of Africans or wanted to be identified with Africa. There was, for instance, E. Frederick Morrow, the first black man to work at the White House in a responsible position. He was representative of black people who wanted nothing to do with Africans and exhibited all the prejudices common with white Americans. During his visit to Uganda, he found Entebbe's Victoria Hotel "loaded with black houseboys and waiters, flunkies who moved about the hotel barefooted," and commended the British for doing "their usual job of making themselves comfortable and developing a splendid civilization in this unique area of the dark continent.... I cannot deny that the British really benefit any place into which they move."[9] By then, however, the British were on the way out.

Independence and Neo-Colonialism

After classical colonialism was terminated in the African continent, around 1960, a period of *neo-colonialism* set in and lasted up to the end of the Cold War, around 1990. Diaspora African leadership went through some dramatic changes. The mutuality of concern between those in the continent and those in the Diaspora seemingly disappeared because the two groups do not suffer the same level of oppression. A few Diaspora Africans penetrated power bases while a few African rulers strode on the continent stamping out dissent while talking of the evils of colonialism and the white man. On both sides, however, the political elite were instruments of indirect control as they tended to ignore the plight of other Africans. This was particularly pronounced before 1980. After 1980, there appeared to be a resurgence of mutual attraction.

The 1960s were volatile in the United States and in Africa. The Civil Rights movement in the United States peaked with some activists who valued Africa being assassinated or becoming disillusioned with their countries. W.E.B. DuBois renounced his American citizenship, declared himself to be a communist and migrated to Ghana where he died an old man. Malcolm X traveled to Africa, founded an organization modeled after the Organisation of African Unity (OAU), the Organisation of Afro-American Unity (OAAU) and was assassinated in 1965. Malcolm X was a Muslim but his better known Christian counter-part, Martin Luther King, was similarly assassinated three years later, in 1968. King believed that anti-colonialism in Africa was akin to civil rights movement in the United States, developed a deep global understanding of international class structure, opposed the war in Vietnam, tried to organize workers in the United States, and was then assassinated. Both men, Malcolm X and King, had inspired numerous youth to take interest in Africa some of who joined the Black Power movement and popularized African and Black studies. As the decade of the 1960s came to an end, some of these activists were dispersed into self-exile, underwent political metamorphosis, or became inactive. Africans in the Diaspora were not as inspiring as before.

Sometimes disillusionment turned into distaste for things African as exemplified in the attitude of novelist James Baldwin. His contact with foreigners, be they Africans, Europeans, or Asiatics convinced him that he was an American and nothing else. In 1970, as the civil rights movement was ebbing and a lot of black Americans still tried to identify with Africa, Baldwin was loathful to such identification. He argued: "The black American is looked down on by other dark people as being an object abjectly used. They envy him on one hand, but on the other hand they also would like to look down on him... It is going to take another generation before the African people become independent of Europe, and European history, *in their minds.*"[10] That being the case, he asserted: "I don't agree with all of these people running around with Afro wigs. And God knows I'm tired of being *told* by people who just got out of the various white colleges and got a *dashiki* and let their hair grow; I am terribly tired of these middle-class darkies telling me what it means to be black. But I *understand* why they have to do it!"[11]

Baldwin was not the only one who did not want to identify with Africa, there was also Carl Rowan who was appointed director of the United States Information Agency (USIA) 1964. USIA, initially called USIS, is a Cold War creation started in the 1948 to counter Soviet and communist propaganda against racism and colonialism. In Africa in the late 1940s, USIS was supposed to post blacks in Accra and Lagos to sell the American way of life, and to emphasise American friendship, understanding and cooperation with Africans.[12] It was such recruitment that led Paul Robeson to complain how the United States uses blacks: "Our government has been employing Negro intellectuals, entertainers, ministers, and many others to play the roles of ambassadorial Uncle Toms for years. They are supposed to show their well-fed, well-groomed faces behind the Iron Curtain as living proof that everyone is free and equal in the U.S. and the colour bar is a myth."[13]

Rowan's appointment to head America's propaganda agency was a first for a black and he considered himself a Negro but not an African in Diaspora and he seemingly extended his low regard for Africa to his close friend, Associate Justice Thurgood Marshall of the US Supreme Court. One of the most interesting aspects of Marshall's legal life is his participation in the 1960 Lancaster House Constitutional Conference where he was the official advisor to the Kenyan African delegation at the invitation of Tom Mboya and Gikonyo Kiano. He was so attached to the Kenyan independence struggle that he felt offended in 1978 when President Jimmy Carter left him out of the official American delegation to the funeral of Jomo Kenyatta, Kenya's first president with whom he identified. Marshall literary forced his way into the funeral delegation. But when in 1992 Rowan wrote a biography of Marshall, *Dream Makers and Dream Breakers: The World of Justice Thurgood Marshall*, published in 1993,[14] not a single word appeared to reflect Marshall's concern for Africa.

The use of blacks to project the interests of the master states was a continuing constant although the type of human instrument to be used would change with circumstances. There is for instance, the story of Mohammed Ali whom President Jimmy Carter in 1980 used as a diplomatic instrument of his anti-Soviet strategy by sending Ali to African countries to persuade their presidents not to send teams to Russia for the Summer Olympics in Moscow. Ali, a one time great boxer, closely identified with Malcolm X, also attracted international attention by being flamboyant, loud-mouthed, and constantly boasting of his skills. He had come to be regarded as a hero of the Third World fighting the white system because he refused to fight in Vietnam. He landed in Nairobi, met President Moi and then announced that Kenya had agreed not to attend the Olympics. Tanzania and Nigeria felt insulted by Carter's decision to send a mere boxer to deal with serious diplomatic and political issues; they did not boycott the games.

Despite the assumption that Africans would agree to side with American policy simply because a black envoy had delivered the message, there were some positive signs that all was not lost on Africa in the 1970s. In part, the disappointment with Carter sending Ali to Africa was because his earlier appointment of Andrew Young to be United States Ambassador to the United Nations had been well received in Africa as he had then pressed for the liberation of Rhodesia and Southern Africa. Young, however, had subsequently been fired for talking to the Palestinian Liberation Organisation (PLO). In being fired, he helped to pave way for Middle East reconciliation and made it possible for other American officials to speak to the PLO. There was also Alex Hailey, inspired by Malcolm X, with his "Roots" television series that captivated public mind and encouraged Africans in the Diaspora to look for their 'roots' in Africa. Such developments were a kind of preparation for the resurgence of interest in Africa by Africans in the Diaspora that took place in the 1980s.

The period between 1960 and 1980, therefore, was one of readjustment in the way Africans in the Diaspora looked at Africa and balanced it with the dynamics of their countries. They were trying to find bearings and got sucked into the American 'me' generation. This tended to split the African Americans into two groups, the disillusioned "revolutionaries" and the mainstreaming of the black elite who were then incorporated into corporate America, sometimes as tokens to divert attacks that institutions were racist.

In the 1980s, there was a resurgence of interest in the activities of those in the Diaspora whose numbers had been supplemented by migrant Africans who were beginning to gain visibility. The most important of these was Ali Mazrui who seemingly went through an intellectual metamorphosis. Before the 1980s, Mazrui could wax Western ideas into the African situation, for which he was accused of pandering to Western interests at the expense of African interests. He then reassessed himself and came up with *The Africans: A Triple Heritage;* a successful television series sponsored by the West. In it he tried to redeem himself by showing the positive side of the African continent, by castigating the West for slavery and colonialism while, at the same time, appearing to exonerate the Arabs. The West, which had sponsored the program, was angry but Mazrui no longer cared much about what the West thought of him. [15] He seemingly cared about what other Africans thought.

The new Mazrui was close to Walter Rodney, a Diaspora African teaching at the University of Dar es Salaam who led the attack on the supposed benevolence of the European colonizer. His argument was that underdevelopment in Africa was a consequence of European exploitation. Rodney had been angry with the way text books, full of distortions, were taught to Africans as history. And that history was that colonialism was benevolent and actually beneficial to Africans. Claiming that he was tired of pointing out to students that various assertions in textbooks were incorrect, he had come up with *How Europe Underdeveloped Africa* as a response to most of the distortions. [16] The book caused disgust in Western circles and those who clung to capitalistic institutions but there was admiration from some Africans and some Westerners who saw it as bold and refreshing. Mazrui's *The Africans* television series also appeared to be bold and refreshing given who the sponsors were.

As Mazrui was causing socio-intellectual consternation with his *The Africans*, the political climate fueled by the Margaret Thatcher and Ronald Reagan's seeming condoning of the remaining racist regimes in Southern Africa, resuscitated pro-African activism in the Diaspora. It reactivated anti-apartheid campaigners led by Randall Robinson and his well organized Trans-Africa and by Rev. Jesse Jackson, a disciple of Martin Luther King. Africans in the Americas took the Thatcher-Reagan policies to be a challenge and they responded by mounting intensified campaigns against apartheid South Africa. It became strategically appropriate for black leaders to be arrested in front of a South African consulate to dramatise political opposition to apartheid. Various state legislatures were inundated with petitions to divest investments from South Africa and the pressure eventually forced Congress to impose sanctions. It was during this campaign that 'progressive' black Americans started calling themselves African-Americans while some went to the extent of asserting that they were Africans, period. This type of pressure led to the release of Nelson Mandela and the dismantling of apartheid in 1990. The Cold War was also over, and *neo-colonialism* had become irrelevant to continued control.

Globalisation and Post-Modern Colonialism

The end of the Cold War forced global readjustments posing interesting challenges to leaders in the Diaspora. These readjustments gave rise to a new form of international exploitation that does not require physical territorial political rule, as in classical colonialism, or indirect control of client states by master states through presidents and other government officials, as in neo-colonialism. The new form of colonialism is globalisation or post-modern colonialism,[17] that ignores borders and governments and uses an assortment of agencies to control people and places intellectually, politically, culturally and economically.

These agencies include multilateral institutions such as the International Monetary Fund, the World Bank, WTO, giant media and publishing houses, and international Non-Governmental Organisations. Some of these agents make strange demands on African governments knowing that they are protected by the master states who do not have to have good reasons before they invade a small country that does not do what the agents want.[18] They are on a number of occasions used on instruments of control in advancing the interests of the master states. They may also serve as shields behind which master states can hide to avoid blame when things go wrong. Significantly, within those agencies are to be found some cultural and intellectual operatives who pass as African leaders in Diaspora.

Africans in the Diaspora, therefore, are caught in a bind as to exactly what they are supposed to do with regard to postmodern colonialism. There is, for instance, increased visibility for a selected few both in politics and in the intellectual arena and as in the previous periods, there is misuse of such leaders to make the case for the interests of the master states in Africa; cases in which Africans in the continent are at times skeptical. There has also been an attempted "rethink" of what the word Diaspora means. In part this is because of the growing presence of recent migrants, born in Africa and who still continue to maintain strong ties to Africa, and yet do not live in Africa. And there are times when Diaspora leaders, whether born in the Diaspora or in the continent, have turned on each other viciously and intellectually on the best way to interpret Africa, or who is responsible for problems in Africa.

Moreover, and there are also those, as in the previous periods, who want nothing to do with Africa. Living in North America and Europe they have been so culturally assimilated that they refuse to think of themselves as Africans, to identify with anything African, and actually disdain their possible African connections. One such a person was *The Washington Post* correspondent in Nairobi, Keith Richburg who wrote a book about his experiences, introduced the concept of the Big Lie Rule, [19] and created the impression that Africa was so hopeless that he was glad that his ancestors had been on the slave ship. He hates Africa and writes, "I'm conscious that some people will say by hating Africa, I am really hating myself." But then he is not an African and therefore cannot hate himself. His stay in Africa was as an alien who may look like Africans but he did not know what it was to be an African. "I am terrified of Africa," he wrote and added, "I don't want to be from this place. In my darkest heart here on this pitch black African night, I am quietly celebrating the passage of my ancestor who made it out."[20] Richburg insisted that he is an American, not an African or an African-American, and as far as he is concerned it is rubbish to talk "about going 'back' to anywhere, in finding some missing 'roots,' in finding a homeland."[21]

There were those black Americans who offered a different type of leadership. Before the mainstream America had embraced democracy in Africa, Diaspora Africans were there, having solidarity with African states against white racism. Among them is Transafrica associated with Randall Robinson, which having dealt with white oppressors in South Africa turned attention "to the violence and tyranny caused by black oppressors in Kenya." Diaspora leaders had then called for tough sanctions to be imposed on African government's that violated human rights. In their letter to President Bush, the African-American leaders stated: "U.S. taxpayers' money must not be used to supply arms and funds to a government that stifles freedom of expression with violence and protects its power through repression."[22] They appealed to Bush, however, as Americans who were concerned with events in Africa.

There was also Jesse Jackson in the 1990s, who had made a name as a civil rights activist and a presidential candidate, and had shown serious interest in developments in Africa, particularly South Africa. He has had such impact that U.S. Ambassador Prudence Bushnell described him as a 'terrific American'. He is a terrific American but not an African and he twice visited Kenya as an emissary of US President Bill Clinton. The first time, in November 1997, was to impress on Kenyans to have a first-class election. He considered it a "good thing" that "there was no violence before the election."[23] The second time, in February 1998, however, was to tell President Moi to stop the killings in the Rift Valley, and to offer consolation to the victims of the political killings. "We simply urge President Moi, who is our ally and who has not been to the Rift Valley, to use his presence and the power of his security forces to bring the people the security that they need and deserve."[24] Within a week of Jackson's urging, Moi visited the clash torn area although he denied that he did so at Jackson's behest. Jackson's pressure on Moi, commented *The Star*, a newly established biweekly newspaper that is critical of the government, "was a slap in our head of state's face."[25]

While many tried to say what was best for Africa often from outside the official officialdom, there are those who operate from within the corridors of power. At the political front, these include political power brokers like Baroness Amos in England, the British Foreign Office Minister for Africa. There was Colin Powell, Secretary of State and National Security Advisor Condoleza Rice in the United States. At the United Nations was Secretary General Kofi Annan who had to bear the brunt of the Anglo-American decision to invade Iraq without a UN Mandate.

The decision revealed some of the challenges that such people in visible positions face. As Carter had done in 1980 when he used Mohammed Ali, these leaders found themselves to be instruments of trying to sell very unpopular policies to Africans. In Britain, Amos became Tony Blair's messenger to Guinea to persuade that country to support the invasion. In the United States, Bush used Powell and Rice to pressure African leaders to support the invasion and in the process, charged critics, the United States "abandoned all its principles," and engaged in "arm-twisting, cajoling and even using tactics that in more moral times it had referred to as 'corruption'"[26] Among the African countries subjected to this treatment, with mixed success, were Cameroon, Angola, Guinea, Ethiopia, Rwanda, Senegal, and Kenya.

The invasion of Iraq by the United States of America and Britain brought out some of the internal conflicts that afflict Diaspora leaders. African-Americans in

Congress were torn between admiring African resistance to Anglo-American threats and pressures and persuading African governments to concede for the sake of foreign aid to Africa. A black Congressman reportedly argued, "On one hand it made us proud of our heritage…but on the other hand it will make it far more difficult for us to pressure this administration into approving foreign aid for African projects … people in this administration are extremely vindictive and the embarrassment caused by Angola, Cameroon and Guinea will not soon be forgotten." And also in the receiving end of the vindictiveness was Kofi Annan who failed to stay in the pocket of the United States.[27]

The infighting also came out in public. Powell was rumoured to have resisted the invasion while Rice was gung-ho and Powell paid the price after the 2004 election when he was shown the door and Rice took his job as Secretary of State. One of the tragedies of Powell was that his record had been exemplary as a soldier, a policy maker and had been touted as a potential presidential candidate. There were other instances that tainted Powell's image but it was the invasion of Iraq that mostly ruined that image. Critics such as Harry Belafonte accused him of pandering to the wishes of the "master" just as in the olden slave days when the "house slave" was happy doing the master's dirty work.[28] And given that the excuses that the Powell presented at the United Nations turned out to be inaccurate, the image stuck.

Belafonte's portrayal of conflicts between modern house slaves and field slaves can be extended to the intellectual arena where a vicious debate, amounting to an intellectual civil war among the Africans, has been taking place. On the one side are Africans who fell into the trap of blaming Africans for everything and exonerating the forces controlling events and thus become agents of post-modern colonialism which tend to blame the victim for the condition he finds himself in. There is a Ghanaian in Washington, George B.N. Ayittey who is regularly a guest of Voice of America programmes on Africa and is very vocal in blaming Africans. The attraction in his two books, *Africa Betrayed* and *Africa in Chaos*, is the blame he puts on African states for the condition that they find themselves in while essentially exonerating the West.[29] There is also a Cameroonian, Achille Mbembe, who, when working in North Carolina attracted attention with a 2002 article published in *Public Culture*, "African Modes of Self-Writing" by asserting that the intellectual capacity of the Africans is not as good as that of the Jews in confronting their unique condition as he dismissed African intellectuals as "nativists" who suffer from a "neurosis of victimization".[30]

Other intellectual peculiarities were seen in the nasty exchanges involving Ali Mazrui, the Kenyan, Wole Soyinka, the Nigerian, and Henry Louis Gates, the

American. All three living in the United States, Soyinka and Gates were on one side and Mazrui was on the other. The subject of the intellectual civil war was the interpretation of two television series on Africa. Mazrui's *The Africans* had essentially blamed the West and seemed to exonerate the Arabs and Muslims. For being soft on the Arabs and Muslims, Soyinka attacked him. Roughly a decade later, Gates was funded to come up with what appeared like a response to Mazrui and he produced, *Wonders of the African World* which critics dismissed as a whitewash. "Shame" is what Randall Robinson of Transafica termed the Gates television program and Mazrui raised serious questions about some of the depictions. The result was public intellectual altercation and the impression that Gates, heading an institute named after W.E.B. DuBois at Harvard University was a hired intellectual gun to shift the blame of slavery to Africans.

Conclusion

The African Diaspora and the leadership therein is therefore complex partly because of the problem of definition. While some black people in the Americas and in Europe want nothing to do with Africa, there others who have an emotional attachment to the continent and struggle to be identified with a lot of things African. Those who do not want to be associated with Africa develop amnesia and emphasise that they are nationals of the countries in which they reside as they imbibe the language of the *master* when talking about Africa and Africans. Some of them do this in the hope of getting promoted for working hard in an anti-African intellectual industry. This is the case whether one is a recent immigrant or a fourth, fifth, or tenth generation Diaspora person.

In the colonial days, there appeared to be some common linkages in terms of the suffering that Africans in the continent and in the Diaspora suffered on account of racism and colonialism. Struggle against racism was synonymous with anti-colonialism and the elite on both sides tended to identify with each other. Such names in the Diaspora as Garvey, DuBois, Robeson, St. Clair Drake, Padmore King, and Belafonte were easily linked to Thuku, Kenyatta, Koinange, Mboya, Kiano, Azikiwe, and Nkrumah. They inspired each other into relative success.

After the end of classical colonialism in Africa and the end of official racism in the Diaspora, common ties appeared to weaken as the leaders concentrated more on being good nationals. They got sucked into the Cold War logic that plunged Africa into a *neo-colonial* condition in which rulers of African states were maintained by rulers of the master states to protect the interests of the master states against the potential demands of their own people. The elite in the Diaspora became tools of persuading Africans to accept what the master states wanted. This is similar to the colonial days when Aggrey had been made part of the Commission to Africa to convince Africans that they should not seek socio-political and philosophical education that was meant for policy makers. As with Aggrey, the results were mixed with defiance being the norm in some places.

Defiance by Diaspora leaders was particularly important in the eventual dismantling of apartheid in Southern Africa and this came at a time when *neo-colonialism* as a controlling mechanism was giving way to a subtle method that requires no individual leaders for exploitation to continue. This was 'globalisation' or *post-modern colonialism*. A characteristic of this controlling method was blame shifting and the use of Africans to beat up other Africans intellectually and policy making. Diaspora Africans in visible high profile positions in Britain and the United States were used to try and sell the invasion of Iraq to the Africans through all sorts of tactics. This led to accusations that those leaders were modern day "house slaves" betraying the interests of Africans despite their positions of influence.

At the intellectual level, there appeared to be a civil war with one group siding with, and imbibing the arguments of, the master states while the other side had difficulties accepting all the blame heaped on the Africans. Whatever the case, those in the Diaspora of many generation continue to agonise over their identity, over the dilemma posed in 1903 by DuBois on what one was primarily a Diaspora African and then a national of the place of residence and citizenship or primarily a national of the place of residence and then a Diaspora African. Those who believe they are primarily African then do a balancing act of ensuring that the national interests of the country of residence are not detrimental to African interests. Those who have little regard for Africa then become very effective tools of fixing Africans.

Recent African migrants to the Diaspora also have problems of acceptability in their new places of residence. They appear to be torn between complete identification with their adopted countries to the detriment of their places of birth and protecting the interests of their countries of birth against the wishes of the rulers of their adopted countries. Some end up joining Africa-bashing in policy making and intellectual industry and are rewarded with appointments and exposure. They become very good in blaming Africans for political, economic, and intellectual problems and then are promoted as "experts" whose version should be accepted because they are Africans.

Others resent this intellectual Africa-bashing and are vocal in their response. As a result there appears to be a civil war among African leaders in Diaspora, sometimes encouraged by the West.

Notes

[1]   Susan S. Silbey, 1996 Presidential Address, "'Let Them Eat Cake': Globalisation, Postmodern Colonialism, and the Possibility of Justice," Law and Society Review, Volume 31, Number 2, p. 219.

[2]   Macharia Munene, "The Idea of Black History as Intellectual Rebellion," KAMESA-Newsletter, Issue # 5, November 1997, pp. 5-6

[3]   Atiba King, "Historic Review of Negro Education in America"

[4]   George G.M. James, *The Stolen Legacy: The Greeks were not the authors of Greek philosophy, but the people of North Africa, commonly called the Egyptians* New York: Philosophical Library, 1954, passim.

[5]   Macharia Munene, "The United States and Anti-colonialism in Kenya," African Review of Foreign Policy, March 1999, Volume 1 Number 1, pp. 5-6

[6]   Jomo Kenyatta, Facing Mount Kenya: The Traditional Life of the Gikuyu Nairobi: Kenway Publications, 1978.

[7]   Mbiyu Koinange, The People of Kenya Speak for Themselves, Detroit: Kenya Publication Fund, 1955; Munene, "The United States and Anti-colonialism in Kenya."

[8]   Macharia Munene, "Leadership: Kenyatta and Nkrumah," in Gerald J. Wanjohi, and G. Wakuraya Wanjohi, editors, *Social and Religious Concerns of East Africa: A Wajibu Anthology* Washington DC.: The Council of Research in Values and Philosophy, 2005, pp.89-90

[9]   E. Frederick Morrow, *Black Man in the White House: A Diary of the Eisenhower Years by the Administrative Officer for Special Projects, The White House, 1955-1961* New York: Coward-McCann, Inc., 1963, pp. 217, 136-137

[10]   James Baldwin statement, in Margaret Mead/ James Baldwin, *A Rap on Race* London: J.B. Lippincott, 1971, p.81.

[11]   James Baldwin statement, in Margaret Mead/ James Baldwin, *A Rap on Race* London: J.B. Lippincott, 1971, p. 95

[12]   Macharia Munene, *The Truman Administration and the Decolonisation of Sub-Saharan Africa* Nairobi: Nairobi University Press, 1995), pp. 105-106, 144, 150.

[13]   Quote in Helen Laville and Scott Lucas, "The American Way: Edith Sampson, the NAACP, and African American Identity in the Cold War," Diplomatic History, Volume 20, Number 4, Fall 1996, p. 565.

[14]   Carl T. Rowan, Dream Makers, Dream Breakers: The World of Justice Thurgood Marshall Boston: Little, Brown and Company, 1993.

[15]   Following the upheavals associated with the Angolan independence in 1975, Mazrui found it necessary to assert his nationalistic credentials after he was accused of treachery for seemingly siding with the United States in the Angolan crisis. His *Triple Heritage* roughly ten years later, however, angered

the Americans so much that an announcer in Kentucky would put a preamble to the show by saying that he did not agree with what Professor Mazrui claimed.

[16] Walter Rodney, *How Europe Underdeveloped Africa* Washington DC:, Howard University Press,1974; Macharia Munene, "Africans and Their Interpreters in International Relations," presented at the 4th Pan-European International Relations Conference, European Consortium for Political Research, University of Kent at Canterbury, September 8-10, 2001.

[17] Susan S. Silby, " 'Let Them Eat Cake' : Globalisation, Postmodern Colonialism, and the Possibilities of Justice," *Law and Society Review*, Volume 31, Number 2, 1997, pp. 219-220

[18] Macharia Munene, "Hazards of Postmodern Colonialism in Kenya," Conference on The Political Economy of Kenya, Oxford University, May 27-28, 2004, Oxford, United Kingdom.

[19] Keith B. Richburg, Out of America: A Black Man Confronts Africa New York: Harper Collins,1997, pp.3-6

[20] Quotes in Keith B. Richburg, Out of America: A Black Man Confronts Africa New York: Harper Collins,1997, pp. 231-233.

[21] *Ibid.,* p.237.

[22] William Raspberry, "Blacks on Black Tyrants," The Washington Post, August 10, 1990

[23] Robert Fullerton, "Jackson Says Violence in Kenya Politically Charged," *External Wireless File: Features for February 11, 1998,* p.1.

[24] Robert Fullerton, "Jackson Says Violence in Kenya Politically Charged," External Wireless File: Features for February 11, 1998, p.1.

[25] *The Star*, February 13-16, 1998, p.19.

[26] Quote in Milan Vesely, "US Word is Not Its Bond," *African Business*, April 2003, p. 25

[27] Quote and Story in Milan Vesely, "Bush's Diplomatic Train Wreck," *African Business*, May 2003, pp. 30-31

[28] Harry Belafonte on Colin Powell, CNN Larry King Live Interview with Belafonte, October 15, 2002, as printed in the *Black Commentator*, Issue Number 14, October 17, 2002

[29] George B.N. Ayittey, *Africa Betrayed* New York: St Martin's Press, 1993 and *Africa in Chaos* New York: St. Martin's Press, 1998

[30] Achille Mbembe, "African Modes of Self-Writing," *Public Culture*, Volume 14, Number 1, 2002, pp. 240, 257

5

Politics and Alternative Leadership in Africa

Eric Masinde Aseka

Introduction

The field of leadership development is beginning to be saturated with a proliferation of new leadership development skills and methods. These methods underscore certain values and norms of democratic practice. This chapter looks at politics and leadership in terms of drawbacks of ideology and social strategies of political governance. It discusses the dynamics of leadership in terms of its poverty with regard to ideological innovation and also the social policy implications of this poverty. It demonstrates how good leadership is founded on clear foundational values and principles. Values ought to be an integral part of a nation's infrastructure of leadership and they ought to provide a good social matrix of responsible public management. Given that leadership development involves more than just developing individual leaders, a growing focus is beginning to be directed at the context in which leadership is developed. It is important to learn about the traits and virtues of effective leaders as studied by a growing number of scholars in order to understand what a leadership of integrity demands. Integrity is a condition of what may be termed as the politesse of social action determined by an assemblage and display of various aptitudes, attitudes, principles and values that go along way in enhancing the required leadership competencies.

Politics without its required politesse can easily be causal to damning forms of social action and public behaviour. *Politesse refers to the development and nurturing of a public morality that is characterized by etiquette, good behaviour, respectability and demureness. Politesse is a competency-producing factor that is critical in the generation of virtuous behaviour in a good leader.* Moral well being of leaders is part of the required normative infrastructure of building a new architecture of political and social security in a nation, an infrastructure that underwrites good political order.

Critical in expediting the development of good leadership is the question of behavioural change in leaders and the development and nurturing of a sense of self-awareness and good character development in them. Good leadership involves the sharpening of personality traits, aptitudes and competencies in those who seek to lead. Again, it requires the development and harnessing of their skills, talents and personality gifting as well as spurring in them a good sense of resource and facilities management.

In view of the importance of national interest, power and nationality in the realm of political realism, it makes sense to state that leaders have to be imbued with sufficient commitment to national and organizational objectives, goals and targets in their national duties. They have to develop habits of widening their decision making environments through consultation and seeking useful professional advice with regard to questions affecting national interest, exercise of power and expression of nationality. Goran Hyden (1992) argues that the alienation of leaders from followers is at the root of Africa's economic and social ills. For him, political will is crippled and social energy is exhausted. The formula of one leader, one ideology, and one party became fractured after it had run its course (Hyden, 1992:ix). Power and influence are described in terms of ability to act, to influence an outcome and therefore to get something to happen or not happen. It also implies the will and capacity to overcome resistance.

Good leaders do not necessarily have all the pertinent traits of personality and character, but they tend to a good proportion of these. Because leaders must have certain dispositions, good leadership is quality leadership. Quality involves a process of measurement, control and the definition of the necessary operational charters for process improvement. Here, I am signifying the primal importance of incepting a leadership quality process in the development of a leadership culture.

Good leadership is driven by certain personality strengths. There is need to learn about the traits of effective leadership personality as studied by leadership scholars and as defined by various cultural communities and social groups. Where possible, we must learn from these the challenges and skills of building excellence in leadership underwritten by a profound attitudinal transformation given that, really, attitude dictates one's performance. A bad leadership attitude will therefore dictate undesirable political behaviour. It is important to measure ourselves against certain profiles of achievers in society.

Social and economic relations and dynamics generated by policies developed within a poor framework of leadership infrastructure and the poor attitudes that this gives rise to are worth serious consideration. These attitudes lead to violation of professional integrity and the rendering of existing policies ineffectual while at the same time contributing to the emergence of organizational cultures of impunity, which characterizes the leadership tyrannies that many African nations and their public institutions exhibit. The absence of proper national foundations of the so-called nation-states is explicable in terms of the disturbing dearth of ideological production so far exemplified by infantile political behaviour of leaders in many African states. Leadership is influence and influence is all about swinging people's choices and commitment to social action. It is not dependent on positions or titles but rather on one's vision. Without a national vision, we can hardly talk of a transformational national ideology given that an ideology is a lived relation; it is, a comprehensive statement vision. Lack of ideological production by leaders merely creates a leadership gap which allows the entrenchment of personality weaknesses.

The political immaturity of many African leaders has made the political economies of many states to be stunted. Political maturity rests on personality strengths. Lack of proper leadership competencies underlies the petulant and despicable behaviour of the political class that is headstrong, naïve, inconsistent, haphazard, indecisive, domineering, manipulative and unpredictable among other negative personality traits. Behaviour is a conscious process and it is driven by perceptions. There must be perception, which animate these negative attitudes. Bad behaviour is driven by poor perceptions and that is why to effect a real attitudinal transformation in leaders, we need some paradigm shifting; an attitudinal transformation. Attitudes reflect inward orientations and readiness to respond in certain predetermined manners to a given situation or concept. That is why it is essential, as part of the creation of a transformational leadership, to examine the role of culture and ideology in defining proper public morality.

Cultures have objectives towards which their practices are geared and which their institutions pursue (Diagne and Ossebi, 1996: 12). Cultures are social matrices within which values, beliefs, standards and norms are defined. Cultures, therefore, circumscribe certain attitudes. Behaviour becomes the outward expression of these inward configurations called attitudes. In other words, cultures are ideological outputs. For this reason, there is need to examine and interrogate the whole question of cultural leadership in terms beyond mere concerns with works of art. We must begin to address the whole question of the role of the intellectual and politician or even the professional public manager in fostering this leadership. Cultural values must be harnessed in the mediation of power and the execution of leadership responsibility. They ought to be apparent in the expression of individual or collective identities and their attendant aspirations in today's 21st century Africa. Negative personality traits lead to negative transactionalist leadership. The transactional nature of politics without its required posturing of politesse merely engrains in the psychology of public actors a transactionalist attitude of business as usual.

Culture, ideology and social policy

A panoramic view of society is germane and should be made possible in terms of what Tade Aina identifies as a wide range of conceptions and contradictions in the practice and politics of social policy (Aina, 1996:13). Society is made up of various cultural repertoires and the whole question of cultural leadership needs to be addressed as a way of creating a new national culture. National culture is a product of leadership mediation to create new political identities that display certain civic virtues embodying a desired national character. Every culture has its derived philosophies and the function of leadership mediation is to reconcile points of conflict, harmonize views and feeling and synchronize certain aspirations into a given national project or agenda. Every culture generates its traditions, customs and mores some of which may be antithetical to the national agenda of national integration. That is why leadership intervention and mediation become necessary. After all, no culture is static. Culture is negotiated and culture can be re-invented. National culture is a product of social and political invention. That is the sense in which I dare talk of leaders as social engineers.

Culture is an arena of struggle and, therefore, organizational leadership culture should be one that transcends myopic transactionalism of tribal millenarian leadership based on personality weaknesses instead of strengths. Transformational leadership demands a kind of political transcendence by which national leaders rise to levels of supra-ethnic culturing in order to address national interests and purposes more meaningfully. Culture is a marker of identity and it therefore circumscribes perceptions of ethnicity. To inscribe a new national motif in culture, leaders need to articulate broader national visions for their societies, and inspire their citizens to work toward achieving those visions. Vision is seeing the future in the present built on the foundation of fundamental lessons from the past. Vision is an informed bridge from the present to a better future. That is why visionary leaders must be people who develop a certain sense of national identity and develop certain personal convictions, values and ethics. Such leaders are transformational leaders who rise above the beneficial and sometimes extortionist exchanges between contracting parties who act in so far as their actions optimize the mutual benefit in a kind of "rub my back and I rub yours" approach. The whole farce of populist politics is based on patron-client networks by which the political class seeks to patronize civil society. This turns inside out ethnicity, making it acquire a political expression called tribalism. Tribalism is simply political ethnicity by which the patrimonialization of the state in Africa has been fomented in despicable transactionalism. Transactional leadership tends to produce predictable but very short-lived outcomes.

Gramsci, a leading philosophy of hegemony was, in particular, concerned with the moral function of culture and he had a meaningful sense of the interplay among traditions and customs in defining political behaviour. That is why he underscored the relevance of moral authority as it is spawned by culture. According to Gramsci then, hegemony is a political situation, a moment in which the philosophy of society fuse or are in equilibrium, an order in which a certain way of life and thought is dominant, in which one concept of reality is diffused throughout society in all its institutional and private manifestations of moral, religious, and customary spheres (Buchanan, 2000:102). The Gramscian pre-occupation with the question of moral authority signified the relevance of values and vision in leadership that have become the focus of transformational leadership sequels. True leaders eventually come to the point where they attract and empower others to their vision and passion for it. Transformational leadership is a leadership that touches on the follower's deep values and it is purpose driven. It is a leadership, which generates high levels of follower commitment and elicits their effort to work towards enduring change. Such a leadership has an emotional impact on followers. It is a leadership whose style should be based on genuineness, authenticity, reliability and credibility (Goleman, et al. 2002).

The question of good leadership is also closely tied to the process of good governance. Good governance must be based on positive personality traits including tenacity, resourcefulness, loyalty, self-sacrificing, obligatoriness, credibility and reliability. Politicians ought to be men and women of appealing personality. Transformational leadership will emanate from a culture created through conscious intellectual intervention and political and social engineering to define a new desirable political character based on a clear social mission. Politicians must provide society with the right national vision and inspire their communities to work in unity to achieve those visions.

A stable society is built on ethical foundations and good leadership is necessary for community development, social and political stability. Given that behaviour is a conscious process, we must begin to work our habit formation processes. Our habits define our behaviour and habits take time to develop. They need to be developed around certain ideals and standards. In any case, character is the sum total of our habits and good character is self-leadership. Good character creates trust in others.

In a situation of competing social and political projects pursuing different ideologies, leadership becomes an ability to transform followers. This is what is supposed to be the case if political parties subscribed to the notion of leadership culture and upheld a leadership ethic. Transformational leaders set out to empower followers and nurture them in the experience of change, personality traits and attempt to raise in them a new consciousness as individuals who can transcend their own self-interests for the sake of societal well being (Northouse, 1997:12). It steers away from *laissez-fairerism*. Laissez-faireism like dictatorship is toxic leadership. Toxic leaders leave their followers worse off than they found them. Both violate basic standards of human rights. How does a given culture condition people by engendering systemic practices and entrenching certain fears that render personalities dysfunctional and make them vulnerable to toxic leaders? As a social matrix culture circumscribes social matrices of standards comprising social rules, values, cultural codes and symbols from which several spaces are said to stem such as political cultures and ethnic, class, religious and gender relations that have a bearing on leadership patterns.

Gramsci talks of moral authority through the creation and perpetuation of legitimating symbols with which ruling groups ought to maintain their domination and hegemony. Therefore hegemony occurs under concrete political and economic conditions that have an ideological justification (Buchanan, 2000: 108). Ideology is a powerful instrument of social organization and as a lived relation its construction and articulation must be a leadership function. Cultural negotiation needs effective mediation and such mediation takes the intervention of good leadership.

Unfortunately there are not many cultural leaders to lead citizens into cross cultural conversations and negotiation despite the fact that Gramsci, having concerned himself with the moral function of culture, emphasized the value of creating and maintaining a deep sense of the need for the interplay among traditions. Neo-Gramscians therefore argue that capitalist rule in the West was secured through hegemony of the bourgeoisie in the ideological and cultural spheres rather than through coercion (Forgacs, 1989: 74, 81). Leadership authority is necessary for the creation and enforcement of order. Talking of responsible exercise of power, the ultimate product of power is the subject himself. Foucault mistakenly argues that the creation of public order in society is not given through consensus since societies are loci of struggle (Keeley, 1990: 100). In my view, there can be no consensus where there is no consent. There is usually lack of consent in states where leaders have virtually become predators on state resources, euphemistically referred to as the national cake.

The façade of Africa Renaissance

Apart from the fibres and ligaments of the national body-politic, there is need to institutionalize wholesome civic education programmes. There must be civic engagement which seeks to demonstrate to citizens how ethical leadership is critical in distilling good leadership from all its organizational, philosophical, psychological and spiritual complexities as to bring out its virtual essence that is the moral force of leadership in society. Leadership must be transformational not only for those who lead but also for those who are led, the citizens of our nations (Torlone, 2004, http://www.collegevalues.org/articles).

The so-called Africa Renaissance is a facade bereft of any motif of personality transformation because it has not laid down the foundational ethics for political, educational and religious leaders. Ethical leadership begins with the formation of a sound framework that requires leaders to undertake the arduous but frank analysis of what principles, beliefs, values and virtues, which constitute the acceptable public morality of a state. How far the so-called African Peer Review mechanism will succeed in establishing and enforcing this facility remains to be seen. The importance of such a framework is instructive in our perception of leadership as a conceptual structure by which moral leadership is engendered as the route to practical action. The leadership question has not been adequately addressed in Africa to the extent that the African crisis is as much a crisis of the state and crisis of leadership. The trend has been the consolidation of a leadership of domination and exclusion.

Leadership trainers must identify the building blocks in crafting a strategy for change in leaders' behaviour both at a personal and institutional level. Bernard Bass defined transformational leadership in terms of how leaders affect followers who are intended to trust, admire and respect the transformational leader (Torlone, 2004). There will always be resistance to change and indeed there are moments when a certain degree of conservatism becomes necessary in order to engender protectiveness of image and compliance to standards. Resistance must be broached on the basis of a convincing alternative if leadership is not to end up as mere self-serving chicanery and surreptitiousness of political participation. Because of the urge to surmount negative resistance, it is necessary to employ personal charisma focusing on the need to increase the awareness of the task and its importance or value, to focus first on team or organizational or community goals rather than own interests and to activate the higher order needs of followers (read citizens). Charismatic leaders can achieve a lot if they positively evoke strong emotions and cause identification of the followers with the leader. It may occur through quieter methods of coaching and mentoring (Torlone, 2004).

The awful political reality of Africa is that of a gravely crippled patient whose condition cannot be improved by sheer sentimental pretence of ideologies such as African Renaissance and the facades of peer review as a means of enforcing good governance. The Renaissance ideology, which has been touted for sometime in absolutely shoddier terms, offers no effective means of positive transformation in all spheres of our existence. In my view, all leadership has to do with interpretation and pursuit of projects that claim to address societal concerns with the essences of human life. The core of the essence of human life is humanity treated with respect and dignity in a just social setting. The leadership of people in a humane and respectable way should be a principal object in the execution of the principle of social justice in the construction of a democratic society.

This construction of society based on the essence of man as a universal attribute must reflect the role of ideology since ideology is a feature of all social relations. Ideology is a powerful tool of social organization, which empowers leaders to be ethical and to act with responsibility and authenticity. It is an effective means to capacity building, and ideology, for Althusser, is not simply a feature of capitalist society (Althusser, 1970:252). It is the means to a just and moral leadership that gives society its basic social structure and ethical leadership framework facilitating expeditious management of its social institutions. The state and its institutional organs must be defined by ideology given that ideology is a system of mass representations. It presents the forms in which people live their lives. It represents a real, lived relation to the world (Althusser, 1970: 252).

The so-called African Renaissance as an African response to the continent's stuntedness does not address in any fundamental sense Africa's imbroglio of political ethnicity. In fact, this concept seems to foreshadow the continent's inability to transcend its pre-teenage instincts, leave alone its adolescence. It is intellectually suspect since it does not tackle the problem of underdevelopment through an insightful and fruitful dialectic between theory and practice. It is befuddled by the material domains of sovereignty as represented by the economic and administrative dimensions of the public sphere more than the ethical domain which emphasizes the importance of our spirituality. Both dimensions of sovereignty require profound intellectual elaboration and the sharing of practical experience across the continent.

It is useful to state that human beings have a dignity whose essence should be the goal of projects of social justice and cultural construction. The essence of humanity deserves respect from all laws and social institutions everywhere in the world. Louis Althusser says that each individual must carry within himself or herself the whole human essence, even if only in principle (Althusser, 1970: 228). Human virtue is the driving force of moral integrity and there can be no moral responsibility among leaders without their resolved commitment to tenets of moral integrity.

An important social dynamic in the management of a community is power, a key force that has different social forms including spiritual forms. Gramsci discusses the social organizing potency of power in terms of hegemony and domination. That is why power is the object of all politics and Gramsci terms hegemony a political situation. It is a moment in which the philosophies of society fuse or are in equilibrium.

The state needs a basis of authentic ideological expression given that the state is an organizational instrument of political leadership. It is a political creation of society to undertake certain functions and serve specific interests and meet material and political needs of the community that has produced it. Those who are in control of the state live in its organizational ideology. This ideology constitutes the relation between the political and social categories in control of the state and their conditions of existence. The state, therefore, occupies a centre stage symbolically and materially over the society for whose interests, needs and aspirations. As an organizational apparatus, the state establishes an organizational hegemony. That does not mean that there are no social struggles against assaults of the ruling ideology. Lenin's definition of the state as an instrument for the domination of one class by another corresponded to Marx's conceptualization of the state (Forgacs, 1989:80).

State building is a leadership function, which is guided by a certain ideological logic in the politics of community change and control. Politics as a form of social struggle is an absolute pre-condition for the development of popular struggles. Community politics cannot find expression in independent organizational forms unless the hegemony of the state is explained, understood and challenged.

Learning from some oral narratives on leadership

Certainly, we should take responsibility for our failures and account for the bad, inept, corrupt, inane, dictatorial and undemocratic practices that characterize the management of public affairs in Africa. In undertaking an ideological and social policy analysis of contemporary Africa, we are concerned with what ought to be done to secure basic structural changes in contemporary African societies in order to generate real conditions of development. The ideas, strategies and tactics in vogue in today's Africa need to be interrogated, alternatively expressed and exchanged, tested and debated, expanded and deepened even by insights from the African past. This ought to be the case in order to secure a more informed basis for radical reconstruction of African institutions.

Leadership culture should draw from our community cultural repertoires and collective expectations and such a leadership culture should define the scope of civility based not only on tradition and custom but also encapsulating acceptable and consensually agreed upon public values and virtues. These values and virtues require to be encoded in law as part of the legal infrastructure defining public leadership ethics that may be relied on to guide leadership behaviour. It is not possible to speak of civil society where there is no organizational principle (Comaroff and Comaroff, 1999: 20). The African pre-colonial rulers played religious and other social functions other than the political (Ubah, 1987: 170).

The cases presented here from pre-colonial East Africa indicate that relations of authority are tied to ideological definitions and demarcation of social practice and hegemonic signification. In any African traditional society the exercise of leadership generated concerns about its legitimacy and that is why ritual practice played a crucial legitimizing role. The question and claims on political loyalty and commitment in cultural and political communities requires a social and cultural analysis of the intricate mechanisms of political super-ordination and subordination. We need a distinctive African ontology in which African leadership processes can be explained adequately. In Kenya, among the Luo, a leader was deemed to be extraordinarily gifted hence the praise of people who exhibited heroic qualities, as was the case of legendary Luanda Magere (Otieno, O.I: 2000).

The emphasis on heroic attributes in a leader was symptomatic of the extent to which the whole society was structured in dominance enforced by ideology and its associated political culture or religion. The social expression of dominance posed as heroism was also evident in the oral accounts from among the Akamba (Musila, O.I: 2000). Nevertheless, this dominance was grounded in moral foundations which Althusser would call "a spontaneously lived ideology" (Callari and Ruccio, 1998:iv). In this field of ideological permutations of values, norms and standards, good leadership qualities elevated the leader above everybody else indicating the importance of the super-ordinate in the emergence of leaders in some of the East African communities.

There is need for alternative ideas that can inspire the setting up of new African organizational codes of conduct and encraft a new moral fibre of social responsibility that can serve as the leitmotif of a new set of whistleblowers for the inauguration of a new quest and effort towards real substantive Renaissance. This is a Renaissance that should expedite the transformation of the African mode of being and the perception of the essence of community or national leadership. It should in effect inspire the transformation of this being from a structurally defined unity of position and identity in cultural settings, expressed in racial or tribal registers, to the perception of being as part of a dynamic process of social encounter and interaction.

The essence of leadership should lead to the re-evaluation of the whole process of representation; that in itself should be marked by the emergence of protective social movements whose leadership is characterized by the pursuit and enforcement of high level of integrity. We need the emergence of social movements, which can continually serve as watchdogs of good public leadership and excellent performance as acts of national political and historical construction. Indeed, public leadership is an exercise in national construction and it is supposed to be steeped in profound ontological inquiry and revelation at most mediated by politics and culture. Ontological introspection should underpin all social policies that are in force in our African nations.

In traditional Africa, leadership was seen as an ability to exercise spiritual functions apart from exercising social responsibilities. It was a key representation process whose discipline was inscribed in ritual practice and a code of behaviour marked by a plethora of taboos that guided one in the exercise of responsibility. The taboos were prohibitions and constraints. They set limits.

At spiritual, economic, social and political levels, processes of domination and social injustice were contested in African traditional societies. The various places of work, worship and recreation had their own leadership forms, including providing for mechanisms of expressing protest, resistance or seeking redress over certain issues or certain discomfitures caused by given ideological assaults. The human environment that is part of our geography is important given that leadership and organizational culture is a learned pattern of behaviour, which is shared from one generation to the next. It includes values and assumptions that are shared by communities of what is good and what is important. Ethnic communities, clans or lineages shared in narratives of heroes, myths and legends of origin and ritual practices, which bound the members together.

In Central and Southern Uganda, there had developed highly centralized systems of government in Buganda, Toro, Ankole and Bunyoro on a monarchical model that the British manipulated. One oral informant, James Serego, states that since the 1900 Buganda Agreement, leadership in Buganda was to be mainly identified with the Anglican and male dominated Mengo establishment (Serego, O.I: 2000). The patriarchal ideology was heavily defined by the Buganda culture. To date, Uganda is still faced with the kingdom syndrome whose instruments of power marginalized women. Yet when talking about alternative leadership, gifts of gender should be harnessed fully in creating an alternative social order. Our cultures have to be renegotiated.

In pre-colonial Buganda, and even more so under colonial rule, the clan heads and the clans as corporate entities were significantly weakened. But still, the commoners continued to voice their political and economic grievances to the king via the clan system. They by-passed the new landowning chiefs who became the real governing elites and against whom much of the grievances were directed (Comaroff and Comaroff, 1999:108). In Buganda the elders held meetings to thrash out thorny social issues at a village level (Ssonko, O.I; 2000). Kinship ideology defined forms of social organization at the clan level or wider ethnic or sub-ethnic levels. Among the Kamba, on the basis of a kin group, a member who failed to be disciplined after being summoned by *Nzama* was expelled from the community. In the Kamba community the state was referred to as *Nthi* and it had provinces called *Kivaho* and counties called *Kisuka*. Below were villages called *Utui* and homesteads called *Musyi* (Muthiani, 1973: 87). Many of these councils had ritual practice and practices of divination that enabled people to transcend their personal biases.

In Tanzania, the religious obligations of kinship in the Nyakyusa communities developed strong social bonds that linked Nyakyusa chiefdoms. The various Watemi participated in common rituals. The chiefdom was a gerontocracy in which the older generation, especially the men had a privileged position. The older men controlled not only political power and the exercise of authority in the determination of political questions, they also controlled wealth embodied in cattle and the social and economic utilization of labour as signified in the assignment of fundamental rights and the domestic execution of the largely gender determined allocation of duties. In the Nyakyusa chiefdoms, along with the control of wealth went religious authority (Masanja, O.I: 2000).

What are the lessons that we acquire from the fading remnants of traditional practice in our societies? In the Highlands, Coastal and Western areas of Kenya, the Kamba, Kikuyu, Embu, Meru, Mijikenda and Luyia lived with various forms of political organization. The Meru gerontocratic ideology was operationalized by the powerful council of elders called **Njuri Ncheke**. The Gikuyu had a different institutional setting of gerontocratic practice where power was embedded in the council of elders called **Kiama** and the Mijikenda had the **Kambi**. The Luyia had **Eshina shia Abakofu** (Council of Elders) and the Kamba had the **Atumia ma Nzama.** Major social tensions and conflicts and crises confronting the Gikuyu, Meru, Kamba and Luyia communities were mediated and resolved through these Councils of Elders meetings. Decisions were made on the basis of consensus.

An account of African socio-economic problems calls for some reconstructed logic in which an alternative theory is put in place as a basis of interpreting, criticizing, and redefining established causal tendencies, propensities and potentialities. There is need to eschew the foolhardiness in our current social practices by seeking to explain and intervene in concrete African realities and devise efficacious means of dealing with even unanticipated situations in the process of formulation of development policy. There is, therefore, a necessity of creating a special social policy bonding between government and civil society organizations by way of empowerment programmes in this era when people are talking about customer bonding (although this is done merely in the language of human resource management and marketing without a clear programme of social empowerment). Social empowerment must be ideologically and conceptually driven, especially since every ontology has an actual reality that it explains. The feasibility of empowerment should be evaluated not just in terms of the ideology defining it but also the leadership style in vogue.

The Leadership Cycle and Qualities of a Leader

A good leader is that person who has the following qualities of personality; self-awareness, relativity, compliance, protective, control, achieving and authenticity. The African state ought to richly harness its repertoire of social capital in developing these competencies. Cultural values and practices must be harnessed in the mediation of power and the execution of leadership responsibility and in the expression of Africanity and its related ontologies. Effective leadership is a leadership that gauges the importance of individual or collective values and canalizes these value orientations in facilitating citizens to meet their aspirations.

Every leader should give himself or herself an assignment to discover his or her talents, potentialities, propensities or tendencies. One has an assignment to discover his or her strengths, weaknesses and vulnerabilities. He or she has an assignment to discover and make use of the opportunities that arise. The leadership circle is based on four points: creative competencies, relationship competencies, reactive competencies and task oriented competencies. These are dimensions, which are increasingly becoming points of discussions in characterology; a method of character reading and character education.

Effective implementation of leadership plans requires discipline and principles. Principles that drive one's sense of loyalty will make that person to endure. Loyalty is faithfulness to principles, to a given plan and to the people whom one selflessly seeks to serve. True leaders are not easily changed but instead have the strength of personality and character to change their environments and the mindset of their followers from mediocrity to greatness, from sheer emotionalism to principled living. Principles are different from values, they are much deeper than values given that even thieves have values but they violate certain fundamental principles of teamwork.

Leadership is, also, a process of follower empowerment. It is part of social empowerment and social empowerment is a process that must entail strengthening civil society in order to enhance its political and economic vitality and provide more orderly paths of access and rules of interaction between state and society, and this must involve balancing the various economic and political opportunities (Johnston, 1998: 85). Followers will be empowered if they can trust their leaders. And trust is a result of honesty and consistency.

Our leaders should be honest and accept positions of responsibility. This will help them make positive contribution to the success of the project for which they are taking up leadership. They must accept responsibility for their input. Unfortunately for us in Africa, we do not have many of such political leaders around. Many of our African political leaders instead, are opportunists who accept positions but want to deny responsibility for their lackadaisical or careless performance. It is a performance whose leadership outcomes are, to say the least, farcical. That is, Africa has its share of a stinking repertoire of poor leadership tendencies and activities that merely exacerbate conditions of stagnation and retrogression in a manner that may be described at best as preposterous. Irresponsibility in our young cadre of leaders who are beginning to take the centre stage is an outgrowth of poor political mentoring.

In much of Africa today, there is too much discussion about consensus building politics without bothering to understand what underlies the very prospect of consensus. In my view, the social dynamic, which belies consensus, is simply consent.

This is the dynamic that erodes away the divisive wall between us humans with different textures of ego. Excellence demands emotional maturity as in the display of various virtues namely prudence, justice, fortitude and temperance which require to be cultivated in negotiators and conflicting parties. Emotional maturity is therefore required in achieving leadership excellence. As human beings, our personality is made up of intellect, will and emotions. Academic achievement is critical for professional achievement and the exercise of leadership. Such achievement and professional excellence are sustained by conformity and display of fundamental moral virtues on whose basis one acquires the necessary moral authority in leadership. Absence of consent creates a crisis of legitimacy. Therefore, the exercise of power by one person over others or by one group over another on the basis of consent should be a basic and recurrent feature of all societies.

Conclusion

In view of the above, national leadership must have an ethical foundation within which tribalism and racism must have neither value placed on them nor room provided for their demagogic expression. What legislative processes have been undertaken in African countries to discourage the growth and spread of tribalism? In my view, tribalism is an ideological production in its most mediocre form. It is a function of ludicrous leadership, which has emerged because of an absence of clear normative structures of national culture and its ideological production. Statesmanship is an output of good leadership and strives for excellence and not mediocrity. Mediocrity is the opposite of excellence and mediocrity denotes ethical and conceptual poverty. Mediocrity expresses abuse of choices and opportunities. The root causes of mediocrity in our society include; low expectations due to failure to set goals and insist on putting in quality effort, lack of faithfulness, lack of resilience to withstand peer pressure and its prevailing attitudes, and of course, lack of a system of effective rewards or motivation and adequate support from key individuals.

We need to have an impact on social behaviour by seeking to re-engineer personality dynamics in leaders. This warrants the inception of a new science of characterology in the African academy. In characterology, self-awareness is composed of leadership considerations to measure the extent to which the leader pursues service over self-interest, where the need for credit and personal ambition is far less important than creating results, which serve a common good. There is need to measure the leader's orientation to ongoing professional and personal development, as well as the degree to which inner self-awareness is expressed through high integrity leadership.

The crisis of leadership, to some extent, is owed to the fact that the political class in Africa has politicized ethnicity in ways that have rendered the continent a hotspot of conflict. Tribalism is dangerous political manipulation and manipulation involves an opportunistic use of people's ignorance. It occurs when the people being influenced are unaware of it, whereby the power of persuasion is used and abused to win consent on the basis of some conjured up and carefully crafted so-called community interests. Africa urgently needs responsible leaders who observe the etiquette of public morality. The new leadership will not be perpetuated with corruption; they will fight it.

Corruption is not a legal matter; it is also a moral question. It is a reflection of personality types that are distorted and lack values of transformational leadership. The ridiculousness of tribalism and corruption makes them some of the most devastating practices in Africa. Tribalism leads to abuse of office leading to violation of principles of justice and fairness. The whole principle of meritocracy is thrown out of the window. African nations are therefore crying for justice.

Some of the violent and punitive or prohibitive activities which are carried out in the leadership exercise of power are absolutist tendencies undertaken in a feat of personal rage that it becomes necessary, in characterological terms, to inquire into the leadership emotions and their various social forms. Electoral processes in Africa are manipulated along tribal lines and victories are declared because there is lack of character education. This is because victories are secured on the basis of euphoria or other forms of scheming mechanisms. We have seen that Africa is faced by many leadership challenges that require innovative and broad based interventions. We might have to understand the past in order to change the present and the future.

References

Aseka, Eric Masinde. *Transformational Leadership in East Africa: Politics, Ideology and Community*. Kampala: Fountain Publishers, 2005.

Aina, Tade Akin. *Globalization and Social Policy in Africa: Issues and Research Directions*. Dakar: Codesria Working Paper Series, 1996.

Althusser, L. "Structuralist Marxism: Political Clarity and Theoretical Distortions" in *Rethinking Marxism*, Vol. 4. No. 4, 1991.

Althusser, L. For Marx. New York: Vintage Books, 1970.

Buchanan, P. "Using Gramsci in the Current International Moment" in *Contemporary Politics, Vol. 6 No. 2, 2000.*

Callari, A. and D.F. Ruccio. "Rereading Althusser" in *Rethinking Marxism,Vol. 10 No. 3, 1998.*

Comaroff, Jean L. and J. Comaroff. *Civil Society and the Political Imagination in Africa Critical Perspectives.* Chicago: The University of Chicago Press, 1999.

Diagne, Suleiman Bashir and Henry Ossebi. *The Cultural Question in Africa.* Dakar: CODESRIA, 1996.

Garland, E. "Developing Bushmen: Building Civil(ized) Society in the Kalahari and Beyond" in Comaroff, J and Comaroff, J. (1999) eds. *Civil Society and the Political Imagination in Africa.* Chicago: The University of Chicago Press, 1999.

Flathman, R.E. *Towards Liberalism.* Ithaca: Cornell University Press, 1989.

Forgacs, D. "Gramsci and Maxism in Britain" in *New Left Review.* No. 176 July/August 1989.

Friedman, J. "Introduction" in J. Friedman (ed) T*he Rational Choice Controversy: Economic Model of Politics Reconsidered.* New Haven: CT: Yale University press, 1999.

Goleman, D. et al. *Primal Leadership.* Boston: Harvard Business School, 2002.

Hartsock, N.C.M. "Louis Althusser's Structuralist Marxism: Political Clarity and Theoretical Distortions", in *Rethinking Marxism,* Vol. 2. No. 1, 1991.

Held, D. *Democracy and the Global Order: From the Modern State to Cosmopolitan Governance.* Stanford: Stanford University Press, 1995.

Hybel, Roberto. *How Leaders Reason.* Cambridge, Massachusetts: Basil Blackwell, 1990.

Hyden, G. "Governance and the Study of Politics" in Hyden and Bratton (eds) *Governance and Politics in Africa.* London: Lynne Rienner publishers, 1992.

Johnston, A. "On Developing Institutions in Africa", Wohgemuth, L. et al eds. *Institutional Building and Leadership in Africa.* Uppsala: Nordiska Afrikainstitutet, 1998.

Johnston, M. "Fighting Systemic Corruption: Social Foundations for Institutional Reform", in *The European Journal of Development Research,* Vol. 10, No. 1, 1998.

Keeley, J. F. "Toward a Foucauldian Analysis of International Regimes", International Organizations Vol. 44, No.1, 1990.

Mafeje, Archie, "Africanity: A combative Ontology". CODESRIA Bulletin No. 1, 2000.

_____. The Ethnogaphy of African Social Formations. Dakar: CODESRIA Book Series, 1991.

Mbembe, A. *On Private Indirect Government*. Dakar: CODESRIA, 2000.

Muthiani, David. *Akamba from Within: Egalitarianism in Social Relations*. New York: Expository Press, 1973.

Mkandawire, T. "Fiscal Structure, State Contraction and Political Responses in Africa" in Mkandawire and Olukoshi (eds.) *Between Liberalism and Oppression: The Politics of Structural Adjustment in Africa*. Dakar: CODESRIA, 1995.

Obadare, E. "Democratic Transition and Political Violence in Nigeria", in *Africa Development*, Vol. XXIV, Nos. 1 and 2, (1999).

Onwuejeogwu, M. A. *The Social Anthropology of Africa: An Introduction*. Nairobi: Heinemann, 1975.

Pennock, J. R. and D.G. Smith. *Political Science: An Introduction*, New, 1964.

Pieterse, J. N., "Going Global: Futures of Capitalism", *Development and Change*, Vol. 28, No. 2, 1997.

Rawls, J. A *Theory of Justice*. New York: Columbia University Press, 1971.

Robinson, M. "Corruption and Development: An Introduction", in *The European Journal of Development Research*, vol. 10, no. 1, June 1998.

Sirico, R. *A Moral Basis for Liberty*. New York: The Foundation, 1994.

Rosengarten, F. "Gramsci and the Twentieth Century", An International Conference, http://wwww.soc.qc.eduu/gramsci/news/newsl7.html, 2000.

Schuurman, F. J. "Introduction: Development Theory in the 1990s", in Schuurman (ed) *Beyond the Impasse: New Directions in Development Theory*. London: Zed Books, 1993.

_____. "Modernity, Postmodernity and the New Social Movements" in Schuurman (ed) *Beyond the Impasse: New Directions in Development Theory*. London: Zed Books, 1993.

Torlone, D. J. http://www.collegevalues.org/articles, 2004.

Ubah, C. N. "Changing Patterns of Leadership Among the Igbo, 1900-1960", in *Trans-African Journal of History*, Vol. 16, 1987.

6

Women and Leadership in Africa: A Case of Deviate or Die

Njeri Kang'ethe

Introduction

As Africa goes through a Second Renaissance, she is looking for quality leadership within her ranks. Unfortunately, women, a critical segment of the society are in a disadvantaged position and have great difficulties occupying their rightful place as national leaders. This is because society, in its wisdom or lack of it, has used sexuality and gender construction tools to disable women from exploiting their full potential. These inequities are manifest in virtually every area of a woman's life, but the most glaring evidence of the underclass status of women is in the area of leadership, especially in the public arena.

This chapter takes the view that for the women of Africa to be relevant in this dispensation, they must create space within which to exercise their God given leadership abilities in order to have an impact on their societies and communities. They must look beyond the horizon of "political leadership" and deviate further afield. In other words, they must deviate or die! The chapter will, wearing a feminist's shoes, walk the reader down the memory lane of Africa's pre-colonial, colonial, neo-colonial and present day experiences, and the impact that these have had on women's participation in leadership. Having laid a foundation, the discussion will take the reader through examples of areas where women in the region have deviated from the conventional "political leadership" and have not only actualised themselves, but have had an influence on their communities. Profiles of these unsung heroines will be interspersed with the substantive narrative in a typical African folklore fashion.

Most history books on Africa read like an almanac of *"things gone awry;"*(Kang'ethe, 1994) a continuum of events that have for centuries dogged and under-classed her people. It is argued in some quarters that most of this history is erroneous having being authored by Europeans whose perspective was tainted with prejudice. However, on close scrutiny, many facts are essentially correct. For instance, one cannot deny the fact that when the West could no longer cope with the demands of an agrarian economy, Africa became a despised breeding ground for slave labour. With the advent of the industrial revolution, the West turned to Africa for cheap raw materials. Neither can anyone gainsay the fact that the infamous 1869 scramble for Africa and consequent colonisation, was an attempt to sanitise the unequal relationship between Africa and the West. Colonisation was indeed a political intervention that facilitated exploitation of the African continent and its peoples within a structured, legitimate, socio-economic, socio-political, administrative framework. Africa did not take this lying down and the turn of the nineteenth century brought with it unprecedented agitation by Africans for freedom and their land. This freedom struggle culminated in political liberation of the 1950s and 1960s.

Today we are looking at a continent at a crossroads. After years of erosion of our hard won independence, first by neo-colonialism, and recently by the thinly veiled re-colonisation by Bretton Woods Institutes under the guise of structural adjustment programmes and difficult to comply with conditionalities, Africa is slowly beginning to see the light and is willing to pay the price for a Second Liberation.

As Africa goes through a rebirth, a Second Renaissance, she is of necessity going through the motions of political, economic, socio-cultural, religious, environmental and technological upheavals. To forestall a still birth, these labour pains must be contained and managed in the here and now, within Africa's borders and in the context of our culture. Rev Ibrahim Omondi (1994), the General Secretary of the Evangelical Alliance of Kenya, states that leaders were God's answer to the needs of his people in ancient Palestine. Today, good leaders are God's gift to humankind. Africa therefore urgently needs good leaders; women and men of vision, integrity and moral uprightness to steer her through the process. Women and men whose vision is a continent, united in diversity, as she seeks to liberate and serve her masses. In essence, therefore, time is up for the lacklustre dictators of yesteryears. Africa needs quality leaders to safely midwife her through this process.

In everyday parlance, the term "leadership" has two key value loaded connotations. First of all, leadership is viewed from the perspective of management of civic and political affairs in the public arena, and secondly, and most importantly for this discourse, leadership is gendered. There is the presupposition that leadership is the domain of the male of the species. Those who are familiar with the Common Law tradition will appreciate that female leaders in the House of Commons or indeed the House of Lords are a rare species, if not virtually non-existent.

This Victorian mindset is not confined to the West. Generally in Africa, leadership is, on the face of it, looked at in the context of the political arena and within the confines of elective, nominative or administrative office. Being predominantly a patriarchal society, leadership is seen as the province of the male. For a society whose construction of gender roles discriminates against women by confining them to the domestic or to an underclass status should they venture into the public arena, it leaves very little to imagination as to the experiences of women vis-à-vis matters of leadership in Africa.

African Women in Political Leadership

It is instructive that one of the earliest records of a female monarchy is the Biblical story of the Queen of Sheba who ruled circa 6000 BC in Abbyssinia, the present day Ethiopia. Moore (1988) states that in pre-colonial Africa, women were the holders of public offices and wielded considerable political power. For instance, the Igbo and Yoruba of Nigeria had dual political systems where women were responsible for women's affairs in matters of commerce and trade, and men for men's affairs [sitting under a tree and discussing political matters?]. In the Igbo culture, structural and formal political power was allowed to women, the most honoured title holders being the *Agba Ekwe* women, who in addition to ritual prerogatives, had vetoing rights in the village and general town assemblies (Amadiume, 1987).

The Queen Mother of the Asante Kingdom of Ghana was responsible for continued fertility and success of matrilineage as a whole. This gave her not only immense political power, but control over the religious and economic life of the Asante. In Kenya, the legendary Gikuyu female Chief and war General, Wangu wa Makeri, posed one of the greatest challenges to the early British settlers (Gakaara, 1968). Was women's leadership only recognised in the public arena? How did women in Africa handle the private versus the public dichotomy in matters of leadership?

By and large in pre-colonial Africa, domestic political relations were well structured and women had a key role to play as leaders of their own households. In the Igbo community aforementioned, families had in place the institution of "male" daughters. These were daughters who remained unmarried, or who, because of their exemplary performance, were favourites of their families. These "male" daughters could take wives and rule over households. Women not in mainstream politics could also acquire titles by sacrificing to Idemili the river goddess (Adimora-Ezeigbo, 2001).

In some parts of Kenya, women were political heads of their own homes. The Gikuyu of Central Kenya practise polygyny. In spite of this, the Gikuyu were and still are a non-pooling economy. Every *Nyumba* (House) in the *Mucii* (Household) was a separate economic and political unit headed by the mother, who had oversight and authority over her children, food and livestock. Leadership in the home was to a certain extent a stepping stone to leadership in the public arena. The Gikuyu had in place the institution of *Nyakinyua* (revered mother). On reaching non-child bearing age, and having given one's children to marriage, a woman ascended from the *Kang'ei* (nursing mother) to *Nyakinyua* status. On attaining the *Nyakinyua* status, a woman qualified to join mainstream politics and sit in the *Kiama* (Council of Elders) that took care of the community's social, commercial, political and war affairs (Kang'ethe, 2002).

One of the criticisms of the West on traditional African leadership is that women were not included in decision-making processes. On close scrutiny, however, one discovers that by and large this claim is erroneous. Although there were instances where women were not physically visible in matters of governance, their latent presence was critical and they would in present day parlance be referred to as the "remote control political bigwigs".

Consultative leadership was a key component of the African socio-political life. A leader knew that for him or her to succeed he or she had to be a good listener. He or she had to be answerable to the people and had to cultivate the culture of dialogue. A leader had to be seen to be able to give direction and to take responsibility for his or her decisions. A leader would make decisions only after lengthy consultations with his or her people, who would in turn be part of the process. A leader never worked in isolation and was expected to reproduce himself or herself by role modelling younger people. Governance was therefore a communal venture that would outlive any one person.

Although by and large men were the visible leaders of the people, women's participation in political leadership was critical at the consultative decision making level, and as checks and balances to counter authoritarianism on the part of the leaders. As mentioned earlier in this discussion, a Gikuyu woman would, on attaining the *Nyakinyua* status, qualify to join mainstream politics and sit in the *Kiama* (Council of Elders) where important decisions touching on the community's social, commercial, political and war affairs were arrived at.

The Kalenjin of the Rift Valley had a bicameral Parliament in the form of a *baraza* (Council of Elders) made up of an inner and an outer circle. The circle was referred to as '**kokwet**' The inner circle was comprised of men while women sat in the outer circle. Although during debates women would speak only on invitation, their opinions were taken into account through a very elaborate process. Discussions at the **kokwet** were held in open court but decisions would be taken a day or two thereafter. During the interim, a referendum of sorts took place. Members of the **kokwet** would talk about matters under discussion to the community, and seek the community's views. During this referendum stage, women's contribution was critical. They would discuss these matters with their husbands, with their peers as they ferried water from the river, cooked together, or thatched huts. Those who were married to members of the inner circle, had the distinct duty of bringing the views of the people to their husbands, thus influencing decisions at the highest level possible. Therefore, although these women were not visible at the circle level, their participation during the referendum, and during the pillow talk, had a direct impact on governance of the people (Chepkwony, 2005).

Women were also critical as checks and balances against totalitarianism on the part of the leaders. Apart from having political, religious and economic oversight over her people, one of the key roles of the Asante Queen discussed above, was that of a check against authoritarianism on the part of the King. The King could be impeached and dethroned if he went against the wishes of the people, and if the Queen agreed. Indeed the Asante Queen was the proverbial power behind the throne.

Why and When Did Things Fall Apart?

Looking at the state of affairs today, it is obvious that participation of women in political leadership is slowly diminishing, much more so on the African continent. According to the 2001 Geneva based Inter-Parliamentary Union Report, women representation to parliaments worldwide was only 13.8%. Of this, 38.8% were from Nordic countries. On the home front, South Africa topped the list with women taking 30% of parliamentary seats followed by Uganda and Mozambique at 15%, and Kenya at a nominal 5%. The others are not worth mentioning.

Five years down the line, the status quo remains. Women are grossly under represented in political leadership. In Kenya, out of 222 elected members of parliament, only 18 are women. Of these, only two are full Cabinet Ministers holding what one would aptly call "soft" ministries. Why have the mighty fallen? Why are there no longer structures within which women mediate their political leadership roles?

Historians lay the blame for this retrogression of women's political power in the continent of Africa on, among many other factors, colonialism and attendant restatement (Kang'ethe, 2003). In an attempt to make the colonies governable, colonial masters particularly the British, introduced the direct rule system. Kenya is a case in point. What the colonial authorities did then was to compartmentalise the then existing African economic, cultural, social and political structures into moulds that they could, or thought they did, understand. These structures would subsequently be used as administrative tools.

For the sake of administrative and political expediency, this compartmentalisation, had to be regularised. To give credit where it is due, the British were careful to give these tools some degree of legitimacy. There was need then to formulate a legal framework, hence the restatement of what they perceived to be the traditions and practices of the people into some form of structured and codified customary law (Cotran, 1968). In restating the traditions, customs and practices of African peoples, the coloniser would look at the structures of African life from his own perspective, and try to translate them into a legal framework that he understood. Needless to say, the colonial master arrived at conclusions based on incorrect assumptions.

The net effect of restatement was to place African socio-political dynamics into a Victorian box, which in essence threw out legitimacy of women's political power and its exercise. Among many other factors, restatement laid the foundation for a new mode of socialisation for political success. It entrenched patriarchy deeper into the culture of the people, albeit without the hitherto time tested checks and balances; a thing that marginalised women further.

Kenya, typical to most former British colonies, is, forty years after independence, still labouring under the yoke of received law; right from statutes such as land laws, to the Lancashire House Constitution. This legal order in essence was an importation of English notions of justice and governance and an attempt at transforming them to suit the native situation. Some of the laws have been repealed or amended and the Constitution is currently going through the gymnastics of a review. However, Kenya is yet to develop a leadership jurisprudence that seeks among many other things, to break barriers that have hitherto marginalised segments of the society, notably women.

Chepkwony (2005) analyses how this imported mode of governance, further derogated from African women, opportunities for leadership in the public arena. It brought with it Victorian norms of governance that embraced the negative aspects of leadership in traditional Africa and discarded those that were all encompassing and participatory. For example, it embraced the notion of a "paramount chief" where the leader alone decided what was good for the people. It introduced the notion of wealth as a tool for acquiring power, where the rich could buy their way into power, amass more wealth and power, and use this power as a tool of suppression. This has degenerated into present day dictatorship and attendant corruption, things that have cost Africa dearly and further marginalised women who are by nature consultative leaders.

Mathu (2001) captures this very well when she propositions that socialisation of the modern day African women does not incorporate traditional skills believed necessary to move on into political leadership, nor does it focus on the importance of the highly patriarchal organisational power structure. This results in women being left out of the mainstream politics, and by extension from important decision and policy making structures.

While concurring with Mathu, Nzomo (2002) warns that there is no shortcut to political success for women, outside of learning the art of *realpolitik.* While affirmative action is highly rated as the way forward, it should be viewed as only one of the instruments for achieving equity and justice. Women must learn to exploit their numerical strength combined with the larger political space occupied by mushrooming women's associations and lobbies. They must translate this sheer numerical strength into political power and influence. Female candidates need to develop staying power and a sense of political professionalism. They must eliminate their low power of incumbency and perennial newness as candidates in electoral politics. Women must learn to keep at it. Those who fail to win at the first trial must not give up but prepare well prior to the next electoral contest. Nzomo asserts that, those who have been in electoral politics longest, or have a long record of political visibility and active participation in public life, stand a better chance of being elected into office.

From Nzomo's assertion, one would rightly (or wrongly!) interpret the art of realpolitik to be synonymous with competing with men in a man's world, where a woman's achievement or non-achievement is measured using the male of the species as the benchmark. Is this the ideal in political leadership? Can a woman work her way through life's challenges as a woman without having to ape a man and be guaranteed of success? Should a woman be denied an opportunity to exercise her God given talents as a leader simply because her testosterone levels are different?

In the case of Kenya, one of the few women who have had a fairly high degree of incumbency is Hon Martha Karua the current Kenyan Minister for Constitutional Affairs. She was voted back for the third time in December 2002 and is among the very few members of parliament who enjoy the coveted over 20,000-vote margins. Karua agrees with Nzomo that visibility and hard work are critical for re-election. Karua begins to strategise her campaign for re-election right from the day she is declared a winner. That is, indeed the way to go, if we are to change women's participation in politics.

Kenya is a member of the international community of civilised nations. She is a signatory to, inter alia, the United Nations Universal Declaration of Human Rights (UNDHR); Convention on the Elimination of all Forms of Discrimination Against Women (CEDAW); the Beijing Declaration and Platform for Action; International Covenant on Civil and Political Rights (ICCPR); International Covenant on Economic, Social and Cultural Rights (ICESCR), Convention on the Rights of the Child (CRC); African Charter on Human and Peoples' Rights (AU Charter); and African Charter on the Rights and Welfare of the Child (ACWRC). All these international instruments outlaw discrimination against women.

At the municipal level, Kenya has enacted laws that domesticate provisions of these international instruments. She has also formulated policies to mainstream gender in virtually every facet of our national life. It therefore beats reason as to why in this time and age, women are still negatively socialised in Kenya, and are marginalised in political leadership.

In her analysis of women's political participation in post Women's Decade Kenya, Nzomo (2005) lays the blame for this state of affairs on several governmental institutional deficiencies.

- Lack of political will on the part of the Kenya Government to comply with the 1975 United Nations Resolutions. These resolutions demanded of all member states to make changes and introduce policies and programs geared towards accelerated advancement of women by creating specific national machineries to serve women and strengthening existing organizations;

- The systematic interference of women's organisations by the then KANU Government. This involved co-option of top group women leaders into party organs and inculcating social welfare orientation into the women's organizations, thus making them toothless bulldogs;

- Gender based discrimination against Kenyan women in almost every aspect of life;

- ¨Discriminatory laws and practices remained in place on such matters as inheritance, marriage and divorce, adoption of children and employment laws;

- Policies that discriminate against women, for instance housing allowance for married women in public service and maternity benefits, remained in place;

- Tolerance of traditions and customs that openly discriminate against women by exposing them to sexual, physical and psychological violence;

- Discriminatory practices and punitive action for women and girls who get pregnant while attending government sponsored educational programs.

There have been indications that since the NARC government took the reigns of power in 2002 governmental support for women will be forthcoming, but there is still a lot of room for improvement.

Deviate Or Die

The Private versus The Public Dichotomy

In his wisdom, God created a woman to reproduce and nurture life. To ensure continuity, God made her a producer of the means and processes to sustain life. These sexual roles elevate a woman to a functional being, whose holistic nature transcends the private/public divide. Therefore, for a woman, any demarcations between the private and the public arena are at best, purely ethereal. Whatever function a woman undertakes be it as mother, wife, lover, caregiver, instructor, professional, occupational or leisure, she brings her total persona into it, thus traversing the domestic and public spheres with equal alacrity. Any structures that would confine a woman to either sphere would therefore limit her. A holistic being can only be effective when these disablers are removed, circumvented, resisted or tamed (Kang'ethe, 1994).

Deviation by Design

How then can a woman who aspires to be political make meaningful contribution to society? Should her God given gifts and talents go to waste simply because she has no avenue where to express them as she serves the community?

Unlike their sisters in the West who place a high premium on the liberal feminist theory that access to political leadership is critical to empowering women, African women are beginning to discover that political leadership is not the only platform from which they can effect change. They have learnt to bloom wherever they are planted, be it at the community level, at Church, at school, at the work place, at the marketplace or at the hearth. They have created safe spaces from where they can mediate their lives, exercise quality leadership without necessarily having to compete with men.

Let us now consider some of the areas in which Kenyan women have created space within existing structures, and using their God given talents, have excelled as leaders and mobilisers of communities, not in competition with men, but as women. In these situations Kenyan women have had the freedom to think with both their brains and boobs.

Education

The Plight of the Girl Child

The right to education is not only a fundamental human right, as articulated in Article 13 of the International Covenant on Economic Social and Cultural Rights (ICESCR), but is a right that has utility value. As a human developmental resource, education has an enabling effect, and in essence is the lynchpin round which access, appropriation and exercise of other rights rotate. Its acquisition, is therefore, critical in guaranteeing, enforcing and maintaining other fundamental human rights, be it at the municipal or at the international arena. It is, therefore, imperative that this right is accessed, appropriated and maintained from the earliest developmental stage of a human person – in childhood.

In Kenya, gross enrolment rate for girls in primary schools is generally much lower than that of boys. In Arid and Semi-arid Land (ASAL) regions, (which account for 69 per cent of the Kenyan territorial landmass), the rate is much lower than that of other parts of the country (Okwach, 1994), sometimes as low as 19 per cent. As the communities who live in ASAL regions are generally poor nomadic pastoralists, socio economic challenges and migratory trends have been cited as key culprits for this gender gap in education (Bloch, 1998).

Kenya enacted the Children's Act 2001 in which the rights of children are enumerated. Section 7 of the Act provides for free and compulsory primary education for all children in Kenya, and further places the obligation for its provision on both the Government and the parents. The Children's Act 2001 received Presidential Assent on 31st December 2001. It became effective on 1st April 2002. It is too early to gauge with any degree of certainty the impact of the Act in so far as it provides for free and compulsory primary education, but there are already indicators that although the number of school children enrolled in class one has increased tremendously for both girl and boy children since the enactment of the Act (UNESCO, 2002), the majority of primary school dropouts are girls, mostly within the first two years of school. One can therefore rightly assume that if this is the case throughout the country, then a girl child in an ASAL region who is already grappling with other disadvantages, is not reaping the full benefit of this statutory obligation.

For the purposes of this discussion we will briefly look at the plight of the Maasai girl child and some of the initiatives that have been undertaken to enable her attain her dream. Efforts to raise the lot of the Maasai girl child are well represented by Priscilla Nangurai.

Priscilla Nangurai - The Lioness of Maasailand

Priscilla Nangurai has held the helm as the Principal of African Inland Church (AIC) Kajiado school since 1972. She was born in Kajiado district where she attended her primary school before proceeding to the prestigious Alliance Girls High School and then to Kenyatta College (now Kenyatta University) where she attained a teaching certificate. Nangurai is an institution unto herself and a role model per excellence. She is a living example of what an African woman can achieve, outside of the glamour of political leadership, but within the context of her socio-cultural, socio-political and socio-economic reality.

According to Nangurai during an oral interview with the writer, AIC Kajiado School was founded in pre-independence Kenya (1959) by African Inland Missionaries from the United States. It was envisaged to be a centre for learning for young Maasai women, who, because of historical administrative factors peculiar to their region, did not enjoy as many developmental advantages as their counterparts in other regions of the country. In the 1920s the then colonial governor declared Ole Kejuado (present day Kajiado district) a "closed district" in an attempt to contain the Maasai uprising which came hot on the heels of dispossession (after being tricked into signing the notorious 1911 Maasai Treaty) and gifting off their prime pastureland to British World War I soldiers by the colonial government.

In addition to giving Maasai girls some basic reading and writing skills, the missionaries' core reason for founding the school was to produce 'educated" wives for the emerging crop of mission educated Maasai men. Thus education was not a right for a Maasai girl by virtue of her being a human being per se, but was dependent on her relationship to the male of the species – as a future wife. Being a Maasai herself and knowing the culture, traditions and customs of her people, Nangurai was a most suitable choice for taking the helm at AIC Kajiado School. She doubled as a teacher, counsellor, mother and role model for the many girls who went through her school.

In spite of enactment of the Children Act which outlaws female genital cutting (FGC) and other oppressive cultural practices, girl children in various communities still undergo female circumcision as an important *rite of passage.* To try and curb this practice, many mission based and Church aided schools especially in the Central Province, would bar any girl who underwent the rite from continuing with school. This is not the case at AIC Kajiado School. The school is home to girls, most of who have gone through female circumcision. Thus Nangurai has been able to create a safe haven for young Maasai girls where they can continue with education, in familiar surroundings and without feeling in any way threatened.

But there is a phenomenon that Nangurai was not prepared for - an escalation of dropout by girls immediately after circumcision. Although for AIC Kajiado School circumcision per se was not a culprit in school dropout for girls, there is a nexus between circumcision and school dropout. Circumcision is a precursor to marriage, **a *rite of passage*** that has expectations – a value tag. Once a Maasai girl is circumcised at around age 13 she is expected to behave like a grown woman and no longer sleeps in the same house with her parents. This puts young girls at risk because away from their parents' watchful eyes, they can get pregnant easily. This is also the time when men come to seek the girl's hand in marriage. Nangurai lost many of her students to early marriages.

In 1989, after having battled with school dropout for nearly twenty years, Nangurai, who by nature is a no nonsense action oriented person, sought the help of the Church and provincial administration to set up a rescue centre in her school. She would organise rescues for girls abducted from her school and the neighbourhood and make a home for them in the centre. This earned her the wrath of the community especially the male relations of the girls she rescued. Convinced that allowing girls to remain in school was the only way of empowering girls in her community, Nangurai was not intimidated (Mathu, 2005).

As a mother and a respected member of the community, Nangurai created another niche for herself and exploited it to the full. She started a campaign to sensitise the community against early marriages. She taught the girls how to recognise early warning signs of impending arranged marriages and how to avert disaster. She encouraged girls who felt threatened to remain in school under her care during school holidays. Using her own example, she extolled the parents to the virtues of educating girl children.

An effective leader is no push-over and Nangurai would resort to strong arm tactics when any of her girls were abducted. Using the police and provincial administration she would rescue the girls and put them back to school under her care. Although this was before the enactment of the Children's Act 2001 that would later give powers to use every means within her reach to ensure that her girls remained in school, Nangurai was never arrested or prosecuted for "abducting" prospective [child]brides from their would-be husbands.

As mentioned elsewhere in this discussion, African women have the rare ability of negotiating their space within existing socio-cultural structures, and mediating change *in situ*. In all her endeavours, Nangurai acts firmly but treats her community especially the elders with respect and dignity. This in turn has earned their respect and support despite dissenting views on her activities. According to an *Ilkishili* (respected elder, usually the leader of an age group and opinion shaper) I spoke to, the Maasai community is happy with what Nangurai is doing and are ready to help her because she respects their culture. As a leader she is focussed and firm. In the *Ilkishili's* words:

> "Nangurai is like a suckling lioness and anyone who plays with the education
> of any of her girls will not know what hit him."

In 1999, in recognition of her contribution to the community, the then President of the Republic of Kenya decorated her with the honour of the Order of the Grand Warrior. A year later, the Lioness turned Moran was awarded the coveted title of Jurist of the Year by the International Commission of Jurists.

As a mother, with a larger than life family, Nangurai is a great mobiliser of resources. She is an active member of the Girls Education Women Lobby Group, which she founded in 1992. This group brings together educated Maasai women who not only act as visible role models for the girls in Maasailand, but as peer educators for the community. Their mission is to make the community understand why girls' education is important and why they should abandon cultures and traditions that subjugate women such as FGM and early marriages.

The Girls Education Women Lobby group is also involved in resource mobilisation activities. Through this sorority, AIC Kajiado school has been able to form long lasting partnerships with organisations having global mandate such as UNICEF, UN World Food Program, World Vision, Forum for African Women Educationalists (FAWE) among many others. Contributions from these organisations have gone a long way into subsidising Government's input into the school. One of the benefits of these partnerships is that AIC Kajiado School has been elevated to a FAWE Centre of Excellence which, among many other things, translates to better facilities and human resources.

One of the distinguishing characteristics of our African culture is the institution of the extended family. A good leader knows that he or she can never escape the responsibility of minding the welfare of others not necessarily within his or her nuclear family. As a retirement gift to the school that she has helped build over the years, Nangurai, a mother of two and grandmother of three, is giving part of her home to the rescue centre. She has also established a secondary school wing in the school.

Indeed these are befitting monuments for the Lioness of Maasailand but Nangurai's contribution to the community as a leader per excellence goes beyond concrete and steel structures. She has shaped lives, changed attitudes and mindsets of a community and empowered girls by giving them a second chance, a future and a hope, thus making an impact for eternity in their lives.

Peace Building and Conflict Resolution

In addition to saving lives by building bridges between warring communities, peace building and conflict resolution are critical tools for preservation, conservation and management of natural resources and the environment. This cannot be truer for the continent of Africa generally, and the Greater East African region in particular, which is threatened by conflicts, wars and rumours of war. It is, therefore, important that we look at what women in the region are doing in the area of peace building and conflict resolution.

Women as Users and Managers of Natural Resources

Eco-feminists and Women in Environment and Development scholars (WED) emphasise the special relationship that exists between women and the environment. This relationship is universal but, needless to say, different cultures have different experiences.

One theory propositions that women in Africa have a multi-faceted role in the use and management of natural resources and the environment (Green, 1998). This role is closely tied to the women's reproductive and productive roles. As breadwinners, women are producers and providers of food. This role entails tilling the land, planting, weeding, manuring, harvesting, gathering, storage and water harvesting. Since it is the women who cook the food, they are responsible for the fuel as well. This involves looking for firewood, animal dung, and processing fuel such as charcoal, warm bricks, biogas, etc. As reproducers, mothers, nurturers and caregivers, women are users of the forests, indigenous plants, animals and insects for medicines and life sustaining herbs.

Women, therefore, have a vested interest in sustainable environment and natural resources and have, as a survival tactic, developed a symbiotic relationship with nature. As they draw food and sustenance from her, they give back something to nature in the form of resource management skills that entail conserving, preserving, protecting, husbanding and sustaining the environment and natural resources. Women can then be aptly referred to as the *de facto* managers of natural resources.

However, because of their underclass status consequent to their productive and reproductive roles, women are more often than not, unable to exercise their management skills effectively over natural resources and the environment.

Factors that Constrain Women as Managers of the Environment

Here are some of the factors that constrain women's management roles:

- ◆ Heavy workload resulting in less time to attend to natural resource management chores or participate in decision making fora;

- ◆ To help manage heavy workload, women result to expanded population, i.e., to having more children or encouraging husbands to take co-wives. This results in depletion of existing resources thus perpetuating abuse of the environment;

- ◆ Gender inequitable property ownership patterns, land tenure systems and governmental fiscal policies that result in dire poverty for women. Women resort to abusing, overusing and degrading the environment in order to make ends meet.

◆   Lack of support from the government and other institutions. For instance, in Kenya, agricultural institutes give priority to big time farmers and women are left to fend for themselves. Efforts by international organisations such as the CGIAR to include women are only fire fighting gimmicks and cannot be sustained for long periods of time in the absence of political will by the national governments (ILRI, 2002).

◆   Lack of appropriate technology means that women spend valuable time doing menial and repetitive chores at the expense of managing resources.

◆   Prevalence of conflicts, civil strife and general unrest in the East African region.

Almost invariably, at the root of any conflict, be it domestic, ethnic, intra or inter-territorial, are domination, control and exploitation of resources by one party to the detriment of another. It follows then that when there is a conflict, natural resources and the environment are threatened. As first line managers and users of natural resources, women then have a right and a moral duty to take up arms and protect them.

At the risk of being overly simplistic I dare suggest that the anti-thesis of conflicts, wars and rumours of war is peace building and conflict resolution. For it to have any tangible effects, peace building and conflict resolution is a science that must be learned over time, practised and internalised. Let us consider briefly the efforts of one woman towards the creation of peace.

Berewa Jommo - Mama Amani

Berewa Jommo is one woman who has given her life to ensuring that peace building and conflict resolution processes in the region become a reality and are autochthonous in character. She has created a niche for herself, where using time tested adult learning processes and working in collaboration with like minded partners, she has been able to engender peace building, early warning/early response methodology and conflict transformation.

Berewa Jommo, is the Regional Director of African Community Education Network (ACEN) headquartered in Nairobi Kenya. ACEN promotes life-long learning based on community needs, knowledge and participation in all aspects, and at all levels of decision making. This is a process driven by a society that enjoys equal rights and opportunities regardless of gender, age, cultural affiliation or lifestyle, fully knowledgeable about its rights and responsibilities.

As noted earlier, whatever function a woman undertakes, she brings her total persona into it. Jommo is essentially an adult educator. As a gender expert, development consultant, linguist, administrator and editor, Jommo brings a wealth of knowledge and expertise into peace building and conflict resolution. As a Pan-Africanist whose ancestry traverses three continents, and having worked with the United Nations in various capacities, Jommo brings with her the requisite international exposure to make her contribution at the grassroots relevant in the international arena as well. One of Jommo's initiative is the mediation and training for women leaders on both sides of the Maasai-Gikuyu conflict in the Maai Mahiu-Satellite-Ololongonot area, in Naivasha, Rift Valley.

The violence between the Maasai and Gikuyu communities in the Maai Mahiu-Satellite-Ololongonot area has antecedents in 1992 and 1997, during the height of multiparty electioneering campaigns. Violence re-erupted since the beginning of 2005. According to various testimonies by victims of the violence, the re-eruption was triggered by a dispute over the use of River Uaso Kedong. Several lives have been lost and property worth millions of shillings destroyed. Many families have been displaced. Jommo's approach is revolutionary in many ways. Unlike the conventional peace initiatives where warring parties face each other at a round-table conference in expensive far away capitals of the world, the Mission and Women's Dialogues For Peaceful Co-existence, as the initiative is called, employs participatory approaches to adult learning and conflict transformation. This is done within the African context, using age-old African tools of reconciliation.

For a woman to mediate her roles as reproducer and nurturer of life, producer of life sustaining processes, manager and custodian of natural resources, environment and traditional knowledge, peace is a pre-requisite. Women, therefore, have a higher stake in conflict resolution than power hungry warlords or clan leaders. Being sensitive to these peculiarities and gender dynamics underlying conflict, Jommo uses women to build women.

Role and peer modelling is a typical African conflict resolution mechanism. A team of women peace builders from the East African region, the Somali Sudanese Kenya Women Solidarity Forum, under the auspices of Coalition for Peace in Africa (COPA), volunteered themselves and were co-opted into the initiative as third party independent facilitators to mediate between the parties to the conflict. To beef up their expertise at mediating in an agrarian/pastoralist conflict, this group was joined by representatives of the Rural Women's Peace Link (RWPL) from Lodwar and

Laikipia. To give it administrative and structural legitimacy, the group consulted widely with key political, administrative, civil society, traditional and religious leaders.

The group made its first contact with both parties on a fairly neutral ground and in circumstances that were conducive to initiating reconciliation. Members of the group attended funeral services for both the Gikuyu and Maasai victims at respective venues. This entry point was critical in that "weeping with the weeping" on the part of the facilitators, elicited trust and openness from the conflicting parties. Thereafter, women from both communities chose representatives to the mediation and training mission.

During the first phase of the programme, the participants using participatory adult learning methods have been able to identify the conflict from their own perspective; its causes, and non-destructive ways of resolving it. They have also formulated their early warning and response methodology. Reconciliation is not a one-off event and by the end of the mission, it is hoped that dialogue between the two parties will ensue as a prerequisite to long lasting peace. As a founder member of the **Baraza la Wanawake la Amani**, a national platform for community-based women's peace initiatives Jommo's name is synonymous with peace building and conflict resolution in Kenya. **Mama Amani** is a well known prophet in her home. On the international arena Jommo was instrumental in initiating UNIFEM's Peace and Conflict Resolution Programme and has been involved in peace building in the Great Lakes Region, Somalia, and South Sudan.

Poverty Eradication

One can hardly talk about poverty in the African context without looking at the effects of neo-colonialism and economic re-colonisation of Africa's peoples. The net effect of the very stringent austerity measures imposed on African economies by the Bretton Woods institutions in the last two decades or so, has been to re-colonise post independence Africa (Nyaga, 2002). Women are the greatest casualties of this economic neo-colonialism. When IMF insists on a lean civil service, the majority of the retrenchees are women who hold junior or middle level management jobs. When World Bank prescribes privatisation of state corporations, it is women who, because of the meagre resources at their disposal, are unable to afford high market prices for commodities and services that are no longer subsidised for by the state. To add insult to injury, when government spending is slashed, (and this is usually a key conditionality of the aid package), budgetary allocations to projects that promote gender equality are the first to go.

When the backlash hits the private sector, the first to go are the so called "soft" jobs in marketing, media and public relations. Because of their ability to pay attention to detail, women are good at communication and public relations and hold top and middle level management positions in those establishments (KPA, 2002). When the axe falls, then the bulk of the victims will be women, especially in Africa. The prevailing world economic order institutionalizes patriarchy in its most oppressive form.

Wahu Kaara - A Leader for All Seasons

In order to achieve development and eradication of poverty, we require more than availability and access to capital, technology and skilled labour. We need value change as well, accompanied by transformed mindsets and attitudes (Kariithi, 2005).

One Kenyan woman who has, by thought, word and deed helped transform mindsets and attitudes of Kenyans is Wahu Kaara, a mother and a grandmother, is one of the 1000 women from 150 countries nominated for the 2005 Nobel Peace Prize. Kaara has learnt to bloom where she is planted and to help others bloom along with her. It is in recognition of this fact that the Nobel Peace Committee nominated her as one of the women who despite their experience, competence and commitment to improving the lives of present and future generations, go unnoticed and unrecognised (KNA, 2005).

A seasoned activist and women's rights lobbyist, Kaara has been in the struggle for social justice for many years. She was born in the height of the Mau Mau struggle and is fondly referred to by her friends as the "daughter of the Mau Mau". Right from primary school in the Rift Valley, through high school and university, Kaara has been in the forefront agitating for social reform. She first came into the limelight in the 1990s, when, together with her fellow Kenyan Nobel Prize laureate the celebrated Prof. Wangari Maathai, fought alongside mothers of political prisoners at the then infamous Freedom Corner. Much later in year 2002, Kaara sought election to Parliament as an independent candidate but lost.

Having gone through the rigours of an election campaign and seen the dark side of elective politics, Kaara realised that her battles would not be won from a political platform. She had seen many of her colleagues in the struggle against the powers of domination and control bend under political and economic pressure, abandon ship and join forces of oppression. Kaara would have none of this and like the proverbial phoenix, rose from the ashes of an election defeat and created space for herself in a novel environment - linkage between a secular and a faith based global organisation.

As postulated elsewhere in, African women have, because of their under-class experience, developed negotiation skills to a very high degree of proficiency. They communicate well, are persuasive and highly creative. Creating a niche in a faith-based organisation was not only a matter of divine providence, but was a work of genius on the part of Kaara. She is currently the All Africa Conference of Churches Ecumenical Program Co-ordinator for the UN Millennium Development Goals, which in essence makes her a link, at the very highest level, between the United Nations and the giant continental Church body. In other words, Kaara's brief is to build some form of consensus between the Kingdom of Heaven and the world governments, as they tackle the nagging question of poverty and its eradication generally, and debt relief for Africa in particular.

As a founder member and former Co-ordinator of the Kenya Debt Relief Network, Kaara is no stranger to the root causes of poverty in Africa - economic occupation by the developed world using debt as a leash. As a woman who has been in the forefront in the war against poverty, Kaara has first hand experience of the impact of under-developed capitalism on Africans generally and the African woman in particular. She has seen on a daily basis the pain and indignity of hunger, disease and illiteracy. Under the cover of the continental Church body, Kaara has comparative advantage over her peers. She is able to breathe hell and brimstone on Pharoah's face from the safety of "hallowed ground", with the same ease she is able to mould young and old alike in her backyard.

A key member of the Global Call to Action Against Poverty (G-CAAP) Task Force, and a co-opted member of the British Make Poverty History Coalition, Kaara has taken her battles right to the doorstep of the "enemy camp". She was an honoured guest at Gleneagles where she was able to articulate Africa's stand on debt cancellation on a one-on-one basis with heads of states of the G-8 Club.

In a recent interview with the writer, Kaara articulated her agenda. As a Christian, she subscribes to the doctrines of the faith. Key among these is the belief that life is sacred and emanates from God. Human beings are stewards unto God for life and must therefore nurture and sustain it in an environment of total liberty, inter-dependence, complementarity, respect for one another, honesty and care. According to Kaara, this is her point of departure with the capitalist economy practised by the G-8 member governments. They employ the market paradigm as their point of reference. Under the market paradigm profit comes before life. It exploits life for expediency. The bedrock on which the West market economy is founded is domination and control of the weak by the mighty. That is why women and children of Africa, nature and environment have been sacrificed at the altar of the god of capital.

According to Kaara there is need to bring about change in attitudes and transform mindsets. We must understand the genesis of poverty and formulate our own ways and means of fighting it. As long as the underlying philosophy of relationship between the West and Africa is that of master and servant, no amount of pep talk on good governance, transparency and accountability will help Africa. As long as corrupt African leaders serve the interests of the West, the West will turn a blind eye to their excesses, gross violations of human rights included. Running to the West, begging bowl in hand, or agreeing to a quick fix prescription by IMF, will not help. African taxpayers cannot continue paying loans and interest for non-existent or worthless development projects that did not benefit them. Debt cancellation without surrender of the country's sovereignty is the way to go, according to Wahu Kaara.

Conclusion

The war against structures that disable women from participating, and taking the helm in the management of civic and political affairs of this nation must be torn down. However, in my view, there is need to strike the very delicate balance between expending one's total energies in fighting structures and systems that might take a long time to bring down, and taking pragmatic steps to meeting the challenges of today. Africa desperately needs quality leaders now.

As reproducers and producers of life, women have of necessity to be pace setters, movers and shapers of human history. They can only do this, in their natural habitat, in circumstances where they are free to live as holistic beings without let or hindrance. Women must create space where they can bring their total persona, brains and boobs as it were, without making any apologies. They must therefore look beyond the horizon of "political leadership" and deviate into areas where they can exercise their God given leadership talents and gifts to bring change and to impact others positively for a better tomorrow.

Nelson Mandela, the icon of leadership in Africa, must have been thinking of the African woman when he delivered his keynote address at the XV International AIDS Conference held in Bangkok, Thailand in July 2004 where he said that leaders must mobilise and inspire people to respond to crisis and that they must lead the response with clear vision and imaginative action. "They must dare to be different and they must be prepared for the course to be difficult. They will be faced with tough decisions and they must come up with bold and innovative responses," he emphasized.

Creating space in order to impact communities cannot be undertaken in a vacuum. Women need governmental commitment and support in pursuit of their leadership goals. To begin with laws that outlaw discrimination must be enacted and enforced. Where need be, affirmative action should institutionalised to level the playing field in all areas of life.. The judiciary and law enforcement agencies must be gender sensitive when dealing with women be they perpetrators or victims of crime. Access to resources such as education, finances, reproductive, mental and physiological health must be enhanced. Gender mainstreaming in all facets of our national life must be a commitment not an empty slogan. Policies and systems that are women friendly must be put in place.

References

ACEN, *Report of Mission And Women's Dialogues For Peaceful Co-Existence In the Maai Mahiu-Satellite-Ololongonot Area*. ACEN, June 2005.

Adimora-Ezeigbo, A. *House of Symbols*. Lagos: Oracle Books Limited, 2001.

Amadiume, I. *Male Daughters, Female Husbands*. London: Zed Books Ltd, 1987.

Bloch, M., et al. *Women and Education in Sub-Saharan Africa: Power, Opportunities and Constraints*. London: Lynne Rienner Publishers, Boulder, 1988.

Chepkwony, A. "Leadership: A Feminine View". *Social and Religious Concerns of East Africa*. Washington DC: The Council of Research in Values and Philosophy, 2005. 116-122.

CNN, Live Coverage reporting from the St Paul's Cathedral, London, Wednesday 6 July 2005.

Cotran, E. *Restatement of African Law, Kenya (Volume 1, The Law of Marriage & Divorce)*. London & Maxwell, 1968.

Fowler, H.W. et al. *The Concise Oxford Dictionary of Current English*. Oxford: Clarendon Press, 1975.

Gakaara, W. "The Unsung Heroes." Murang'a Today, 1968.

Green, J. et al "Gender Sustainable Development, and Improved Resource Management in Africa". *Africa's Valuable Assets*. New York: World Resources Institute, 1998.

ILRI, *Sustaining the Future Harvest*. International Livestock Research Institute, Annual Report. Nairobi, 2002

Kang'ethe, N. "Courage Sister Do Not Stumble". *PARENTS Magazine*, 1994. 17-18.

_____. "Distinguishing Characteristics of African Feminism". Unpublished, University of Zimbabwe, Women's Law Centre, Harare, 2003.

_____. "Arise and Shine Africa." *Insights Magazine*, 43, St James, NSW, (1994) 143-147.

_____. "Women and Devolution of Property Under the Law of Succession Act: Why Law Reform Without More Is Inadequate" Unpublished, University of Nairobi, 2002.

Kariithi, K. et al. *Building a Prosperous Kenya*. Nairobi: Christians for a Just Society, 2005.

Kenya Psychological Association, "The Developed Mind" Psychology Beat; Nairobi: English Press, 2001.

KNA Press Release, "Kenyan Activist Among 1000 Nobel Peace Prize". Nairobi, June 29, 2005.

Mathu, E. "Celebrating Our Heroes". *PARENTS Magazine*. July 2005. 20-22.

Mathu, E. "Confronting Barriers To Women's Rights" Women's Edition. Washington DC: Population Reference Bureau, 2001. 143-145.

Moore, H. L. *Feminism and Anthropology*. Cambridge: Polity Press, 1988.

Nyagah, N. "Woman Be Thou Loosed". Unpublished, a Keynote address delivered by the Governor of the Central Bank of Kenya to a Women in Christian Leadership Conference Held in Nairobi in September, 2002.

Nzomo, M. "Beyond the Women's Decade: Women's Political Participation in Kenya". *Social and Religious Concerns of East Africa: A Wajibu Anthology*. Washington DC: The Council of Research in Values and Philosophy, 2005. 123-129.

Nzomo, M. "Women in Politics: What Prospects?" Election Platform, *Daily Nation*, December 5, 2002.

Okwach, A. *Household Based Factors as Determinants of School Participation in Kenya: The Case of Nairobi and Siaya Districts*. Abridged Research Report No. 20 African Academy of Sciences, 1994.

Omondi, I. "It is Time For An Overhaul." *Christian Media*, No. 9 (1994) 1-2.

United Nations, *The Worlds Women 2000 Trends & Statistics*. Geneva: UN Publications, 2001.

UNESCO, "Opportunity 21 For Kenya". *Daily Nation*, 12 July, 2003.

The Holy Bible. King James Version

"Karua's Ten Year Wait" Commentary. *Daily Nation* Friday 17 January 2003.

7

"Bodily Contrariness": Some Preliminary Questions on Disability and Leadership in Kenya[1]

Mbugua Wa- Mungai

An autobiographical note

It is somewhat of a dilemma to discuss a problematic in which one's subjectivity is directly implicated yet this quandary can be turned into a unique vantage point in at least two key ways. In the first place I am able to speak for myself—and for others in conditions like mine—rather than being spoken *for* or *about*, as is usually the case, and thereby defy misrepresentations that often occur when "*the disabled*" are referred to. In a sense then, my narrative here is also one of resistance not just to the dominant metaphors about which disabilities are spoken but, even more fundamentally, to the continuing silence that inhibits serious discourse about such issues in Kenya.[2] The lack of an agentic role for people with disabilities, as we shall see later, is the function of a number of institutional structures—cultural, linguistic, economic, social, even political—and is firmly inscribed in everyday forms of exclusivist behavior. Indeed, as I demonstrate later, amongst a majority of Kenyans it is near impossible to conceptualize the terms disability and leadership in the same context.

People in this category are understood, and preeminently figured, in terms of tragic/ diseased bodies. There is overwhelming evidence of this in traditional African social practices, for instance among the Pokot and Samburu nomads of Kenya who either kill off their infants with disabilities at birth or leave them behind as they move on in search of greener pastures. The exclusion of persons with disabilities from mainstream society in Western cultures is also well documented (see Wilson and Lewiecki-Wilson 2001:1-6). Thus whether thinking about Aristotle's exhortations against "deformed children", the Gospels and their discourse on disability as contamination or the 'elimination' of children with disabilities in nomadic societies, PWD are not only seen and treated as a drain on material resources, but are also more crucially regarded as a direct threat to the survival of society. As such conventional meanings of the term disability "restrict[s] thinking about disability in any other way" (Wilson and Lewecki-Wilson *ibid*: 2).

In this regard, when disability in Kenya is spoken about it is often in association with marginal social spaces (special schools, rehabilitation institutions) that are hidden from view, and when disabled bodies appear in the center, they are often thought of as scars on the social fabric for instance street beggars or general inconveniences on the sidewalk. Indeed, widely documented incidents where disabled hawkers are beaten up and forcibly removed from Nairobi city center streets by municipal authorities lend credence to this view (see, for instance, Ayieko 2005). Thus, for instance, as I limp along the city pavement on my crutches, I often wonder whether the people I encounter and who usually give me a wide berth, literally, do so out of consideration to my condition or perhaps because of their unspoken horror at coming into contact with a 'strange-looking' body. I notice too how they stop and stare as I enter my car, many unspoken questions about my ability to work the machine etched onto their faces; the parking boys dutifully collect their tip from me—they show no prejudice against disability—as I ease my car into the traffic mainstream where I instantly become and I am treated as just another anonymous motorist, one of those Nairobians that is considered to have 'arrived' at the economic center, and nobody notices my physical condition. As this anecdote demonstrates, identity can hardly be a fixed mode, and one can slip into multiple identities contingent to particular material realities. Therefore, to perceive and talk about disability as a permanent state of inability and dependence is in itself a flawed way of thinking the biological body. Unfortunately, these are some of the assumptions that inform the exclusion of persons with disabilities from leadership roles.

Secondly, and derived from the above, owing to my being uniquely placed at the junction between experience and theoretical discourse, I can unpack and question some of the misrepresentations about disability without inhibitions. Disability is a taboo subject, at best spoken about in undertones; but then discussing in the open an unsettling subject forces people to confront their own assumptions and biases. By way of illustration, does the term 'disabled' even remotely describe me? The imperatives of social correctness have moved us from the word "cripple" to "handicapped" to "impaired", "challenged" and finally to the catch-all "disabled". There is even the term "differently-abled" which smirks of an inferiority complex that finds it necessary to legitimize its own existence (See Mairs, 1998:382). All these attempts at correctness are in essence semantic nonsense given that they inadequately predicate identity upon only one aspect of the body that is so described. For example, even though I am a victim of polio, I make good use of whatever remains of my limbs. Most significantly, I utilize my brain and mouth and earn a living teaching literature and folklore at Kenyatta University. How then can the term disabled adequately describe me? I am a lecturer, a husband, a father, a son and a brother as well as a person to many other people with whom I am situated in socio-economic relations defined by a set of parameters where my physical condition is a non-issue. I do not deny the fact that I can't run, but the fact that such a thoroughly inaccurate term like ' a disabled man' can be purported to define my social worth and identity is a telling comment about the inability of language to capture and reflect reality fully.

As becomes apparent from the foregoing, language can and does obfuscate more than it uncovers and names, and part of the reason Kenya's persons with disabilities remain largely invisible—whether in mainstream leadership in particular or in public space generally—is that the terms by which such persons are described/discussed seem to have been accepted uncritically. Thus, one of my key arguments in this chapter is that disability has no space within public discourse and that when it occurs it is not about disability *per se* but about other factors surrounding it. When there is a semblance of discussion, as seen in the publication of the Persons with Disability Act 2003, it is often misguided by treating disability as a homologous space. As such, despite its phenomenal prevalence in society, disability in Kenya remains one of the least debated issues. In fact, the Kenyan Vice President has recently admitted that the government— or anyone else for that matter—really does not know how many PWD there are in Kenya and that no single post-independence government has ever factored them in national planning (see *Daily Nation* 2005). Incidentally a similar omission is evident in the world of Kenyan NGOs where rape, "rights of the girl child", domestic violence and road traffic accidents have recently emerged forcefully; disability rights seem to be of only peripheral interest. To understand better this silence , it is necessary to examine the construction of disability in Kenya.

The discourse of 'abnormality': confronting the disabled body in Kenyan society

"Couple kill and eat own child,"[3] states a news headline in one of the local dailies. But even as it emphasizes on the rather touchy subject of cannibalism, this headline simultaneously obscures the fact that the victim in question was a six-year old boy with a disability. Indeed this news item underlines one of the most dominant methods—silence—with which Kenyans have traditionally approached disability. Thus to the news editor, the parents' cannibalistic act, with its whiff of 'backwardness' / 'primitive' behavior, forms the juicy bit of the story while to the local administration and law enforcers, this incident is merely a criminal act. Without in any way trying to minimize the magnitude of their deed, a closer look at the story reveals that the couple seems to have a rational explanation that "allows" them to cut up their son with a disability and serve him up as meal for the rest of the family. In their own words, the boy could not fend for himself especially in a situation where the family faced collective starvation and he was thus a "burden" to be shed. To understand how such cold logic erases any parental instinct for the nurture and protection of the socially vulnerable, I suggest that one has to look at concepts of disability within the broader Kenyan context since they condition how persons with disability are viewed vis-à-vis leadership.

In Kenya, as indeed in any other society, people that are in one moment considered 'normal' are often ushered into the unfamiliar topos of 'abnormality' as they acquire one form of disability or the other; from limb injuries sustained in road traffic accidents to the "dimming of lights"[4] (blindness) occasioned by the consumption of methanol-laced brews. Disability can strike from any number of sources, none of which is easily predictable. In other words, there is nothing natural about disability, a fact that perhaps underlies most of anxieties and attitudes that people harbor towards disabilities and those who have them. Hence, it should be clear that the ranks of persons with disabilities are ever-increasing and even if for no other reason this fact alone ought to make Kenyan society to begin an appraisal of its understanding of and approaches to persons with disability. What is important for our purposes then is to consider how people confront disabilities. I offer in this regard what deems to be an exceptional case that amply illustrates how one person who has learnt how to cope with his disability has in an unheralded way been offering effective alternative leadership, particularly for persons with disabilities but also more generally to the youth in this country and abroad.

Swarzenegger's Other; Running into visibility

One day soon after Sidney 2000, I got a call from Swarzenegger's office. The governor had himself tried to get in touch with me but had failed. He said how much he felt inspired by my athletic ability and he keeps abreast of my activities on the field…you see he was in the crowd that cheered me on to victory that day in Sidney.[5]

In these simple words, Henry Wanyoike, the visually impaired Kenyan marathoner and paralympics champion, captures an interesting encounter between two oppositional concepts of the body—an "imperfect" body and a "perfect" one. There is a distinct irony in Swarzenegger's cheering on a blind man. His vast film career has cast him as a one-man army, an individual endowed with the ideal physique—and is thereby presented as the epitome of physical fitness—and who by employing a combination of raw physical power and intellect relentlessly conquers a myriad obstacles. Yet here was Swarzeneger applauding the astounding achievements of a man who, even though gifted with physical stamina, could not see but only merely sense whatever (foe) it was that he had conquered. Whatever must have flashed across the mind of this Western icon of bodily-masculine perfection as he stood in thrall of the excellence of a 'flawed' body, an antithetical representation in its entirety of what his was not, we can never tell. However, one can say with certainty that in the heat of that track in Sidney, Henry Wanyoike presented to the thousands of spectators present an excellent example of what can be achieved within and beyond the limitations of the physical body. This involves a considerable effort in self-acceptance as well as in will power to overcome obstacles. As Henry states:-

> One night in 1994 I went to bed as usual but when I woke up the next morning, my sight was gone. I couldn't see a thing! Believing that my life was effectively over, I sunk into a deep depression and I often considered suicide as an option…But after many months of soul-searching I asked myself "Is it really true that I am now entirely useless?" That was the turning point in my life. It was difficult to adjust to my new life but I decided to face up to the challenge. You see, I was the same Henry Wanyoike but one who had now discovered another part of himself. I discovered abilities that I had never even imagined I possessed. As ironic as this may sound, I consider my loss of physical vision as an entry point into another mode of perception and now I appreciate things, colours and people that I otherwise used to take for granted. I feel that I am more useful to society now than I was before my blindness.[6]

Narrating his travels and track exploits across the globe, one senses that Wanyoike considers himself a marathoner on a mission. What is however even more fascinating listening to his narrative is the countless times in which he uses the verb "see"; one might expect that anyone that has only experienced loss of vision in recent adulthood might shun any reminders to the previous state of sightedness. But as Wanyoike's case illustrates, a lot of the things that persons with disabilities do or do not do, or the things that are done or not done to/for them stem from attitude; perception is key, the 'turning point' in dealing with disabilities in Kenyan society. Rather than being obsessed with their physical condition, PWD ought to be more bothered by how to make their disabilities work both for them and for society. Disability, as Wanyoike has demonstrated, can and should be turned against itself.

Inspired by Wanyoike's example, young people I have talked to are now willing to try a hand (and a leg!) in athletics. At one level, from the vantage point of his visual impairment he has offered an excellent opportunity for Kenyan young people to discover their abilities; "I can now see that success does not just lie in politics", one of them told me. It is doubtlessly in this capacity that Standard Chartered Bank sponsors his participation in various races across the world. The Bank has also facilitated his motivational lectures to schoolchildren in Kenya, Indonesia, and most recently in the UK. In similar manner the United Disabled Persons of Naivasha (UDPN), a local Community Based Organization (CBO), has also recently recruited him into its disability-sensitization campaign amongst Naivasha schoolchildren.

At another perhaps even more critical level Wanyoike's case has helped to make disability visible; his being awarded the Sportsman of the Year 2005 medal speaks to this fact. However, this is not to suggest that people are now more inclined towards accepting PWDs more easily but that it is still possible for merit to shine through the veils that shroud disability in order to achieve a different take on leadership. Thus Wanyoike is of the opinion that persons with disabilities who exhibit outstanding qualities should be seen as leaders in their own right.

> A leader is not necessarily that individual who is the wealthiest or the loudest amongst us. A leader is that person, not only a politician, who through personal example and dedication, influences others to follow him [7]

In this regard, Wanyoike fits very well within his own understanding of leadership.

Contrasting the above notion of leadership to prevailing leadership models might enable a better understanding of why PWD have hitherto rarely been considered for leadership roles. A number of relevant questions might be asked in regard to this scenario. First, why is it that PWD are near invisible in Kenyan social-economic leadership spaces? Second, why is it that PWD seem underrepresented among the professional classes? Finally, how do PWD understand themselves vis-à-vis leadership? In order to attempt answers to these questions, it is necessary to examine specific aspects of mainstream Kenyan life in order to understand how the politics of exclusion works to keep PWD at the very margins of society.

The "*Saidia maskini*" syndrome: The Discourse of charity

Within the Kenyan public understanding of disability, there is perhaps no better enduring image of PWD than that the portrait of dependence. The "saidia maskini [help the poor]" refrain chanted by the many supposedly disabled street beggars across major Kenyan towns has been instrumental in etching the image of dependence upon the collective public psyche. Consequently, few people can dissociate disability from charity as the constant use of phrases like "the less fortunate", "the less privileged", and "maskini wa Mungu" [God's poor creatures] in relation to PWD indicate. The commonly deployed 'wasiojiweza' [unable] and 'walemavu' [the disabled] point to a conception of disability as both a state of vegetativeness and a blight, a scar on the 'normal' surfaces of society.

Such popular phraseology of disabilities not only marks the subjects so figured as helpless but also maps them as a burden on society. As Appadurai (1986) has shown in his discussion of the social negotiations that are enacted through commodities, there is no such thing like an innocent gift. In this vein, it is possible that some of the charity extended to PWD is a cynical quest for a feel-good effect. Indeed elsewhere, disability has evolved into a vast industry in its own right (Albrecht 1992). While giving alms has its merits, especially as a function of Kenyan Moslem and Christian traditions, charity remains a double-edged sword and its long-term effects are at best questionable as witnessed by the fact that more pity towards PWD than understanding of them seems to have emerged from Kenya's deep rooted alms-giving tradition. For instance, a 1988 fundraiser conducted by then president Moi in aid of the National Disabled Fund set the tone in which the welfare of PWD would henceforth be addressed[8]; once a donation for the helpless (wasiojiweza) is made, the giver is absolved of any other obligations- social, political, economic- towards such persons. This is also reflected in the way disability organizations in Kenya operate.

To illustrate, few disability-work organizations can be ranked alongside the Association of the Physically Disabled of Kenya, an NGO established in 1958 and which sources mobility aids (wheelchairs, white canes, crutches etc) and facilitates access to them. However, by virtue of being one of the more readily recognizable disability organizations, the APDK perhaps more than any other institution has been instrumental in crystallizing the donor-dependant paradigm that conditions thinking about disability issues in Kenya. The crucial advocacy component is glaringly lacking from APDK's activities; it is necessary to sensitize 'donors' towards needs other than mobility aids. At the same time, dependence on charity has led some PWD to internalize and accept helplessness as a normative condition, thereby remaining unable to tap into their internal resources, especially the personal. Often such persons gripe about what society "owes" them- and indeed there is a measure of truth in such claims- but this particular attitude might also be seen as a critical impediment to personal progress since it leads to the abdication of their own agency.

The Disability ghetto: Special schools

Quite correctly recognizing the diversity of disabilities existing in Kenya, various church-based NGOs have set up "special schools" to cater for particular disabilities; Joyland *Special* School-Kisumu, Joytown *Special* primary and secondary schools-Thika, Thika School for the *Blind*, Ol-Kalou *Disabled* Children's home, Machakos School for the *Blind* etc are some of the more notable examples that come to mind. The establishment of such schools springs from the assumption that PWD require facilities that are specially adapted to their needs and that it is easier to cater for such persons if they are brought together into a central location. Without trying in any way to minimize the contribution of such church-based schools/institutions, especially in view of the government's inability/unwillingness to provide the same, it can still be legitimately asked whether these schools do not end up instilling an us ('disabled') vs. them ('normal') attitude amongst their pupils.

The 'special' tag in the schools' names, or the deliberate accenting of a particular category of disability that is being catered for in such institutions gives the impression of an alterity, a group of persons set off and apart from the rest of society. The special group thus 'shielded ' from the 'normal' other is in this manner taught to view itself as distinct and different from the rest of society. What effects such seclusion/exclusion causes in an individuals' identity-formation process might be debatable. However, it suffices to observe that environment plays a key role in shaping an individual's understanding of their world, more so if that world seems to be predominated by leg braces, crutches and braille machines! It should not amaze then that a large number of PWD are acutely self-conscious about their physical state. Similarly, those living in the outside ("normal") world never really get to know what goes on in the locked-up/secluded other world of PWD. In the end, both those on the inside and outside of these institutions never get to understand one another or, at the very least, meaningfully learn how the other lives. Arguably, these circumstances conduce for the growth of a culture of silence and the formulation of taboos about disability. This in turn forms suitable ground for mistrust and suspicion as well as the formation of negative attitudes towards PWD which, once they take root, become extremely difficult if not impossible to confront. In these circumstances, it is hard for PWD to be seen as leaders regardless of their particular abilities or professional qualifications.

"I got the cash!": The ethos of Kenyan politics

Political office is the most dominant way in which Kenyans conceive leadership. Yet looking at the political landscape, one notices that it is heavily imbalanced against PWD. Indeed few such persons have played key political roles. The visually-impaired Chomba Munyi's failed quest for a parliamentary seat in Nairobi is memorable as indeed is the remarkable career of Muthoni Kihara, a woman with a disability who at 21 in 1992 became the youngest councilor ever in Kenya. She has been actively involved in civil society activities since losing her seat and she now heads the NARC disability desk. Josephine Sinyo, a blind lawyer, had a brief stint in parliament as a nominated MP before she went back to her legal practice and Lawrence Mute has served as a commissioner in the Kenya National Human Rights Commission. His blindness has not stopped him from writing poetry and agitating for the rights of all Kenyans. What is striking however is the fact that few PWD are keen to venture into careers in public life especially in the field of elective politics. This might be explained in two ways.

Firstly, few people are willing to even consider a PWD as a serious contender for office simply by the fact of their disability. As Muthoni observes:-

> Many people were put off by the fact that I was then "only a small girl" and some said loudly that I was a prostitute. But what horrified them most was that I have a disability with some declaring in my hearing 'I can never vote for a cripple! The irony was that they were still expecting some largesse from this "crippled girl"!'"[9]

The refusal to vote for a cripple is a play on the more common Gikuyu phrase "*ungioyana na kionje gigutware ku?*" [what would you possibly do with a cripple?] normally used by mothers to chide their daughters against marrying suitors with a physical disability. The assumption usually is that such a PWD is incapable of fulfilling his conjugal duties. The contemptuous view of disability vis-à-vis leadership expressed above seems to be prevalent in mainstream Kenyan politics. For instance, in a publicly documented case in October 2001 then-president Daniel Arap Moi loudly wondered where and how a blind man like the late Oki Ooko Ombaka, then a Commissioner on the Constitution of Kenya Review Commission, could lead Kenyans. That few voices of criticism were raised against Daniel Moi leads to the probable conclusion that his sentiments resonated well with a great number of Kenyans. Clearly, widely held misconceptions about PWD and irrational fears of disability generally militate against a productive public sector life for persons with disability.

Secondly, success in Kenyan politics often depends upon one's ability to command and hand out vast amounts of fiscal resources. As Haugerud (1997) has observed it is often impossible to marshal such resources if one is not well connected to the political elite based in Nairobi and other major urban centers. In turn, politicians create patronage networks that fan outwards to the grassroots in the countryside. Doubtlessly, for reasons already discussed above, PWD are not encouraged to come too close to the mainstream and because they cannot access finances from the political center they can only raise funds for their political projects from their own private resources. Ironically, few even have the jobs from which to raise this money owing to the fact that potential employers often discriminate against them, a fact that the Persons with Disability Act 2003 (see *Kenya Gazette Supplement* no.111) identifies and seeks to redress. Again, where PWD engage in informal sector economic activities such as street vending, it is impossible to raise much funding owing to the unstable nature of such micro businesses. Thus the economic emasculation of PWD or their inability to participate meaningfully in the economic domain for whatever reasons means that they nearly always set off from a point of disadvantage.

"According to our people...": Disability in Kenyan cultures

At another level, many of the reasons that ensure that PWD are shunted from visibility might be found in traditional practices. One way of trying to understand this is to establish how diverse Kenyan communities generally regard disability. The practice of killing off infants with disabilities among nomadic communities has already been alluded to (see also Albrecht 1992:40-41). This is doubtlessly an extreme form of literal erasure which means that other non-nomadic people have subtler ways of dealing with PWD. One such method is abandonment; if people get a disability in adulthood, they could always be put in a hut and left to starve to death since they were now a burden. Similar logic informs the parents' decision to get rid of their six-year old 'disabled burden' in the newspaper article cited earlier. Elsewhere, during a recent outreach visit with the CBO I work for, a father to a PWD bluntly stated, "this child has become a big burden and a bother! I am totally fed up!" Whereas one might understand the frustrations of bringing up a child with severe cerebral palsy, it seems clear that few parents are disposed to accepting such children as their legitimate responsibility. In the latter case, the father stridently sought to place his "burden" on the CBO as he particularly chided the government for not helping him.

Folklore is an extremely rich repository in which traditional attitudes towards disability are archived. These are not always negative, as Franks (2001) reports in her study of disability in Grimms' fairy tales. Unfortunately, as any examination might reveal, there is hardly any positive representation of disability in Kenyan folklore. At any rate disability in folklore and culture in Kenya has not been seriously thought about. As Franks (*ibid*: 244) has argued, despite the abundance of disability imagery in much art, it passes as unnoticed 'background' because it is never analyzed. Proverbs are perhaps one such fields in which research might yield telling results. Disability is amply represented in the everyday idiom of Kenyan cultures; "Why beg as if you are a cripple?", "You do not fight a cripple", "Poverty cannot be equated to being crippled". Additionally, popular music has been crucial to the dissemination of images of disability, e.g. the perfect wife ought not to be a PWD (see for instance Peter Kigia's song '*Ciku Kiwete*'). On the whole, Kenyan cultures construct disability as a portrait of negativity, a state of pariahdom to be shunned determinedly. Given the ease with which such portraits circulate within the flows of popular culture (music, TV, cinema, newspapers and magazines), it becomes easy to prey upon pre-existing/latent culturally conditioned negative predisposition towards PWD/disability. As a consequence, it is almost a given that the public will turn away from such persons, whatever else they might represent, let alone accept them in leadership positions. Thus, even though there is in place now in Kenya a legal framework to guard against the marginalization of PWD, particularly with regard to workplace discrimination, it remains to be seen how the cultural structures that inhibit the realization of such persons' leadership potential will be dealt with.

Conclusion: Whither Disability Discourse?

In the light of the foregoing I suggest below a number of ways in which persons with disability might be enabled a space in which to play some leadership roles. Admittedly, in her handling of disability issues Kenya lags far behind other societies such as the US and the UK which have got more resources and better established structures. Notwithstanding, it is becoming clear that the Kenyan political class is finally paying serious attention to the predicament of PWD as attested to by the enactment into law of the Disability Act in 2003. The challenge that remains is two-fold.

First, the government has to supervise the implementation of the articles of the Disability Act. In this regard little work if any has been seen since the passing of this law. Secondly, and perhaps this is the more fruitful area of engagement, civil society groups ought to firmly inscribe the disability agenda into mainstream human rights discourse. This can be a partnership where such groups supplement government efforts to conscientize society about its legal obligations to PWD as well as educate the latter about their rights. While not denying that affirmative action for persons with disabilities is a good idea, real gains can only be realized when society reaches a true understanding of what disability is and how it can be harnessed for social good.

At another level, the special schools/institutions system needs to be re-examined. One way of doing this might be to conduct pilot projects on integrated schooling; a few schools have already opened up in this way (e.g. Ol-Kalou Children's home, Joytown Secondary School and Thika School for the Blind). However, what is envisaged here involves children with disabilities on a large scale being facilitated to attend schools in their immediate social environment. Children with mild disabilities can easily fit into such a model of schooling. This ensures that such children are not uprooted from their social networks and other support bases at the same time as it enables them to learn and grow up in a natural environment. This would no doubt help overcome the self-consciousness that being placed in special schools imposes upon them and thereby enable the cultivation of the independence and confidence with which to face challenges in life. Furthermore, children without disabilities will get to learn that there is nothing strange about disabled bodies, after all.

The media also can be brought to effect a change of attitude about disability. It is possible to sing or write about persons with disability who have made a positive impact in diverse fields in society. Indeed, one of the cardinal problems in addressing the challenges of disability in Kenya today is that few people speak about the issues at all; the media is well placed to foster dialogue and thus help to break the taboos surrounding this subject. In doing this, it is necessary for media practitioners in whichever field to deliberately emphasize that political leaders constitute only one aspect of leadership and that alternative leaders might be found in other fields such as sports, the creative arts, academia etc. The leadership stories of people like Henry Wanyoike need to be told and retold as they offer valuable beacons of hope for both PWD and others. In this way young persons will have a diversity of role models from which to choose.

Notes

[1] Observations raised in this paper are derived from conversations with persons with disability (hereafter PWD) whom I encounter in my work with United Disabled Persons of Naivasha (UDPN), a CBO, as well as from my own experience as a person living with polio.

[2] Though slow in coming, once in a while self-narratives by PWD appear e.g. Njuguna Githagui's Don't Worry My Son (1985) and Esther Owuor's (1995) *My Life as a Paraplegic*.

3   See *Sunday Nation*, July 24 2005,p 5. Col 2,3.

4   "*Nitaendelea kukunywa hata mkizima taa!*" [I will continue drinking despite the fact that you have put out the lamp] was a common phrase heard during FM radio call-in shows as listeners sought to describe the reactions of those who went blind following the consumption of illicit brews first in Maai Mahiu in 2002 and in June 2005 in parts of Ukambani, Kenya.

5   Interview held with the author, February 2005,Nairobi.

6   Interview with the author February 2005,Nairobi.

7   Interview with the author, July 4th, Nairobi

8   To most Kenyans I talked to during the writing of this paper this fundraiser is a bitter memory which tends to color their perceptions of PWD. Indeed, and quite a few wondered; "Was the 89 million we were forced to donate in 1988 not enough to solve your problems?"

9   Conversation with the author, June 4th 2005,Nairobi.

References

Albrecht, G. *The Disability Business: Rehabilitation in America*. New Delhi: Sage Publications, 1992.

Appadurai, A. (Ed.) Introduction: *Commodities and the Politics of Value. The Social Life of Things*. Cambridge: Cambridge University Press, 1986.

Ayieko,O. Lives and limbs lost during raids by cruel askaris. *Daily Nation, Outlook Magazine*, September 19, p.8 Col. 1, 2005.

Daily Nation. State to use 150m on census for Disabled. April 1, p.5 Col. 1, 2005

Franks, B. "Gutting the Golden Goose: Disability in Grimms ' Fairy Tales". In James C. Wilson and Cynthia Lewecki-Wilson (Ed) *Embodied Rhetorics: Disability in Language and Culture*, pp.244-258.Cabondale and Edwardsville: Southern Illinois University Press , 2001

Haugerud,A..*The Culture of Politics in Modern Kenya* . New York: Cambridge University Press , 1997

Mairs, N. "On being a cripple". In Lillian Bridwell-Bowles (et al) *Identity Matters Rhetorics of Difference*, pp.383-391.New Jersey: Prentice Hall, 1998

The Kenya Gazette Supplement No. 111(Acts No.15) of January 9, 2004

Wilson, J. C and Lewiecki-Wilson, C. *Embodied Rhetorics: Disability in Language and Culture*. Cabondale and Edwardsville: Southern Illinois University Press , 2001

8

Religion and Leadership: The Creation of a Just Society

Philomena N. Mwaura

Introduction

Africa is a continent of diversity and division based on religion, culture, ethnicity, language and a wide range of manifestation of the colonial experience. It has predominantly three major religious heritages namely, African traditional religion, Christianity and Islam. Available data shows that most of West Africa is Muslim and that traditional religion is still a vibrant force. Christianity is dominant in countries like Equatorial Guinea, Gabon, Togo, Nigeria, Ghana and South West Cameroon.[1]

In East Africa, and especially in Kenya and Uganda, Christians account for 80% of the population, while Islam is 15% and African traditional religion 5%.[2] Central and Southern Africa have predominantly Christian populations. There are large Muslim populations in Tanzania, a few in Malawi and South Africa with still a smaller percentage adhering to African Traditional Religion. Nonetheless, despite the prepondence of Christianity and Islam in different parts of Africa, the influence of African religion is not diminished for it still colours people's imagination and impacts on various aspects of their social life. African spirituality influences people's values, concepts of self identity and behaviour.

The last three decades of the 20th century witnessed what has been described by scholars of religion, theologians and missiologists as a shift of the center of gravity of Christianity from the west to the south, in Africa, Asia and Latin America.[3] This rapid growth of Christianity in Africa has occurred in a context of pauperization of the continent due to poor leadership, militarilization of the society, collapse of economies, abuse of human rights, corruption, foreign debt, debilitating disease, including HIV/AIDS, and rising poverty. The period between 1975 – 2000 saw an intensification of the return of the Christian churches into the public space providing leadership in the recovery of democratic practice. During the same period, other components of civil society such as trade unions, academic and students' professional bodies, judiciary and traditional rulers and any other restraining social forces had been compromised or destroyed[4].

Religion, Christianity included, is a catalyst for change because it can be used to provide leadership in times of social upheaval, though it may also be used as an oppressive tool. This chapter explores religious leadership in the African context drawing from the institutions of African religion and Christianity. It addresses the following questions: What is religious leadership? How does religious leadership contribute to transformation of society? How can religion be used as a mobilizing tool for good governance and development? In what ways can religions be used for evil? We shall begin by defining the concept, religious leadership before exploring the other variables. The central thesis of this chapter is that Kenyans attach great moral value to the religious institutions to which they belong for these serve as the custodians of the moral fabric of society. They expect religious institutions and leaders to provide guidance not only in matters of faith and morals but also in political, social, economic and other spheres of society. But to what extent are the religious institutions equipped to provide this guidance?

The chapter also argues that at various stages of Kenya's history, religion (whether African traditional religion, Islam and various expressions of Christianity) have challenged oppression, inculcated democratic ideals and championed human rights. At other times too, churches collaborated with oppressors and hindered, rather than helped prepare, the way for democratic rule before and after independence.

Conceptualizing Religious Leadership

Mircea Eliade defines religious leadership as "the process by which leaders induce followers to act for certain transcendental goals that embody the value, motivation and aspirations of both leaders and followers."[5] The concept is related to other concepts such as power and authority. Authority is legitimate power to require and receive submission and obedience and it is found in all religions. Power on the other hard, according to Max Weber is "the probability that one actor with a social relationship will be in a position to carry out (his or her) will despite resistance, regardless of the basis on which this probability rests."[6] People with power know that they will be listened to; they do not hope that someone will listen to them.

Power can be achieved or lost. It is resisted when it works for human downfall. Effective power, long term power, depends for its energy on three factors: the opportunity to make the rules, the right to sanction those who break them and the means to control thought and transmit ideas.[7] A distinction can be made between power understood as physical force or might and power as moral right. Physical power accomplishes its ends by force and it can be used for good or for evil. Moral power, on the other hand, is the right or the legitimate ability to make decisions in matters of social or religious significance. It follows, therefore, that one can have power without authority but not vice versa. The sources of this authority can be social, political, religious or supernatural.

Religious leadership involves the exercise of power in religious collectives. Religious leadership has been recognized by scholars as an important vehicle of religiosity and social change. Research into religious leadership in the pioneering works of Max Weber and Joachim Wach[8] attempted to classify religious leadership into prophet priest, magician, founder, reformer, seer, diviner, saint and religious. This approach focused on the personality of the leader, his/her traits and the situation of the followers. Other recent research has shown that leadership occurs in an immensely complex social network of structural and patterned relationships. In small groups leadership adheres not in an individual but in a role that is embedded within some specified social system; "variations in the social context within which religious leadership is deemed to be critical represent an important historical variable."[9]

Religious leaders as reformers, revolutionaries, founders or conservationists challenge, revitalize or maintain existing social and religious order. What is the basis of legitimation of religious leadership? According to Weber,[10] validity of claims of legitimacy are based on a number of things which include:

(i)   Rational grounds resting on belief in the legality of enacted roles and the right of those elevated to authority under such roles to issue commands that is, *legal authority*.

(ii) Grounds resting on an established belief in the sanctity of traditions and the legitimacy of those exercising authority under them, that is *traditional authority*.

(iii) *Charismatic grounds* resting on devotion to the exceptional sanctity, heroism or exemplary character of an individual person and on the normative patterns or order revealed or ordained by him/her. For religious leaders, *charismatic authority* is said to have its source in the supernatural.

The right of the leader to rule is determined by the followers recognition of the godlike qualities either imputed to him/her or through ascension to a charismatic office. Charismatic leaders like prophets, are agents of change who take personal responsibility for breaking with the established normative or declaring this break to be morally legitimate. Prophets claim definite revelation and are able to challenge social and cultural practices and political governance. Prophets and charismatic leaders in new religious movements in Africa, both traditional and Christian, have served this purpose at various epochs of Kenya's history. Let us now examine religious leadership in African religion and Christianity.

Religious Leadership in Traditional African Societies

In most traditional African communities the state (community), its rulers and institutions were set within a sacred cosmic order. The "political organizations were often derived from a religious cosmology and the mythology that expressed and supported it."[11] The political leader or head, in most societies was the channel through which ultimate cosmic forces operated for the welfare of the society. Radcliffe Brown makes the following observation in regard to leadership in African societies:

> In Africa it is often hardly possible to separate, even in thought, political from ritual or religious office. Thus, in some African societies it may be said that the king is the executive head, the legislator, the supreme judge, the commander in chief of the army, the chief priest or supreme ritual head and even perhaps the principle capitalist of the whole community. But it is erroneous to think of him as combining in himself a number of separate and distinct offices. There is a single office, that of king and its various duties and activities and its rights, prerogatives and privileges make up a single unified whole.[12]

This observation clearly demonstrates that sharp distinctions between religious and political institutions and activities was very rare. For example among the Abagusii of Western Kenya the chief (*Omugambi* or *Omuruothi*) embodied in his office political, social, religious and economic roles. He publicly executed these functions within his areas of jurisdiction. Chiefs were regarded as living representatives of their original lineage founders. The clan chiefs were the automatic political heads of their clans and they led them in religious functions like communal sacrifices, arbitrated in disputes and supervised social activities. They were also men of integrity and beyond reproach.[13]

Among the Akan of Ghana, the chief is the final authority in the land and is responsible for the spiritual well being of the people. As a spiritual leader, he has the obligation to maintain a link between his people and the ancestors, to maintain law and order within his division or town, and to ensure that the people are well protected against attack from enemies. He embodies the moral and ritual purity of his people and leads them into prayer during ancestral rites and important festivals. He symbolizes the value of hospitality, good company, consideration and justice. These are all characteristics of God in the African worldview. As Magesa observes:

> The life of the chief must be exemplary because as the head custodian of the people's moral tradition, he must be in constant contact with the power of God, ancestors, spirits and the earth to guide and sustain him.[14]

This is because in the African moral universe, power is not an abstraction, it does not exist apart from relationships. Relationships establish power and give it meaning, purpose and specific identity. A powerful relationship exists between God, ancestors, spirits, human beings and the whole cosmos. God sustains all these elements who share in the sustenance. Power "in African Religion is therefore 'incarnated' or 'personalized' in the sense that it can only be realized in relationships between and among autonomous realities or forces."[15]

Inspite of what has been said about "abuse of power" in traditional systems of government, this principle of interdependence, sharing and relationships was key and constituted the controlling consciousness. Abuse of power, was seen as abuse of these relationships. The maintenance of these relationships was the religious imperative. Its distortion or destruction was the worst form of evil. African leaders who distorted this relationships by being dictatorial, unjust and oppressive, brought disaster to themselves and the whole community. Among the Akan of Ghana, abusive leaders were *destooled*. Right power relationships, however, create and nurture authority, the characteristic most admitted in a leader. What does all this mean as far as the use of power by leaders in contemporary Africa is concerned? This is an indictment to African civil and religious rulers who have used power entrusted to them by their communities as an instrument of oppression, injustice and self promotion.

African religion can provide resources to establish structures with life enhancing authority and, to replace power that has been misused. This can enable leaders to guide with authority and become enablers of people rather than their brutalizers and oppressors thus alienating them.

This holistic view of religious leadership in Africa was disrupted by the intrusion of western ideas and power which accelerated the pace of secularization thus catalyzing the separation of the religious from the secular. Today, especially among the elite, religion is beginning to lose its hold at the level of social institution and human consciousness.

Consequently religion has just become a mere department of the social order. One of the consequences of this change was a shift from religious to military power as a basis for political authority. In this regard, Gecaga notes that "under Western rule the colonial areas were held together by vastly military, technological, economic and administrative power. However, with its demise, the states of the South were faced with the legitimacy crisis. To counteract this, Europeans introduced secular ideologies to assure the legitimizing functions of religion."[16] These included various theories on democracy and marxist / socialist ideologies that were utilized to entrench authoritarianism.

The Western missionary enterprise with its assumption of the inferiority of African religion and depravity of the African psycho and moral status, challenged indigenous religious belief systems and structures, thus replacing them with the supposedly superior religion of Christianity. Religion became a faith to be converted into rather than a way of life. It was no longer the thread that wove the social, political and economic fabrics of society together. It was something external imposed on individuals.

Due to the ensuing upheaval, indigenous religious ideology shifted from the center and became available to inspire new religious movements of the indigenous kind: it questioned Christian ideology. Religious based organizations in the colonial period inspired by indigenous and Christian ideologies of justice and universal brotherhood, mobilized people to resist foreign rule. For example, the Church of Jesus Christ on Earth through the Prophet Simon Kimbangu (Kimbanguism) in the Democratic Republic of the Congo, the Dini ya Musambwa of Elijah Masinde, Mumboism and the whole host of Gikuyu independent churches of the 1930s and the Holy Spirit movement among the Abaluhya in Kenya were religious quests for transcendental justice and order and a protest against white hegemony in culture and church. These religious movements had political undertones and served the function of mobilizing people to resist injustice and redefine and restructure their religious, social and political set up. Since colonial times to the present, Kenya has experienced invasion of the public space by religion and this has intensified since the 1990s. Religion has become an object to provide moral and spiritual support amidst rising social-economic inequalities, poverty, disease, political instability, crime and gender violence. Having examined how religious leadership is perceived in traditional African society let us explore how Christianity has envisaged, embodied, and provided spiritual leadership in Africa, with specific reference to Kenya.

Christianity and Leadership in Africa

Christianity is a founded religion. Like all founded religions, authority is derived from the founder of the new community of faith and or his/her religious experience. It has its own structure of authority and authoritative tradition vested in the scriptures (both Old and New Testaments), oral tradition, apostolic authority (sacerdotal priesthood, which has instutionalized charisma) and charismatic presence of the Holy Spirit, depending on the form of Christian expression.

Christian presence in Africa dates from the first century with the spread of the church to North Africa and Alexandria. Ethiopia, the Maghreb and Nuba were significant enclaves of Christianity since the earliest times and some forms, like the Ethiopian Coptic Orthodox Church, have survived to this day. However, Christian presence in the rest of the continent was established in the fifteenth, nineteenth and twentieth centuries in different epochs and was usually part and parcel of the imperial and colonial enterprise. As already mentioned, Christianity in Africa has grown at a tremendous rate especially in the last half of the 20th century. David Barrett in his ground breaking work on statistical analysis of world Christianity shows that the number of Christians in Africa grew from 8.75 million in 1900 to 117 million in 1970 to 335.1 million by 2000. He projected a figure of 360 million for mid 2003 and 600.5 million for 2005.[17]

Though missionary Christianity has been criticized for launching an onslaught against African cultural, religious, social, economic and political institutions there is no doubt that it had a great appeal among African converts at its inception and today. In Jesus Christ, converts found new hope and clung to that hope in the face of great challenges which would otherwise have broken their lives, especially in situation of extreme oppression, exploitation and dehumanization during the colonial period.[18] To what extent is this function of Christianity based on its concept of religious leadership? How has Christianity in colonial and post colonial Africa provided leadership not only in religious matters but also in socio-political and economic realms? How does Christianity conceptualize leadership and how does it implement it? It is to this that we shall now turn.

The Christian Church conceptualizes leadership as servanthood. In both the Old and the New Testaments, those who are depicted as qualified for appointment as leaders among the people of God are always appointed to serve. Whether appointed as prophets, priests or kings, they are not expected to lord it over God's people but to serve. Biblical characters like Moses, Aaron, and Solomon, saw their roles as not an opportunity for self aggrandizement but as one requiring special enablement for service to God's people. Likewise, prophets were called servants because they were to serve for the benefit of the Lord's people. As Osei Mensah avers:

> It was the service of the prophet, by oral message and by written word, to teach God's people his truth, to rebuke their errors, to correct their faults and to instruct them in righteous behaviour, so that God's people might be thoroughly equipped for every good work.[19]

In the New Testament, Jesus sets forth the same model in both word and deed. He taught his disciples what type of leader they should aspire to be. He rejected the dominant leadership style of his time under Graeco-Roman influence which was based on domination and control. He insisted that Christian leadership should be characterized by humble service:

> You know that the rulers of the Gentiles lord it over them, and their high officials exercise authority over them. Not so with you. Instead, whoever wants to become great among you must be your servant, and whoever wants to be first must be your slave.[20]

Throughout his ministry, he consistently exemplified this type of leadership as servanthood in his relationship with the disciples. He required that this principle should characterize his followers, "the son of man did not come to be served but to serve."[21]

Several important principles for leadership are illustrated by Jesus in his ministry with his disciples. These include:

(i) Dignity and humble service. "By washing his disciples feet at the last supper, Jesus illustrated clearly that humble service in no way detracts from the essential dignity of any office or role to which the lord may call us in the church"[22]

This means that humble service to one another, out of love of God, is the mark and dignity of the true disciple. This is contrary to worldly expectations.

(ii) God gives gifts to office bearers in the church to equip them for service to others which must be mediated in the context of love. These gifts are for ministering to God's people, equipping them and serving them. They are not status symbols about which we boast or use to exploit or oppress God's people.

(iii) Leadership is for encouragement and inspiration of God's people to experience fullness of life.

(iv) Christian leadership should show concern for other persons. People should be accepted as persons and be helped to meet other needs. Some mainline churches have become too preoccupied with institutional development and forgotten that concern for the person should be a hall mark of their leadership. It is no wonder that Christians keep shifting alliance to the up and coming new Pentecostal churches which are loosely structured and privilege individual participation, spiritual experience and fulfillment.

(v) In line with the Old Testament prophetic tradition, Christian leadership is also expected to be prophetic. Jesus Christ embodied this characteristic in his denouncement of the Jewish political and religious leaders and rejection of their authority. He denounced their hypocrisy, existing social injustice and proclaimed liberation for the oppressed, good news of salvation to the poor, sight to the blind and physical health to the sick.[23]

These principles of Christian leadership are supposed to inform and influence the perception of the church's mission in the world. The church perceives her mission as a mediator of the promised abundant life in all its varied dimensions, "in season and out of season." Hence the church regards herself as the conscience of society and has consequently challenged social, political and economic injustice.

Discussing the justification for Christians and the church to get involved in social, political and economic issues of their nation, Gitari argues that every Christian is called by God, and that by virtue of this call every person is called to leadership. Christian leadership according to him, therefore, requires several components among which are vision and hope.[24] Vision enables a leader to see new possibilities while hope is a form of faith that tends to produce what it sees.

Has the church in Africa exemplified this biblical vision of leadership? We shall now briefly examine how the church in colonial and post-colonial Africa has provided leadership or failed to do so.

The Church and Leadership in Colonial and Post-Colonial State

It has been argued that during the colonial period, the mission churches which were extensions of their mother churches collaborated with the colonial authorities in their oppression of Africans. Except for a few individual church ministers like Archbishop Owen of the Church Missionary Society in Maseno, who initiated development projects to uplift Africans' livelihood and a few others who opposed forced labour of women and children, the church as an institution did not provide the required leadership in the context of denial of human rights, detention, unfair taxation, alienation of land and oppressive rule.[25] The church thus functioned as a social and ideological arm of the colonial and imperial powers. Other scholars like de Gruchy argue that the churches emerging out of colonial rule were infact equipped to provide leadership because preparation for democratic rule was nurtured within missionary institutions.[26]

Nevertheless, it is within the African Instituted Churches which emerged during the colonial period and were pejoratively labelled as nativistic, schismatic, neo-pagan, heretical and movements of rebellion that nationalism was nurtured.[27] Independent religious movements like the Ethiopian churches in South Africa, Zionist churches in Zimbabwe and Gikuyu independent churches in Central Kenya, acted as mobilizsing forces to facilitate African agitation for self rule not only in church but also in the nation. The agitation for human rights and self-rule was coached in theological and political language.

Leaders of some of these movements like Isaiah Shembe of the Nazareth Baptist Church, among the Zulu, Simon Kimbangu of the DRC, Engenes Legkhanyane of the Zion Christian Church in South Africa were perceived as messiahs who would not only midwife a new religious dispensation, but a political one as well. In this model of leadership we see a reinterpretation of indigenous African leadership models. Even today, African Instituted Churches that have their roots to the period before independence have replicated this model of leadership. Their founding archbishops, whether men or women function as both indigenous chiefs, patriarchs and elders in administration of their churches, management of resources held in common, dispensing justice and providing spiritual leadership and social, economic and moral support to their members.

In the post-colonial period it has been alleged that "churches that colluded with the colonial enterprise and waltzed with nationalists had lost relevance in their public space."[28] The period between 1960 – 1985, was "characterized by the implosion of the state, the attack on the dominant role of the church in the public space and the churches' various strategies for survival."[29] In West Africa and nations that were aligned to marxist/socialist rule, the politics of nationalism turned against the church. Dictatorial military regimes, and alliance with socialist ideologies reflected efforts to dislodge the vestiges of the colonial heritage. In such countries, "Christian churches were imaged as neo-imperialist symbols. Churches lost control of schools, hospitals and other charitable institutions."[30] In Kenya the church, in this period, was perceived as supporting the status quo. Paul Freston argues that in some African countries,

> mainline churches feared the new states might turn to communism or African traditions and were happy to accept requests for help in state-defined development. The state was seen as the key actor and churches enjoyed precarious legitimacy.[31]

This observation aptly describes Kenya where the church became a department of prayers, judging by the presence of leaders in national functions, usually performing the role of offering prayers and blessing these occasions.

It is important to point out that the Kenyan church is divided into three broad categories, namely **Ecumenical** or **mainline** churches (which include major protestant denominations who are members of the National Council of Churches of Kenya and the Roman Catholic Church); **Evangelicals** and the **Pentecostals**. The African Instituted Churches which are members of the Organization of African Instituted Churches (AICs) find themselves oscillating between the Evangelicals and Pentecostals. All these churches have a different political theology which is exemplified in their relationship to the political authorities of the day. It has been observed that before 1988 the mainline churches in Kenya supported the status quo though they provided much needed leadership in interventions to alleviate poverty and provision of social services like education, health and pastoral care. Several things happened in the 1980s to propel the churches, especially the mainline churches, to the public space. Due to international economic policies of globalization imposed on the developing world, most economies collapsed; poverty enveloped communities; abuse of human rights and the political legitimacy crises followed suit. Coups and counter-coups, destabilized most African nations and despotic rulers clung to power by force through manipulating the electoral process. But,

> it was however the change in the geo-political front that catalyzed the rapid
> series of events that would bring Christianity to the center again. The collapse
> of the Berlin Wall, the collapse of communist Russia and the ends of the cold
> war made democratic ideology popular again.[32]

What leadership did the church provide in the democratization process and what was its justification for doing so? Archbishop David Gitari, former head of the Anglican Church in Kenya observes that Kenya is one of the few nations in Africa where church leaders have taken issues with those in authority and provided much needed leadership in times of social and political upheaval.[33]

Nevertheless, in Kenya, the patterns of church-state relationship since the 1980s have been unstable and variant depending on the religious tradition and the regime powers. As Gifford observes, "mainline church leaders oppose one party regimes, but evangelical, charismatic and Pentecostal churches support tottering dictators."[34] Whereas as we have noted between 1960 – 1985 the state and church had an amicable relationship, this turned sour when the Erastian doctrine of subordinating the church to the state was taken to great lengths in the Moi regime in Kenya.

This development saw sychopathic support of the dictatorial regime by some Evangelical, Pentecostal and independent churches in return for political favours and the demonizing of mainline churches as opposition parties. Moi was praised as a God fearing leader and some churches like the Africa Inland Church left the National Council of Churches of Kenya. The Catholic Church and the protestant churches (Presbyterian Church of East Africa, Methodist Church of Kenya and Anglican Church of Kenya) issued joint statements condemning corruption, social and political injustice especially the emasculating of the electoral process during the 1988 queue voting nomination process by KANU which saw popular leaders "voted" out and weak, sycophant leaders being "voted" in. The Evangelical churches (ACK and PCEA) had a limited theology of secular power, but a well developed evangelical biblical hermeneutics. The Evangelicals in the ACK, especially -

> believed themselves obliged to measure any state's actions by the standards
> of the scriptures and to compel the state to attend to the scriptures by
> preaching. But they only critiqued the consequences and not the theory of
> Nyayoism.[35]

However, significant leadership in defence of democracy and human rights came from individual church leaders rather than institutions. While Catholics issued collective pastoral letters, the ACK and PCEA, had courageous individuals like the late Bishop Kipsang Muge of Eldoret, David Gitari and Timothy Njoya. The international connections, resources and a strong constituent base facilitated these church leaders to resist oppression, offer a primary challenge to Moi, and to generate a public discourse on democracy and change. They covered a definition of politics and legitimate exercise of power as well as questions of corruption and local conflicts.

These church leaders were at the forefront of political change and their churches supported them. These challenges continued even after multiparty democracy was achieved in 1992 and the Moi regime dislodged in 2002. Throughout this period, the anti-establishment churches were prominent in the civil society movement advocating for a review of the constitution, human rights, and providing civic education to sensitize the masses about their role in the electoral process. It is a well accepted fact in Kenya today that churches as institutions and as individual leaders provided focused and transformational leadership that ushered in a new government in 2002. However, today the same churches have ambivalent attitudes towards the National Rainbow Coalition (NARC) regime. They are still polarized with the Pentecostals and Evangelicals playing a half-hearted opposition role and the pre-2002 anti-establishment appearing to support the status quo.

What has been the justification for the churches providing this leadership? Gitari argues that -

> the church (has a) heavy responsibility to remind a nation … of the standard of righteousness and justice which alone can exult that nation…Christian leaders must come out of their ecclesiastical Ghettos and ivory towers to lead the citizens …in giving active practical moral support to the state when it upholds the standards of righteousness…if however those in authority depart (from such standards), the church should follow the footsteps of the prophets and the apostles in declaring boldly the righteousness and judgement of God.[36]

Gitari's sermons during the period 1988 – 2002, have become a homiletic form of doing theology. The theological roots of his involvement in leadership are based on the biblical doctrines of creation, humanity, incarnation and the kingdom of God. These doctrines stress the fact that God creates all systems and the universe. Human beings were created in His image and likeness and that God took residence in human history through the process of incarnation and that Jesus was involved in the social, political, economic and spiritual affairs of his world.

Therefore, the mission of the church in the world is to provide leadership in the transformation of cultures, socio-economic and political conditions of the world. Human beings, are also called to be co-creators with God, transform the world, rule justly and remind decision makers that the world belongs to God and they are just but custodians or stewards. Likewise, church leaders are servants to humanity and stewards. For politicians to deny Christians the chance to be involved in the welfare of their communities is tantamount to rejecting to follow Jesus' example of servanthood and bringing salvation to the world.

At this point, it is worth noting that although AICs (African Independent / Instituted Churches) and Neo-Pentecostal churches do not visibly appear to be providing leadership, their approach has been focused on personal transformation which Kalu describes thus:

> The trend (has been) towards internal critiques, maturity and radical perfectionism, not as a means of escape but as a means of transcending life's difficulties.[37]

In Pentecostal churches, leadership is dependent upon proved worth and charisma and not inherent right. Furthermore, with the belief in the doctrine of the priesthood of all believers, every convert is a potential leader. It is this ideology of individuals as actors that renders the movement to focus more on individuals and their cumulative impact on society in attempts to transform it. Again as Kalu notes:

> Pentecostal political theology moves from rebuilding the bruised self perception of the individual to empowering him with new hope and confidence, to assisting him to garner the rich promises of the Gospel and finally to enabling him to reclaim, redeem and liberate the land."[38]

One may conclude from this that contrary to the common view that Pentecostals, especially the latest variety of charismatic or Neo-Pentecostals have no theology of socio-political engagement and are more interested in preparing souls for heaven, and interpret structural evil in spiritual terms that, they are involved in special transformation but through a different approach. More studies in this area require to be done.

Conclusion

Having discussed how religions have, within their ethic, values that promote leadership, one may ask: What spaces exist today in the church to nurture leadership that may be transformational and would embody integrity and other values? How can young people, women and other marginalized groups be empowered for leadership at the individual, family and community levels? A common misunderstanding of leadership as domination, suppression of divergent opinions and as self-aggrandizement, has permeated not only the secular domain but religious spheres as well. Violence, lack of humility and accountability and exploitation of public resources are vices that have also infested church leadership.

Nevertheless, it is not religions *per se* that are wrong; but the human leaders who misinterpret religious texts and their supposed link with the supernatural through abuse of authority. Usually, the hierarchal structures of religious institutions with God at the top, spiritual agents next, then clergy and finally lay adherents at the bottom, have been inimical to the promotion of democracy. Religious leaders therefore pose as demi gods, usually controlling the minds of their followers and abusing them.[39] While we may not say with certainty that this is the lot of many religious institutions there are some which, if not checked, can degenerate into cults or sects or operate like them. However, religious institutions, especially churches, have spaces that may be utilized for nurturing leadership potential in the young and old. These spaces include youth groups, women's groups and other spiritual movements like the Charismatic Renewal Movement, Fellowships of different age groups and gender and other movements like the Grail, Focolare (in the Catholic Church), Women's Aglow, Full Gospel Businessmen's Fellowship, Student Christian Fellowship and other para church organizations.

In all these spaces, focus is given to nurturing the spiritual lives of the members, empowering them for Christian leadership and equipping them with skills relevant for personal development and transformation of communities. Many Kenyan church leaders were formed and trained in these organizations. What is required is to utilize these spaces to equip citizens for more than leadership, beyond the spiritual level. This should include prophetic leadership that perceives the link between, personal integrity and social, political and economic concerns. Like Jesus Christ whose message and leadership was holistic covering all realms of being from the personal to the communal; so too, modern church leaders and those they nurture should continue seeing the relationship between all realms of being and all sectors of societal life.

The following recommendations may be considered in an attempt to nurture holistic leadership in Kenya today.

♦ The church and other religious institutions should continue to join other civil society groups operating in the country to nurture responsible leadership by making adequate use of the resources she has at her disposal, both human and material.

♦ The organizational structures of some churches and religions are hierarchical. This renders them incapable of operating democratically and could therefore oppress adherents with dogmas and practices that are not challenged due to their appeal to divine authority. The church should therefore make efforts to democratize her structures if she has to be in a position to critique injustice in society, or be a mediator of justice to her adherents.

♦ The church and other religions are in a position to champion democratic value for they are the channels through which morality is inculcated. They are also agents of socialization. They can utilize these avenues to provide spaces for leadership training at individual and community levels.

From the foregoing, we can conclude that, religion has a perspective on leadership. This is not only leadership in terms of organizing and managing religious institutions but also in the secular realm. Because of its function in society, religion is often used to give legitimacy to many activities in society. It is invoked to give legitimacy to individual and communal decisions, an activity or ceremony. Religion has been used by politicians to achieve their narrow interests, especially for purposes of seeking consent and acceptance from constituents.

Religion has also been used as a tool for mobilization of the oppressed to dethrone despotic leaders and advocate for human rights, the democratic process and social transformation. In pre-colonial and post-colonial Kenya, this has been spearheaded by the AICs and mainline churches respectively. It has been seen in this chapter that this function has been adopted differently by the various Christian traditions in Kenya. Those who, however, see the religious institutions and individuals having a role in transformation follow in the tradition of African religion and biblical Christianity where there was no demarcation between the sacred and the secular. Religion was part and parcel of the social and cosmic order. Religion should therefore remain in the public discourse on social transformation and leadership provision.

Notes

[1]   Ogbu, Kalu, "Jesus Christ where are you? Themes in West African Church Historiography at the end of the 21st century," Missionalia 30, No 25 (2000): 237.

[2]   These figures are not authoritative for there has not been a census survey on Religions in Kenya since 1973. The figures are based on the assumptions of David B. Barrett, Kurian G.T. , & Johnson T.M. (eds.) World Christian Encyclopedia. A Comparative Survey of Churches and Religions in the Modern World. New York: Oxford University Press, 2001: 465.

[3]   Osei-Mensah, Gottfried, Wanted: Servant Leaders Theological Perspectives in Africa Achimota: African Christian Press, 1990: 60.

[4]   Hofmeyr, J.W., "Mainline Churches in the Public Space, 1975 – 2000," Kalu O.U. African Christianity: An African Story. Pretoria: University of Pretoria Press 2005: 362

[5]   Eliade, Mircea, The Encyclopedia of Religion vol 8 New York: Macmillan Publishing Company 1987: 485.

[6]   Weber, Max, The Theory of Social and Economic Organization. New York: Free Press, 1947: 152 - 153.

[7]   Butterfield, Herbert, History and Human Relations.

[8]   Cited, in Eliade, Encyclopedia of Religion, 488

[9]   Eliade, Encyclopedia of Religion vol 8 488

[10] Weber, cited in Eliade, Encyclopedia of Religion vol 8, 487

[11] Gecaga, Margaret,: "Religious Movements and Democratization in Kenya: Between the Sacred and the Profane." Unpublished Research Paper, 2005; 1.

[12] Radcliffe, Brown, 1940: xxi

[13] Ochieng, William, R. A Precolonial History of the Gusii of Western Kenya from c. A.D. 1500 to 1914. Nairobi: East African Literature Bureau

[14] Magesa, Laurenti, "Power in African Religion," Wajibu: A Journal of Social and Religious Concern, 14, no. 3 (1999): 3.

[15] Magesa, "Power in African Religion," 2.

[16] Gecaga, "Religious Movements and Democratization in Kenya," 2.

[17] Barrett, Kurian, & Johnson (eds), World Christian Encyclopedia; 25.

[18] This continued to be true for African Christians under the yoke of apartheid in South Africa and Namibia till the 1980s and 1990s and is still prevalent in post independent Africa due to the oppressive political regimes; and other manifestations of oppression like disease, poverty, abuse of human rights, gender violence, insecurity etc.

[19] Osei Mensah, Wanted: Servant Leaders, 10, see also 2 Timothy, 3:16- 17.

[20] Matthew, 20: 25 - 27

[21] Matthew ,20: 28

[22] Osei-Mensah, Wanted: Servant Leaders, 10

[23] Luke, 4: 16 - 20

[24] David, Gitari, Responsible Church Leadership. Nairobi: Acton Publishers, 2005, 14. See also Proverbs 29: 18.

[25] Caroline, Elkins: *Britain's Gulag: The Brutal End of Empire in Kenya,* New York: Oxford University Press 2005.

[26] J.W. de Gruchy, *Christianity and Democracy.* Cambridge: Cambridge University Press, 1995, 168.

[27] Adrian, Hastings, *The Construction of Nationhood: Ethnicity, Religion and Nationalism,* Cambridge: Cambridge University Press, 1997,166.

[28] Hofmeyrn Mainline Churches in the Public Space, 364

[29] Hofmeyrn *Mainline Churches in the Public Space,* 364

[30] Hofmeyrn *Mainline Churches in the Public Space,* 364

[31] Paul, Freston, *Evangelicals and Politics in Asia, Africa and Latin America* Cambridge: Cambridge University Press, 2001, 110.

[32] Hofmeyrn *Mainline Churches in the Public Space,* 364

[33] Gitari, *Responsible Church Leadership*, 14-10.

[34] Paul, Gifford, "Some Recent Developments in African Christianity," *Africa Affairs,* 93, 1994 528.

[35] Freston, *Evangelicals and Politics,* 148

[36] Cited in Freston, *Evangelicals and Politics,* 157.

[37] Kalu, Ogbu, "The Third Response: Pentecostalism and the Reconstruction of Christian Experience in Africa 1970 – 1995." *Journal of African Christian Thought* 1 No. 2, (1998), 8.

[38] Kalu, "The Third Response," 13

[39] Religious movements like the Mungiki, which is also quasi political and cultural have been accused of violence and intimidating not only members but also non-members as well. Other Christian religious movements that have cultic tendencies also exploit their members especially financially using what they call a "Seed Theology." This means that spiritual and material returns depend on giving generously to the church.

References

Barrett, D., G.T. Kurian, and T.M. Johnson. (eds.) *World Christian Encyclopedia: A Comparative Survey of Churches and Religions in the Modern World*. New York: Oxford University Press, 2001.

De' Gruchy, T.W. *Christianity and Democracy*. Cambridge: Cambridge University Press, 1995

Eliade, Mircea. *The Encyclopedia of Religion 8*. New York: Macmillan Publishing Company, 1987.

Elkins, C. *Britain's Gulag: The Brutal end of Empire in Kenya*. Nairobi: Transafric, 2005.

Freston, P. *Evangelicals and Politics in Asia, Africa and Latin America*. Cambridge: Cambridge University Press, 2001.

Hastings, A. *The Construction of Nationhood: Ethnicity, Religion and Nationalism.* Cambridge: Cambridge University Press, 1997.

Gitari, David. *Responsible Church Leadership.* Nairobi: Acton Publishers, 2005.

Gecaga, M. "Religious Movements and Democratization in Kenya between the Sacred and the Profane." Unpublished Paper, 2005.

Gifford, P. "Some Recent Developments in African Christianity," *Africa Affairs*, 93, 1994.

Kalu, Ogbu, U. "Jesus Christ Where Are You? Themes in West African Church Historiography at the end of the 21st Century." *Missionalia* 30, No. 25 (2000).

_____. *African Christianity: An African Story.* Pretoria: University of Pretoria Press, 2005.

_____. "The Third Response: Pentecostalism and the Reconstruction of Christian Experience in Africa 1970 – 1995." *Journal of African Christian Thought*, 1, No. 2 (1998), 3 – 16.

Magesa, L. "Power in African Religion" *Wajibu: A Journal of Social and Religious Concern* 14, No. 3 (1999) 2 – 3.

Ochieng', W. R. *A Precolonial History of the Gusii of Western Kenya from c. AD. 1500 to 1914.* Nairobi: East African Literature Bureau, 1974.

Osei M.G. *Wanted: Servant Leaders Theological Perspectives in Africa.* Achimota: African Christian Press, 1990.

Weber, Max. *The Theory of Social and Economic Organization.* New York: Free Press, 1947.

9

Leadership and Economic Development in the Informal Sector

Mark O. Ogutu

Introduction

Business leaders, government officials, economic developers and other key community and regional leaders need to better understand the processes involved in developing a supportive environment for entrepreneurs. Kenyan's future as an entrepreneurial state remains promising. Only a few years ago, the state's economic development discussion focused almost exclusively on attracting new firms and rarely included growing new firms. Today, the mounting interest in entrepreneurship as an economic development strategy has set the stage for future growth. Although risk aversion and lack of capital are still strong in Kenya, the growth of new firms, the increased focus on innovation in existing firms, and industry diversification should make many regions more resistant to economic downturns than in the recent past.

In Kenya, leadership in the informal sector is dwindling because of lack of entrepreneurial culture. Leadership itself emanates from management, even though there is a difference between the two. Management is doing things through and with others, while leadership is the ability of an individual to take others through enthusiastically (Follet, 1999). Small businesses as the breeding grounds of entrepreneurs need proper and effective leadership. Like in other countries, leaders in the informal sector are entrepreneurs, who can turn around the performance of their economies. From the classical economics to the post- Keynesian analysts, the topic of entrepreneurship has been surveyed, and observations, theories and pronouncements advanced. In general, contemporary economists agree that an entrepreneur is a business leader and thus his/her role in fostering economic growth and development is a pivotal one.

Cole (1995) views entrepreneurship as the purposeful activity of an individual or a group of associated individuals, undertaken to initiate, maintain or organize a profit oriented business units for the production or distribution of economic goods and services. In addition, for McClelland (1945), entrepreneurship involves doing things in a new and better way. This is lacking in our small informal sector. Entrepreneurship is an integrated approach surrounded by the characteristics in figure 1 below:

Characteristics of entrepreneurial leadership

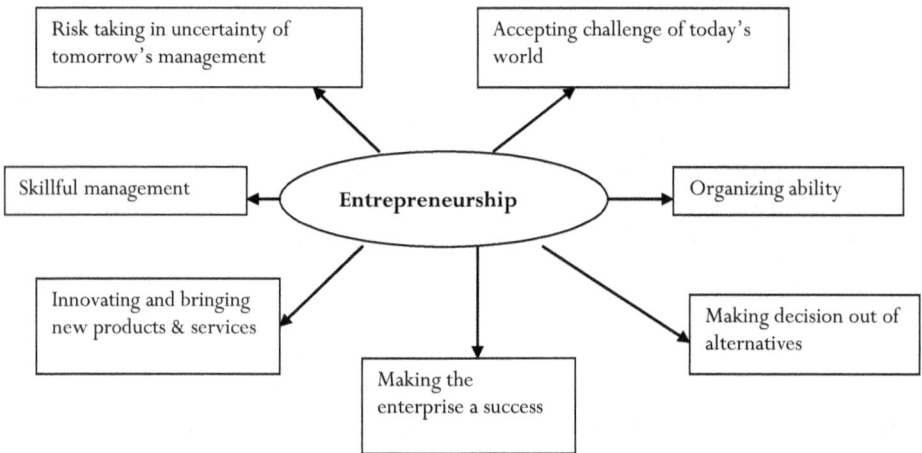

These are also other critical factors that affect entrepreneurship and they include: overpopulation, food shortage, shortage of natural resources, energy shortages and lack of technology. These automatically call for both effective political leadership and entrepreneurial leadership. In addition, entrepreneurship should benefit the individual and community.

Community Economic Development

When entrepreneurial skills are well developed, they can contribute to 'sustainable development.' Although the phrase sustainable development has been defined in many ways, the original description is still among the most popular: "development that meets the needs of the present without compromising the ability of future generations to meet their own needs" (WCED, 1987). Sustainable development recognizes that there are limits to economic growth and levels of human production and consumption. It emphasizes qualitative development rather than quantitative growth, thus adding a third dimension to considerations of environment and economy – social development. Ecosystem preservation will not occur unless poverty relief and economic health for communities of all nations can be provided (Rees 1990). For example, it is already clear that most less developed countries will not become party to environmental controls unless the North accepts responsibility for current problems and is willing to pay the costs of their mitigation" (Rees, 1990: 443). Regional economic disparities present similar problems. Resource workers, for example, resist having to bear the cost of wilderness preservation when the majority of the benefits of the resource consumption and profits are received by urban dwellers (Brown, 1995).

The implications of qualitative development include the redistribution of economic benefits and the development of the spiritual, social and cultural qualities of human beings rather than simply the creation of material wealth. Finally, sustainable development recognizes the importance of local issues and actions which when combined, determine our global situation. Thus, the importance of the concept of community to sustainability. Sustainable development requires sustainable communities (Roseland, 1994) and communities require sustainable development if they are to continue from generation to generation (Ommer in Muzychka, 1996).

Despite widespread recognition of its importance, there is still significant debate about the meaning and environmental, social and economic implications of sustainable development. The debate is founded in the existence of different sustainable development paradigms or worldviews (Pierce, 1992). These paradigms range from "ecocentric to technocentric" and from "sustainable development" to "sustainable growth/utilization" (Feagan, 1993; O'Riordan, 1977, 1988; Pierce 1990, 1992).

These views demonstrate that continued growth and "business-as-usual" practices cannot be sustained in the long-term and that viable alternatives that bridge the gap between the "theory" or paradigm, and practice of sustainable development are needed. Community economic development (CED) may provide one such alternative. But what is community economic development?

Like sustainable development, community economic development has been defined in a multitude of ways. Each of these definitions, however, shares common characteristics which distinguishes it from traditional forms of economic development activity. In a 1987 report, McRobie and Ross synthesized the various definitions of CED into the following; "Community Economic Development is a process by which communities can initiate and generate their own solutions to their common economic problems and thereby build long term community capacity and foster the integration of economic, social and environmental objectives" (McRobie and Ross 1987; 1). This description emphasizes local involvement in, and control of, the development process. CED is recognized as distinct from forms of economic development where, for example, a consultant from outside of a community comes in to complete a study and then makes recommendations on what the community should do, or when senior governments initiate and implement a development program based on broad policy directions, rather than local realities. CED is also distinct from conventional economic development because it gives precedence to communities over the more narrowly defined interests of consumers or shareholders. Finally, it is distinct from local economic development (LED), which is focused on local communities but tends to have narrowly-defined, purely economic objectives (Blakely, 1989) and is less participatory and dominated by local elites (Boothroyd and Davis, 1991; Burkey 1993; Bryant, 1999; Gill and Reed, 1999). McRobie and Ross (1987) point out that their definition is purposely broad taking into account the full range of local initiatives and practices that may be defined by communities themselves as CED. "It is not the theoreticians to define CED; it is up to the local communities which are struggling with new ways to create employment" (McRobie and Ross 1989;1). Community economic development should also be sustainable.

In the past, the notion of sustainable development has gained increasing recognition within the field of CED; just as the need for healthy local economies is acknowledged by a growing number of individuals and organizations within the environmental movement. Sustainable community economic development (SCED) is a brand of CED that combines the principles of both sustainable development and community economic development. In doing so SCED emphasizes the realities of the natural world (e.g. limitations of our ability to utilize the environment as a source of resources and as a waste disposal site), but also the local social, cultural and economic realities that are brought into the development process through meaningful public participation. The overall goals of SCED are ecosystem and community health. When used in this context the word 'health' is meant in its broadest sense: "health as wellness rather than absence of disease "(Roseland, 1997:1).

Sustainable CED attempts to balance the best interests of both local communities and the broader society (Bryant, 1999). It is equitable, community based and does not threaten the integrity of global or local ecological systems. While it could be argued that CED is intrinsically sustainable and therefore that CED and SCED are one in the same, in the past CED initiatives have tended to focus on human centered aspects such as social justice and self reliance (International Institute for Sustainable Development, 1994; Vodden 1997; Bryant 1999). For example, the definitions of community provided above are those most commonly cited in CED literature. They describe human communities. Ecologists broaden the definition of community to include all of the species that occur together in space and time (Begon et al, 1990). Like ecologists, practitioners and researchers of SCED seek to understand the interactions of human and other species by considering the impacts of human development on other species dependent on the same resources.

Bryant (1999) argues that CED is evolving from a 'war on poverty' to an integrated approach that includes environmental values. In Kenya this hasn't been well focused. Despite this apparent progress the author prefers to use the term SCED as a matter of emphasis on the primary importance of ecological integrity to sustainable development and because, for many practicing in the field, the term CED does not necessarily imply a movement towards ecological sustainability and environmental responsibility, along with social and economic change.

Creating a Framework for Sustainable Community Economic Development

The practice of community economic development (CED) has existed for well over a century. Along Canada's eastern coastline for example, the earliest cooperative enterprises began in the 1860s. True to the spirit of CED they focused not only on economic but also social, cultural and educational initiatives (Wismer and Pell, 1981). However, the field did not receive the attention of "mainstream" Canada until the recession of the early 1990s when, in the search for alternatives to failing economies, CED gained popularity among communities and governments alike. Both the Ontario and British Columbia provincial governments for instance, formed CED Secretariats at this time. The Yukon 2000 Development Strategy grew out of both a recession and the realization that previous "top-down" approaches had not been successful (Decter and Kowall, 1989). In 1990 the Economic Council of Canada released a statement that described community based economic development as a "new approach" that may be "precisely what is needed" to fully mobilize the human and physical resources of local economies (Economic Council of Canada, 1990).

Despite a relatively long-lived history as a practice, no unified set of guidelines for successful CED has been developed. This is partly because diversity is a key tenant of CED and characteristic of the communities it serves (Schultz, 1996). The practice of CED differs in every location, according to the unique situations histories and peoples within communities and the ecosystems of which they are a part.

In attempting to build a "theory" of CED and to establish best practices despite this variety, researchers have searched for commonalities in case studies. Some researchers contend that not enough of this synthesis has been done (personal communications, Roseland, M. and Pierce J. 1997). Out of the research of this kind that has been conducted to date, as well as dialogue between communities and practitioners, a number of guiding principles for CED have been identified. Perhaps the most fundamental of these are self-reliance and community control. Equity and broad based public involvement in economic development planning and decision-making also are key. Further principles include; capacity building, collaboration; integration; collective benefits; long term planning and action; and community building (Schultz, 1995; Lauer 1993, Dauncey 1988; Boothoyd and Davis 1991; Wismer & Pell, 1982).

To put the principles of CED into practice various strategies for economic renewal and enhancement of community well being have been employed by communities and identified in the literature, as outlined below:

Strategic options for CED
- plug the leaks (outflow of resources)
- initiate and encourage new enterprises (business and social entrepreneurship)
- support existing enterprises/business retention
- develop human resources
- share work
- strengthen the informal economy
- recruit compatible new businesses
- increase local ownership
- develop physical infrastructure
- manage community resources
- make improvements to the local environment
- undertake other quality of life improvements (health, social, recreational amenities)
- celebrate local identity and culture

Blakely (1989) points out that these alternative strategies can, and will in most cases, be combined, with those strategies most appropriate for the socioeconomic circumstances being employed.

Because of the diverse circumstances within communities, the development of a set of rigid, prescriptive rules for successful implementation of CED initiatives is not an appropriate or realistic goal. Mitchell (1989) describes prescriptive models as difficult to implement when the problem being confronted is not clearly defined, the necessary data are not available or "intangibles" exist that require consideration. These conditions are often rampant in communities. He points out, however, that despite the fact that "real world processes do not usually approach the prescriptive ideal" (Mitchell, 1989; 272), comparison with prescriptive models can highlight process weaknesses (e.g. missing information). It is generally recognized that by establishing process guidelines and determining favorable conditions for success based on the past experiences of communities, researchers can provide useful information for communities engaging in CED.

The conditions for success are daunting, particularly for those communities with little prior CED experience. Further, even if these conditions are met success cannot be guaranteed."… an individual community can only influence and guide its development path. Other factors such as international markets, environmental conditions and shifting demographics (among countless others) also have their roles in molding a community" (Hussmann, 1993; 8). Technological change and government policy can also have a profound effect on local economies. It is doubtful that any community has all of the conditions for success outlined below. However, many of them can be created. Capacity building initiatives, for example, may be needed to create the ability of community leaders to coordinate the process of citizens to participate effectively.

Success factors for Community Economic Development

- ◆ a sense of community identity, history and culture;
- ◆ a dynamic leader or "sparkplug" (often an elected public official, e.g. the mayor and /or a core group of committed individuals who, together, have the necessary skills, know-how and community acceptance);
- ◆ a crisis or major concern motivating local leaders to act (a felt need);
- ◆ a realization that if things are going to happen they (community members and leaders) have to do it themselves;
- ◆ the ability of local leaders and the community to work together and mobilize

broad-based support;

- available local resources such as a specialized yet flexible, young and/or educated labor force, information and trade networks, infrastructure, healthy, productive renewable natural resources or other features, such as a tourist attraction, offering a competitive advantage;
- existing education, training programs and learning opportunities (includes adult education, conventional educational institutions, informal learning options);
- senior governments that are willing and flexible enough to follow the community's lead, to provide advice and cost-share development initiatives.
- investor confidence (where lacking, community seeks to rebuild);
- entrepreneurial spirit (number of new enterprises, participation in business development programs and services, business success rates, local ownership of local firms and resources);
- willingness and ability to collaborate. may involve a regional approach among neighboring communities (e.g. cooperative marketing, shared services);
- existing range of CED related businesses, community organizations and, in resource communities, of community resource management and planning initiatives (CED experience);
- supply and demand networks among local enterprises (e.g. equipment suppliers, harvesters, value-added manufacturers) – existing and opportunities for development;
- social and cultural amenities;
- health and well-being (current levels and related services);
- a long-term approach (willingness and ability to sustain development efforts over the long-term);
- availability of internal and external funding/financing mechanisms;
- a base of informal economic activity;
- availability of professional support and technical services for local organizations and entrepreneurs, marketing expertise;
- willingness and ability to utilize a strategic planning and evaluation process in CED efforts;
- ability to adapt to changing circumstances;
- an innovative idea, plan or solution.

(Sources:Young and Charland, 1992;Ameyaw, 1997: Kinsley, 1996; Economic Council of Canada, 1990:Wismer and Pell, 1981; Pierce, 1995; Stacey and Needham, 1993.)

The absence of a number of the conditions listed above, should not be viewed necessarily as a recipe for failure. When assessing community capacity, in the case of absent conditions, two questions must be asked: How critical are these conditions to the success of CED in the community or of a specific CED initiative being considered? And two, is it likely that the community can create those conditions that are absent (or weak) but considered to be important? Such a checklist of "ideal conditions", consequently, also serves as an assessment of training and development needs and can help communities decide which CED strategies to pursue.

Capacity Building

While capacity-building initiatives are often invaluable, they are not always sufficient. Not only do external factors such as those referred to above (e.g. international markets and environmental conditions) come into play, but several of the conditions for success listed above are difficult to create or enhance. The existence of: a) a crisis of major concern; b) appropriate leadership (with the right skills, community support and "we'll do it ourselves" attitude); c) willingness of the community to get behind their leaders and participate; and d) available natural resources are specific examples. These factors, therefore, are among the most important pre-existing conditions to look for in a community when launching a CED process.

Leadership

While resources that can be drawn upon for economic development can be found in many communities, appropriate leadership skills are especially critical and institute a challenging human resource requirement. The Report of the Commission on Employment and Unemployment in Newfoundland (1986;380) notes that most success stories examined by the Commission came about "because a small group of dedicated people worked hard to put in place the organization and institutional framework that made local development possible". Yet in many of our communities this small group of dedicated people is not readily identifiable or even present.

Exacerbating the challenge of finding "a leader", is the range of skills that are required of community leaders to facilitate a CED process. These skills are not often found in one individual. Blakely (1989), for example, describes an effective economic development manager as a visionary, risk-taker, innovator, motivator and coordinator. For CED additional skills and characteristics are required: cross-cultural sensitivity and facilitation, for example. Wismer and Pell (1981) identify two often conflicting skill sets that are required in CED – that of the initiator and that of the manager.

Finding an initiator and a manager, either in one person or in a team that works well together, is a difficult but critical task. An appropriate leadership style for the community in question is also important. "In some of the most successful initiatives, one person has given a clear and committed lead, saying. 'This is the vision: now let's achieve it'. That is one way forward" (Dauncey, 1988; 110). In many cases leaders who are facilitators, helping citizens to generate the vision themselves, are more appropriate and better aligned with the self-help nature of CED.

Communities, particularly those lacking in leadership capacity, may need to be willing to accept newcomers in leadership roles. Schmidt et al (1993) point out that newcomers with a wider range of experiences and greater social ties with outside organizations often initiate CED projects.

Barriers and potential pitfalls

While some conditions can create success, others can become barriers or "conditions for failure". The Economic Council of Canada (1990) identified five factors that can stand in the way of a successful CED program in small communities. These five handicaps include: high unemployment, eroding skills and entrepreneurial energy, provoking migration of younger and better educated residents and leading to a decay in social amenities that help attract new businesses; shortage of information available to residents in urban centers; lack of basic social services; inadequate access to capital; and cost disadvantages. Two additional barriers are: lack of physical infrastructure required for development; and conflict or divisive power struggles within the community that act as a barrier to cooperation and movement towards a common goal.

The access to capital barrier

Inadequate access to capital is among the most frequently cited barriers to the success of CED initiatives. These initiatives often do not meet the requirements of mainstream capital sources, in part because economic returns are not the sole objective and, therefore, may be lower than alternative investments. Further, those involved may be considered a credit risk (e.g. low income and unemployed citizens). Therefore, a range of alternative forms of financing have been devised as the practice of CED has grown. Canada's Calmeadow Foundation, for example, launched a program of micro-enterprise lending and borrowing circles in First Nations communities, initially in Ontario and then across the country, in 1987. Loans of up to $3,000 were made through a bank and guaranteed by Calmeadow. The Foundation also helped subsidize bank transaction costs and provided training for responsible officers. The Calmeadow Program was based on the success of Micro-credit Schemes in Latin American countries, where experience had shown that jobs could be created at one-tenth to one-twentieth of the cost of job creation in the formal sector. Another frequently cited example of micro-credit is Grameen Bank in Bangladesh. The Bank has lent to over 500,000 people and has a loan repayment rate of 98 percent (Jackson and Pierce, 1990).

Community loan funds are another source of short-term lending capital formed to support CED. Loans may be larger than those of Micro-credit Programs. Most accept below-market interest returns and many offer technical assistance to borrowers (Community Economics, 1987). Community loan funds rely on community-oriented investors, both individuals and organizations such as churches, foundations and even private business. In some cases government agencies have provided loan guarantees to ensure security for loan fund investors (Vodden, 1997; Jackson and Piece, 1990). Local credit unions, community banks and business development centers/community futures programs are also sources of capital for CED. By obtaining funds from such sources it is sometimes possible to lever additional capital from conventional sources.

Debt financing, however, is not the only option discussed in the CED literature. Share purchases and other equity arrangements, including worker ownership, have also been employed. In Chicago, for example, South Shore Bank runs the Neighborhood Fund (Meeker-Lowry, 1988). The Fund finances minority-owned businesses with venture capital. Socially and environmentally responsible investment options do not only provide funding for CED initiatives but also give alternatives for investors concerned with the implications of their investment decisions (Meeker-Lowry, 1988). Such investments can also result in higher financial returns than those that are "non-screened". (Dauncey, 1988).

Joint ventures with private firms have also proven to be an effective method of accessing financing. The Great Northern Peninsula Development Corporation (GNPDC) in Newfoundland, for example, worked with a group of local saw millers, forming a consortium capable of supplying Newfoundland Hydro's wood chip facility (Sinclair, 1989). Grants can also be obtained from government, Foundations and corporate donors (Wismer and Pell 1981). Despite this range of options, however, obtaining project financing remains a significant CED challenge, particularly in communities where few of these mechanisms exist.

Dependency and the Role of Government

Willingness of senior government officials to support local development initiatives can also be a very important factor in success and is difficult to create in the absence of a supportive policy framework. Roseland (1994) argues that local initiatives must be accompanied by appropriate federal regulations and incentives if they are to succeed. Decter and Kowall (1989;1) suggest that the commitment of senior levels of government was among the most important elements of the Yukon 2000 Consultation Process put in place to "take control over the future direction of the Yukon economy and to enhance the region's quality of life." In Ontario, a provincial election in the early 1990s resulted in a change in government and the subsequent cancellation of a provincial CED strategy and supporting programs. The change also caused the demise of many fledging local CED initiatives in the province. While this example further illustrates the importance of government assistance, it also serves as a warning against reliance on governments for financial and other forms of support (Vodden 1997). Reliance on government leaves a community open to many of the same risks as reliance on externally owned and operated corporations; with, for example, decisions being made to satisfy the needs of outside agencies rather than the community and the risk of program failure if the supporting government agencies "pull out" (Blakely 1989).

Dependence on one or few employers can also be detrimental. Dependency may result in reluctance to take on initiatives that threaten the status quo, particularly if major employers resist the direction proposed by a CED strategy (Halseth, 1989). Locally owned businesses may, however, be more likely to support activities that will enhance the well-being of their communities. Local ownership and economic diversity, therefore, tend to create conditions more conducive to CED.

Implementing the Community Economic Development Process

A flawed development process can destroy a community's chances of success. Potential pitfalls include reliance on government; letting the tools (e.g. government program) determine the strategy; ignoring local labor supply realities; following a development fad (high technology, convention centers and tourism are examples) not suited to community's unique attributes and capabilities; and overlooking the capacity of an organization or community to undertake and manage projects (Blakely, 1989). Blakely (1989) believes that these pitfalls often occur because civic leaders are too anxious about getting results quickly. Lauer (1993) identifies three common process "traps" in CED also related to the tendency to look for fast results: the study syndrome (outside consultants prepare reports treating locals as spectators instead of participants, sense of ownership is not instilled); the quick fix (inadequate discussion and planning); and the autocratic leader (the loudest voice wins the public debate and gets his/her way but the people aren't really behind the idea and/or it has not been well thought out). Leadership pitfalls can also include reliance on the "local elite" (insufficient public participation).

Building community involvement is a particularly important step in the CED process, one that is ongoing throughout all remaining steps. Participation and getting people "behind an idea", however, can be difficult task. Many people choose not to attend meetings or join coalitions because it means pulling away from their lives "to join a high pressure environment with few rewards," particularly when so-called experts dominate the agendas of interminable meetings and demands on time, energy and money seem endless" (Brown, 1995: 258). As a result, the participation of rural working people in economic and political decision-making is minimized. One way of dealing with this is collecting narratives from working people and providing effective representation for less powerful interests (e.g. through labor unions) as ways of capturing these people's input.

Steps in a Community Economic Development Process

1. Identify issue, need, and opportunity
2. Identify leader/core leadership group
3. Build community involvement
4. Create/select development organization
5. Research other communities experiences
6. Design and implement planning process
7. Ensure resources are in place for process.
8. Establish a vision
9. Create/update community profile
10. Identify issues and opportunities
11. Assess local capacity/readiness for change
12. Set long term goals and objectives
13. Determine how success will be measured
14. Create a strategy (with targets, goals etc.)
15. Create local partnerships

16. Raise funds locally
17. Generate additional capital/resources as required
18. Implement project action plans
19. Develop human resources
20. Evaluate progress and if necessary, adapt strategy
21. Build on success

Beyond providing input, community members are also needed to perform volunteer roles in many CED initiatives. Volunteer as well as financial resources are often limited, particularly when increasing demands are placed on existing volunteers. "Volunteers burnout" is frequently cited as a barrier to community involvement. Thus, ongoing volunteer recruitment, recognition and support programs are often offered by development organizations. Bollman and Biggs (1992) point out that more people in Canada's small, rural towns volunteer their time than do urban residents. Publicity and outreach for CED initiatives can help encourage participation, voluntarism and generally build awareness and support. Newsletters, local television spots and newspaper columns, for example, have been used by community groups and local governments to disseminate information and generate local interest.

It is now widely recognized that environmental sustainability is required for communities to have healthy economies and healthy citizens over the long term. In resource-dependent communities the link between healthy resources, healthy economies and healthy communities is particularly apparent. As natural resource stocks are depleted due, in large part, to exploitation at levels exceeding the resources ability to renew itself, communities that have relied on these resources for decades, even centuries find their access to these resources restricted and their employment and income opportunities reduced. While local communities are greatly impacted by the restructuring that results when previous levels of harvest can no longer be maintained, they are often not the ones primarily responsible for the damaging practices of the past. Resources degradation and consequent economic impact can have a series of far reaching negative effects on a community and its members. Crime, marital breakdowns, poor health, family, drug and alcohol abuse, for example, have all been linked to job loss (Economic Council of Canada, 1990; Brown 1995). The decline of a resource sector upon which a community has been built can also result in a loss of community identity and culture. In summary, resource and ecosystem sustainability is inextricably linked to economic sustainability and to community well-being.

Several authors have explored the intersection of the concepts of ecological sustainability and CED and devised new principles for sustainable, community economic development (SCED), a unique brand of CED which recognizes that long-term community health and viability depends on healthy local and global ecosystems. SCED shares the principles of CED while placing paramount importance on ecological sustainability.

For the most part, SCED shares the strategies, success and process steps of CED, adding an emphasis on the importance of maintaining ecosystem integrity and in the role of human action in meeting this objective. Sustainability requires an ongoing effort to meet the first and primary principle of living within ecological limits, with individuals, organizations and communities continually seeking new ways to practice stewardship and environmental responsibility (Aspen Institute, 1996).

Adding an emphasis on ecological sustainability in CED also requires modification of the strategies, process steps and success factors for CED listed above. SCED strategies include, corporate environmental management (minimizing the environmental impact of existing enterprises) and environmental entrepreneurship (developing businesses that offer environmentally responsible products and services as a consumer alternative).

Some of the principles of sustainable Community Economic Development include:

- Living within ecological limits;
- Ongoing action toward environmental protection and restoration;
- Self-reliance and community control;
- Equity and social justice;
- Marginalized and disadvantaged groups;
- Broad based public involvement in CED planning and decision-making;
- Economic viability;
- Capacity building;
- Long term planning and action;
- Diversity;
- Collaboration;
- Integration;
- Qualitative development;
- Recognition of the value of the voluntary/informal economy;
- Collective benefits;

- ◆ Community building/community mutuality;
- ◆ Entrepreneurialism.

(Sources: Schultz, 1995, Coodland et al 1993, Lauer 1993, Dauncey 1988, Nozick 1993, Boothroyd and Davis 1991, Renner 1991,Wismer & Pell 1981, Jacobs and Munroe 1987, Gardner 1988, Dovers 1990, Byrant 1999).

Conclusion

In view of the above, how can leadership in the informal sector provide the engine for rural development? It needs to learn from entrepreneurship and so set key goals such as:

- ◆ Make entrepreneurship an important part of the state and regional economic development toolkits;

- ◆ Develop an entrepreneurial strategy that demonstrates that entrepreneurs are valued as engines of local and regional economic development;

- ◆ Place a greater emphasis on increasing supply of leadership oriented entrepreneurs;

- ◆ Tap into the wide range of public, private and nonprofit resources to identify ways to connect and support entrepreneurs.

Leaders who seek success for communities will do the following:

(i)   Create an "entrepreneurial-friendly" environment;

(ii)   Develop a common vision of the future and local plan of action to sustain the momentum;

(iii) Develop a critical mass of entrepreneurship in order to spawn greater level of innovation;

(iv)   Make available networks and capital;

(v)   Entrepreneurial firms;

(vi)   Organize networking events such as luncheons, awards events, after-hours get-togethers and other opportunities for firms to interact;

(vii) New firms typically spin off in niche areas, often becoming suppliers to the regional firms, or providing secondary or tertiary products, processes and services. Encourage the clustering and spin-off process;

(viii) Connect existing programs and resources to entrepreneurial needs;

(ix) Establish benchmarks for measuring progress.

The informal sector is key to development in Kenya. It is populated by the youth and women and offers a great opportunity to spur economic growth. But this will only happen if there is total support, mobilization of resources, linkages and network, and capacity building in entrepreneurial skills.

References

Economic Development Commission (ABEDC), Economic Restructuring Strategy, Alert Bay, BC., 1996.

Blakely, E. J. *Planning Local Economic Development; Theory and practice.* California: Newbury Park: Sage Publications, 1989.

Bollman, R. and Biggs (eds.) *Rural and Small Town Canada.* Toronto: Supply and Services, 1992.

Boothroyd, P. and C Davis. *The Meaning of Community Economic Development.* Vancouver: School of Community and Regional Planning, University of British Columbia, 1991.

Brown R. "Opening Remarks" In *Exploring Cooperative Management in Fisheries. Pacific Fisheries Think Tank Report No.2*, Gallaugher, P, K. Vodden and L. Wood (eds.) Proceedings of Exploring Cooperative Management in Fisheries workshop held April 21-22, 1997.

Bryant, C. "Community Change in Context" In *Communities Development and Sustainability Across Canada*, Pierce, J. and A. Dale (eds.). Vancouver: UBC Press, 1999.

Coastal Community Network, *The State of B.C's Coastal Economy: A 1999 Regional Status Report,* Ucluect, B. C.: Coastal Community Network, 1999.

Cole G A "Personnel Management: Theory and Practice" London: Ashford Color Press, 1993.

Commission on Resource and the Environment (CORE), Public Participation, 1995.

Community Economics, 1987.

Community Economics, Vol. 5, No. 1 (spring) 1995

Davis, H. C. and T. Hutton. *Structural Change in the British Columbia Economy: Regional Diversification and Metropolitan Transition*, BC Round Table on Environment and Economy, 1992.

Drucker, P.F. *The practice of management*. Heinemann Professional, P.156.

Drucker, K., B. Nixon, and R. Travers (eds.), Madeira Park, BC.: Habour Publishing, 1989.

Drucker "Forest Ownership and the Case for Diversification"' In *TouchWood: BC Forest at a Crossroads*, Drucker K. B Nixon, and R. Travels (eds.) Madeira Park, BC.: Harbour Publishing, 1993.

Economic Council of Canada. *From the Bottom Up: The Community Economic Development Approach*, 1990.

Feagan, R. *Interpretations of Sustainability: World views of Environmental Activists of Save Georgia* Straight Alliance of British Colombia, Ph.D. Thesis, Simon Fraser University, 1993.

Follet, Mary. *Management and Leadership; A Contemporary Approach*. London: Prentice Hall, 1999.

Gallaugher, P. and K Vodden "Trying it Together along the BC Coast", In *Fishing Places People: Traditions and Issues and in the Canadian Small-Scale Fisheries*, Newell D. and R. Ommer (eds), Toronto: University of Toronto Press, 1999.

Halseth, G. *Community Economic Development Strategies in Resource Communities Under Stress-Illustrations from British Columbia*, talk given at 1998 CAG Meeting, 1997.

Higgins, *Entrepreneurship Theory and Practice*, London: Higgins and Bros, 1911.

Hussmann M. M. "Small Town Revitalization through the Main Street Approach", In *Community-based Approaches to Rural Development: Principles and Practice* Bruce, D. & Mc Gregor, D. *The Human side of Enterprise*, Penguin, 1987.

McClelland. *Management and Entrepreneurship*, Bombay: Prentice Hall, 1945.

McRobie, G. and D. Ross. "What is Community Development?" Excerpt from A Feasibility Study for a Centre for Community Economic Development at Simon Fraser University, Community Economic Development Centre. Simon Fraser University, Burnaby, BC. 1987.

Meeker-Lowry, S. *Economics as If The Earth Really Mattered: A Catalyst Guide To Socially Conscious Investing*. New Society Publishers, 1988.

Mitchell, B. *Geography and Recourse Analysis*, (Second edition), London: Longman, 1989.

Mitchell R "The Howe Sound Round Table: Working Towards a Common Goal", National Round Table Review p. 12, 1994.

Mullins, L.J. *Approaches to leadership*; The British Journal of Administrative Management, Vol 32, No 8, Nov., 1982.

New Founded and Labrador Round Table on Environment and the Economy. *The Report of the Partnership on Sustainable Coastal Communities and Marine Ecosystems in Newfoundland and Labrador*, 1995.

Ngovi Kitau. *Franchising Uchumi*, Standard Newspaper pg 13, 4th August 2005.

Phaland, N. *Forest Sector-Development Communities in Canada: A Demographic Profile* Ottawa. 1988

Parker, P. 'The shape of Leaders to come'. *Management Today*, July 1994.

Pierce, J. "The Conservation Challenge in Sustaining Rural Environments" *Journal of Rural Studies*, Vol. 8, No. 3, 1995.

Rees, J. *Natural Recourses: Allocations, Economics and Policy*, London: Routledge, 1990.

Roseland, M. *Personal communication*, 1997.

Roseland, M. "Dimensions of the Future", In *Eco-City Dimensions: Healthy Communities, Healthy Planet*, Roseland, M (ed). New Society Publishers, 1997.

Schulz, E. (ed) *Sharing Our Stories: Community Economic Development in British Columbia*, Vancouver: BC Working Group on CED, 1995.

Travers, O. R. "Rhetoric and Reality". In: *Touch Wood: BC Forests at Crossroads*, 1993.

Taylor, F.W. *Scientific Management*. Harper and Raw. (1947) comprise shop management, *Principles of Scientific Management*, 1911.

Vodden, K. *CED Sectors and Strategies: Opportunities and Action on Cormorant Island*. Alert Bay, BC.: Inner Coast Natural Resource Centre, 1996.

Vodden, K. "Working Together for a Green Economy", In *Eco-city Dimensions: Healthy Communities, Healthy Planet*, Roseland, M. (ed), Gabriola Island, BC.: New Society Publishers, 1997.

Wismer, S. and D. Pell. *Community Profit: Community-Based Economic Development in Canada* Toronto: Is Five Press, 1981.

Young, D. and J. Charland. *Successful Local Economic Development Initiatives*, ICURR Press, 1992.

10

Leadership and Economic Development: What Type of Leadership Facilitates Rapid Economic Advancement?

Sunny Bindra

Introduction

The famous American economist John Kenneth Galbraith said this about leadership: "All of the great leaders have had one characteristic in common. It was the willingness to confront unequivocally the major anxiety of their people in their time. This, and not much else, is the essence of leadership." The failure of economic development, reflected in widespread poverty, is undoubtedly the major anxiety facing the Kenyan people. Successive governments since independence in 1963 have failed to deliver economic advancement to the great mass of the people. Kenya's GDP per capita in 2005 stood at just US$ 360 – a level largely unchanged in real terms over 40 years. The economy grew promisingly in the years following independence, but this turned out to be a false dawn: annual growth rates were very low from the mid-1990s onwards. The economy enjoyed average real growth rates of 5 per cent from 1963 to 1970, and as much as 8 per cent from 1970 to 1980. However, the following two decades brought sharply lower rates: 4 per cent from 1980 to 1990, and just 2 per cent from 1990 to 2000.[1] In addition, what little growth has been realised has not had widespread economic benefits. In 2005, nearly six out of every ten people are estimated to live beneath the poverty line. In addition, Kenya is afflicted by a very high level of economic inequality: recent statistics showed that the country's bottom 10% households control less than 1 per cent of the total income. Kenya is believed to be among the top 10 most unequal countries in the world.[2]

The Narc government, elected in 2002 on a wave of resentment against the economic stagnation that characterised the final years of its predecessor, promised to raise Kenya's economic game. Its original Economic Recovery Strategy, published in June 2003, promised to achieve real GDP growth of 7 per cent by 2006, and to reduce the poverty level by at least 5 percentage points by 2007.[3] The government has indeed managed to achieve higher levels of growth in the economy, recording 4.3 per cent growth in 2004 (albeit on an adjusted formula for recording economic activity) and 5.8 percent in 2006. It is widely acknowledged, however, that an economy needs to hit 8-10 per cent growth over a long period in order to make any meaningful impact on poverty. Achieving 5 per cent annual growth in Kenya, with its diverse and open economy, is relatively easy; achieving 10 per cent is another matter altogether.

Consider the experience of India and China, the two countries that held most of the world's poor within their borders in the 1970s. After 1980, both 'sleeping giants' awoke to adopt an export focus and economic liberalisation: China aggressively so; India, until more recently, at a more modest pace. According to the World Bank, China grew at an annual average of 10 per cent and India at 6 per cent during the two decades ending in 2000. In 2003, India, too, hit the 10 per cent mark. Poverty in China fell dramatically, from an estimated 28 per cent to just 9 per cent over a similar period; India's poverty rate fell from over 50 per cent to a more tolerable 26 per cent.[4]

A consensus appears to be emerging amongst development economists regarding the factors that stimulate high levels of economic growth and development.[5] These would include:

1) *Free markets*, which generally give most economic players the incentives to use resources efficiently and produce products and services actually demanded by consumers;

2) *Political democracy*, which empowers citizens to select governments and leaders who operate in their interest – and reject and remove those that fail to deliver;

3) *Technological capacity*, which enables a society to keep producing (or adapting) technical innovations that boost productivity and unlock new markets and industries;

4) *Social facilities*, primarily education and heath care, which allow individuals to have access to the basic building blocks of a productive life;

5) *Transparency guarantees*, which allow people to transact in a climate of mutual trust, based on the necessary institutional safeguards against fraud, corruption etc; and

6) *Protective security*, which provides a general safety net to the populace to reduce vulnerability to natural disasters, crime and national emergencies.

Growth and development take place when a society has the correct *freedoms and incentives* to achieve them. This applies to governments as well as individuals. Governments must have the incentive to promote private-sector growth; to enable technological innovation and adaption; to provide high-quality schooling. These things happen when a government is held accountable by the institutions of democracy and governance, and invests in collective goods like education and health in the interests of its citizens. Equally, growth happens when individuals and businesses, protected by robust property rights, are able to participate in their own development. They can engage in stable employment protected by law; invest in entrepreneurial ventures in an environment of trust and reliability; and have physical and institutional access to markets. This requires a robust judicial system, physical infrastructure that aids transactions (such as good transport linkages and efficient telecommunications networks), and the absence of artificial barriers to entry in most markets.

It should be obvious that the factors outlined above work in concert. Free markets require healthy and educated individuals to operate them. Health and education are easier to provide when economic growth is high and the population grows at manageable rates. Large investments in technology are easier to make when economies are stable and the returns accrue largely to the investors bearing the risk.

It should be equally obvious that different societies have placed varying emphasis on the six factors described here at different times. Both China and India, for example, emerged from socialistic structures and tightly controlled markets and undertook programmes of economic liberalisation, involving the opening up of the economy to competition, an international outlook and an emphasis on market-led provision. China's early success, however, far outpaced that of India. This can be put down to China's social preparedness to benefit from liberalisation: in 1979 (when its reforms began), China already had a highly literate population and an impressive universal health-care programme. In contrast, India had neglected its educational and health facilities and was therefore poorly prepared for a widely shared economic expansion. India, however, has always been a vibrant democracy, whereas China lacks democratic freedoms even today. This reduces China's economic flexibility and the accountability of its government, and limits the participation of the general public in policy making. This, more than any other factor, may put a limit on China's future growth.

It is clear that good government and leadership have a vital role to play as an enabler and facilitator of economic growth – even though private enterprise is the primary engine of growth. Governments must provide the institutions that regulate the economy; protect the rights of all the players; regulate certain markets in the collective interest; and manage a taxation framework that balances equity with the need to provide adequate incentives for investment and entrepreneurship. Leadership can, therefore, make or break a country's drive towards growth and development. What role has leadership played in Kenya's fitful and inadequate performance in the development race?

Leadership and the Economy: Kenya's dismal record

If the measure of success for the leadership of a developing country is the economic well-being of the general population, then the quality of Kenya's leadership since 1963 has been sorely wanting. As indicated above, the common Kenyan has seen very little of the fruits of development. Severe economic inequality suggests that the limited gains from economic growth have traditionally been expropriated by a very small group of elites. The roots of this dismal record are not hard to find.

Successive governments have shied away from the opportunity to build a participative economy that shares opportunity and wealth, and instead have built institutions and markets based on *exclusion*. Access to key markets was limited, for as long as was possible, to a very small number of players who then proceeded to extract monopoly rents and make Kenya a high-cost economy. Multi-party democracy was not permitted for a large proportion of the country's years of independence. Basic facilities (good quality schools, health clinics, access roads, piped water, electricity) were not available to the vast majority of people. An oppressive regime of permits and licenses for every economic activity stifled business activity. All of these exclusions produced a country in which a small group of politically connected politicians and businesspeople enjoyed a disproportionate share of the rewards, while the greater mass of citizens continued to wallow in underachievement. To date, there is little evidence that a participative approach to development is being considered or introduced.

Because access to opportunity has been based on patronage, the incentive to emphasise performance has been removed. Access to resources, markets and economic institutions was often given as a political reward. The need to manage resources efficiently and instil effective management frameworks was systematically eroded. In turn, the incentive to invest in skills, education and technology was weakened. Why invest in those things, when a network of political contacts would do just as well, if not better? Kenya's leaders have produced an economy of low productivity and high production cost, and the country has seen its international competitiveness undermined as a result.

The tribal agenda has dominated the politics (and economics) of the land. Successive leaders have given disproportionate amounts of development capital to members of their own ethnic groups, leading to distrust and acrimony across tribal boundaries. A 'my tribe first' culture has been allowed to take root, in which the primary goal of development is the furtherance of the interests of tribe before country. This culture in turn has a negative effect on productivity: when recruitment decisions are swayed by tribal background rather than experience and qualifications, a meritocracy cannot develop. A national social and political fabric, so vital to ensuring unity of purpose and effort in economic development, has been sorely missing in Kenya.

All of these factors were made far worse by the outright plunder of national resources that took root during the 1970s and 1980s and reached monstrous proportions in the 1990s. The various scams and scandals that resulted in massive misappropriation of public funds are well documented elsewhere, and need not be repeated here. The new Narc government pledged to reclaim large sums of money allegedly stashed abroad by senior figures from the previous regime; these efforts, however, appear to have reached an impasse as the new government has become embroiled in fresh corruption scandals of its own. Precise estimates are naturally difficult to come by, but many observers believe that the amount of money that left the economy illegally over the past two decades runs into tens of billions of dollars – or several years' national product. With such a drain on the country, economic stagnation ceases to be surprising.

In short, Kenya's leaders may well have kept the country free of wars and serious ethnic strife in a region characterised by both. But using the key criterion of providing economic growth, development and wellbeing to the ordinary citizen, Kenya's leadership over several decades can be adjudged an abject failure.

Leadership and Development: case studies

To understand the powerful effect that strong, visionary leadership can actually have on economic development, this paper will consider two individuals from different corners of the world, both of whom left office in 1990: Lee Kuan Yew in Singapore, and Margaret Thatcher in Great Britain.

Lee Kuan Yew and the Singapore story

Lee Kuan Yew was the tiny Republic of Singapore's first Prime Minister, reigning from 1959 to 1990. Singapore is a set of Islands lying off the southern tip of the Malay Peninsula, with a land area of just 639 square kilometres. It is low-lying, hot and humid, and singularly lacking in any mineral or energy resources. Most food needs to be imported, and there is no natural source of drinking water. Yet this is the country whose GDP per capita today is comparable with the likes of France and Britain. Singapore achieved one of the fastest economic transformations seen in world history. To many, the Singapore 'miracle' is synonymous with the name of Lee Kuan Yew.

Lee was always an internationalist, and saw the benefits of being part of the global community soon after he took power in 1959. In 1963, Lee took Singapore into the Federation of Malaysia to take advantage of a larger economy and resource base. This was short-lived, and Singapore became a totally independent sovereign nation in 1965. Singapore joined the United Nations immediately after this, and the Association of Southeast Asian Nations (ASEAN) in 1967. Wary of Singapore's military vulnerability, Lee courted strong relationships with Malaysia and Indonesia, and with Britain, Singapore's former colonial master. He also spent a great deal of effort cultivating a unique Singaporean identity, fully aware of the divisions that could arise in a nation of diverse ethnic identity. Nevertheless, the government always stressed the importance of maintaining religious tolerance and racial harmony, and used the law to counter any threat to incite the ethnic and religious violence that has been the bane of Singapore's neighbours.

In the early 1960s, Singapore faced all the problems of a poor, small country. Lee's early years were spent grappling with the entrenched problems of poor education facilities, inadequate housing and widespread unemployment. The separation from Malaysia led to the permanent loss of a common market and an economic hinterland. In addition, the British withdrawal from the area meant the elimination of 50,000 jobs. One of his first acts was to establish the Housing and Development Board to begin a massive public housing construction programme. This happened in tandem with the launch of an ambitious plan to industrialise the country. The Economic Development Board was set up to attract foreign direct investment (FDI) into the economy, offering tax incentives and access to a reasonably skilled, highly disciplined and relatively low-paid workforce. A large programme of infrastructure development was initiated, focusing on an international airport, capacious port, good roads and excellent communications links. All of this led to very significant job creation, allowing Singapore to reduce its unemployment rate from 14 per cent in 1965 to just 4.5 per cent by 1973.

Singapore in those early days was not immune to the problem of corruption. But Lee was a stickler for maintaining a "clean house", and set up the Corrupt Practices Investigations Bureau with powers to conduct searches, investigate and address any citizen. Several ministers were later charged with corruption. Lee also believed that government officials should be well paid in order to attract the best people and reduce the temptation to engage in corruption. Salaries of top civil servants were linked to comparable rewards in the private sector. This emphasis on a corruption-free state led to great future benefits and allowed Singapore to attract a steady stream of foreign capital. Singapore is today routinely listed amongst the world's least corrupt nations on international surveys of perceptions about corruption.

Singapore followed a vigorous economic policy under Lee: pro-business, pro-FDI and with a heavy emphasis on export promotion. Singapore's early success was as an importer of raw goods for refinement and export, using its strategically located seaport. Lee used a mandatory savings scheme known as the Central Provident Fund to promote high levels of savings and investment, which gave every citizen a stake in the system. Much of this capital was channelled into education and technology. That is still the case: 21 per cent of Singapore's budget in 2005 went to education (compared with 4 per cent in the USA). Lee's emphasis on skills also meant he was not afraid of importing them: more than a quarter of the labour force in Singapore is traditionally foreign, filling the gaps in various sectors of the economy.

Singapore's economic strategy proved to be a real success. Growth rates averaged 8 per cent from 1960 to 1999 – a remarkable trajectory that took the small state to first-world status in one generation. Today, its skilled workforce, clean government and first-class infrastructure have attracted nearly 3,000 multinational corporations, accounting for nearly two-thirds of manufacturing output. Singapore's own investments abroad are now very sizeable. Singapore is ranked amongst the top nations in the world in terms of global competitiveness and business environment. It operates at close to full employment, and has little or no poverty to speak of. The country is virtually crime-free and boasts one of the finest health and education systems in Asia.

Singaporeans generally agree: Lee was the visionary and architect at the centre of this remarkable success. A man gifted with a powerful mind, driving energy and a strong personality, he established himself as one of the world's great leaders. He showed a relentless dedication to his work (not even keeping a diary, as he feared it would distract him). Many of his peers, such as Mao, Suharto, and Marcos left their countries in ruins with no obvious successor, and had to be forced out of office; Lee relinquished the leadership of Singapore voluntarily, and left it in the top tier of nations with a strong team of second-generation leaders ready to take over.

Lee is not without his detractors. Critics point out his record of political intolerance, his elitism and autocratic nature. He himself stated that he would rather be feared than loved. His measures against political opposition and the curbing of a free press brought international criticism. Paradoxically, he created a country that is today rated in the top two in the Economic Freedom Index – which measures the extent to which government inhibits economic relations between individuals. So Lee stifled political freedoms while granting unprecedented business freedoms – and a citizenry whose average income was growing so rapidly did not complain.

Lee also recognised the necessity of social facilities. He has often stated that Singapore's only natural resources are its people and their strong work ethic. But he boosted this resource by investing deeply in health and education, and by providing the strongest of role models in terms of hard work and dedication to duty.

In 1999, Time Magazine included Lee Kuan Yew in its list of 100 Most Influential People of the 20th Century. This reflected his internationalist vision and his status on the world stage. The Singapore story is truly inseparable from the personality of Lee Kuan Yew.[6]

Margaret Thatcher and the revival of Great Britain

Margaret Thatcher is probably the world's most famous grocer's daughter. Prime Minister of the United Kingdom from 1979 to 1990, she is to date the only woman to serve in that position. The "Iron Lady" came into office when Britain's economy was in remarkable disarray. When she left, its position amongst the world's richest nations was secure again. But her path was never an easy one.

As leader of the Conservative opposition from 1975 to 1979, she was seen as a strident figure, arousing controversy for her unbridled attacks on the Soviet Union and for stoking fears about immigration. Most opinion polls at the time showed that she was trailing Prime Minister James Callaghan in personal ratings. However, the latter's mismanagement of the economy led to the humiliating "Winter of Discontent"

(1978/79) when widespread strikes crippled public services throughout the country and inflation seemed out of control. A fed-up electorate gave the Conservatives a handsome election victory in April 1979.

Thatcher soon showed that she was the consummate "conviction politician" – holding unflinching views about what needed to be done to Britain and leading from the front. She quickly set about implementing the main thrusts of her economic policy: breaking the power of the trade unions; rolling back the involvement of the state in the economy; reclaiming Britain's role and voice in world affairs; and instilling a sense of self-help in a country that she felt had become soft and weak in the warm embrace of the welfare state.

Her immediate priority was to increase interest rates and drive down the money supply. She preferred indirect taxes to taxes on income, and VAT was increased sharply. British business was hit hard by these measures, and unemployment quickly rose to over 2 million. The early 1980s were a period of severe recession in Britain, and Thatcher was widely blamed. She faced vocal opposition from both the Confederation of British Industry and the economics profession. In 1981 she received an open letter from 364 prominent economists, opposing her policies. Mrs. Thatcher did not blink: she repeatedly stated that she would not change her policies ("You turn if you want to. The lady's not for turning."). Unemployment kept climbing to unprecedented levels, topping 3 million in January 1982. By this time Thatcher was extremely unpopular, with an election to come the following year.

Then history played a decisive card. In April 1982 Argentina invaded the Falklands Islands, a British territory long claimed by the Argentines. This was to become Thatcher's defining moment. As resolute in global politics as in matters of the economy, she did not procrastinate. She despatched a huge naval task force to recapture the islands, and after a short campaign, succeeded in driving Argentine forces out. Her popularity soared on a wave of patriotic fervour. The "Falklands Factor", as it was dubbed, took her from Britain's least popular serving leader to a landslide victory in 1983, in the space of little over a year.

Her popularity assured, Thatcher set about implementing the rest of her economic programme. She increased her popularity in working-class areas with the "Right to Buy" policy that allowed residents of council housing to buy their homes at a discount. She launched an unprecedented attack on the unions, and turned a politically motivated strike by the National Union of Mineworkers into a personal crusade. The strike lasted a full year, but Thatcher had built up coal stocks and no loss of power was experienced. As the miners became desperate and violence began occurring on picket lines, public opinion gradually swung in Thatcher's favour. Against all expectations, Thatcher refused to brook any consideration of the miners' demands. Their spirit broken, the miners went back to work with no agreement. Symbolically, Thatcher had tamed the trade unions, and labour reform followed in many other industries.

Thatcher's economic policy emphasised free markets and entrepreneurialism. After 1983, a bold privatisation programme began to unfold. Most large utilities, which had been in public hands for more than 40 years, were sold off to the public via well-marketed share offerings. Privatisation became synonymous with Thatcher, and most large publicly-owned organisations (such as British Telecom and British Airways) prospered under private ownership, providing better service to customers and investing in much-needed infrastructure and new products. The only casualty of Thatcher's privatisation programme has been the railway system, which is widely viewed as a failure. Thatcher's privatisation policies have nevertheless been successfully exported across the globe, reviving moribund organisations and improving government balance sheets.

Thatcher won her third consecutive election in 1987. Britain was by now thriving again economically. Tight monetary policies had allowed inflation to stabilise at a low level, and unemployment had fallen consistently over several years. A newfound confidence was afoot, reflected in an entrepreneurial spirit that led to many new businesses, small and large, being established. However, the gap between 'haves' and 'have-nots' was believed to be growing, particularly in the north of the country that had suffered the loss of many old manufacturing industries and mines, and had not made the transition to new industries and sectors requiring different skills.

By 1989, Britain was believed by many to be a victim of its own success, caught in the grip of an unsustainable economic boom: house prices had spiralled out of control and general inflation was creeping up again. Thatcher and her Chancellor, Nigel Lawson, repeated the monetarist prescription of raising interest rates and reducing the money supply. Her popularity began to wane again as the policies began to bite. In addition, deep divisions began to emerge within the Conservative party over the vexed issue of deeper integration with Europe. Thatcher disagreed publicly both with Lawson and her Foreign Secretary, Geoffrey Howe. Howe was soon demoted and Lawson subsequently resigned, feeling undermined by Thatcher. The loss of her close colleagues was to prove crucial.

Thatcher had also reformed the local government rates system, replacing it with the Community Charge, widely derided as Thatcher's "Poll Tax". This was the most universally unpopular measure of her premiership. Protests and riots began occurring, and millions refused to pay the new tax. Thatcher, unbending as ever, refused to compromise. Interest rates were now at very high levels, hurting both businesspeople and homeowners, once a core part of Thatcher's constituency. Geoffrey Howe resigned suddenly, precipitating a leadership challenge. Thatcher won the first ballot, but not convincingly. On 22 November 1990, she was forced to resign, having lost the confidence of her own party. She was jettisoned by her party; yet she had never lost a general election.

Even today, Thatcher evokes wildly different points of view. Some regard her in messianic terms for having rescued Britain from the economic stagnation of the 1970s, and for having re-instilled entrepreneurial vigour into Britain. Others see her (like her compatriot Lee Yuan Kew) as autocratic and egotistical. She was a divisive figure who nevertheless transformed Britain from being the "sick man of Europe" into a strong and vibrant modern economy. She returned the City of London to a leadership position as an international financial centre, and exposed many a protected industry to invigorating competition. While she undoubtedly increased the efficiency of British markets, many observers believe she simultaneously eroded long-term competitiveness by reducing research and education spending.

At bottom, her core values were focused on self-help, hard work and personal responsibility for success. She is said to have stated at age nine, when receiving a school prize: "I wasn't lucky. I deserved it." During her tenure as premier, she put it another way: "Pennies do not come from heaven. They have to be earned here on Earth."[7]

Leadership Lessons

Lee Kuan Yew and Margaret Thatcher were both leaders of a certain breed: visionaries who saw a particular future for their countries very clearly, and who pursued their dream with relentless fervour. Both hauled their nations up by the bootstraps and instilled values in their citizenry that they themselves demonstrated in their daily lives. Yet they cannot be said to have achieved this on their own. Both cultivated strong teams of like-minded ministers and advisors: Lee had Goh Keng Swee and Hon Sui Swen; Thatcher was ably assisted by Keith Joseph, Nigel Lawson, John Major and Geoffrey Howe. In addition, both leaders had aspirations beyond their domestic agendas: during their time, both straddled the world stage with authority and became respected international leaders. Neither suffered fools gladly.

Is this the only model of leadership that can create rapid economic wealth? Certainly not. Lee and Thatcher have been highlighted here only because they epitomise the type of leader that is often needed when a nation is stagnating and the standards it sets itself are unnecessarily low. In circumstances like those, a strong personality practicing conviction politics often provides exactly the right elixir.

Yet a quiet leader can also produce similar results. India's Manmohan Singh, as Finance Minister in the early 1990s, is credited with being the father of India's economic reforms, a programme he followed with great dedication despite much initial opposition from vested interests. Today, as India's Prime Minister, he is following a more balanced "growth with equity" programme that nurtures wealth creation without losing sight of *Aam Aadmi* (the common man). A humble and soft-spoken man who avoids unnecessary confontation, Mr. Singh is not a consummate politician; he has always relied on the political support of others to allow him to do his good work.

Seretse Khama took charge of a Botswana that was amongst the world's poorest countries at independence in 1966. Today it is the envy of sub-Saharan Africa, with a relatively high GDP per capita (it has enjoyed remarkable rates of growth in both GDP and per capita income) a stable economy, and little or no foreign debt. Khama's achievement as a leader lies in using the country's vast diamond wealth wisely and judiciously, channelling it into infrastructure, health and education. Like Lee in Singapore, he developed strong measures and institutions against corruption, which has blighted the economies of so many of his African neighbours. Unlike Lee, Khama nurtured a multiparty democracy and held free and fair elections without fail every five years. This political openness has played a large role in Botswana's economic success. Since the 1990s, Botswana has been reducing its dependence on diamonds by allowing unrestricted foreign investment and management.

A common theme emerges: leaders who have successfully guided their economies towards sustained development have all paid attention to most (if not always all) of the six drivers of economic development introduced in section 1 of this chapter. Giving economic freedoms to the wider population to participate in its own success is a particularly important ingredient in creating sustained success. The freedom to exchange is now widely viewed as a necessary part of the way human beings live, and constructing workable market mechanisms is something that most countries are engaged in today. The degree of freedoms, and the role of state intervention, often differs. Lee's Singapore invested heavily in state-owned players in the economy; Margaret Thatcher tried to divest as many as she could in her years in charge.

Nevertheless, creating an essential level of economic freedom is a central part of a leader's role.

Sustained development also demands an emphasis on collective goods which require state provision – particularly in the areas of health and education. India has in the past neglected these essentials relative to China – but is belatedly catching up. Botswana's leaders were unique in Africa in channelling the proceeds of mineral wealth into schools, universities, hospitals and clinics. Singapore's Lee had an almost obsessive fixation on developing human capital. Only Margaret Thatcher of the leaders considered here is regarded as having diminished the importance of commonly provided social facilities. Yet it must be remembered that she was dealing with a developed country where the minimum necessary level of such provision had long been exceeded, and that her 'assault' on the universities and the National Health Service was more concerned with introducing efficiency and a missing focus on consumers and users.

The role of political freedoms also raises interesting questions. It is often claimed that the denial of certain basic political or civil rights actually aids the process of rapid economic development, and that political liberty is something a poor country somehow cannot afford. Lee's Singapore and post-reform China are often cited in this regard. Amartya Sen disputes this position, stating that "the empirical evidence very strongly suggests that economic growth is more a matter of a friendlier economic climate than a harsher political system." Botswana, an oasis of democracy on an otherwise intolerant continent, provides a strong counter-example.

Professor Sen argues that the list of "helpful policies" that led to the success of the East Asian economies is pretty well understood and generally agreed, and includes: openness to competition; the use of international markets; a high level of literacy and school education; successful land reforms; and public provision of incentives for investment, exporting and industrialisation. He concludes: "There is nothing whatsoever to indicate that any of these policies is inconsistent with greater democracy and actually had to be sustained by the elements of authoritarianism that happened to be present in South Korea or Singapore or China."[8] By this reckoning, those relatively intolerant countries would have achieved *more* development, not less, by reducing the level of political authoritarianism present in them. More political freedoms would have enforced economic and other freedoms (by providing more checks and balances), not hampered them.

So the historical evidence is reasonably clear: leaders who allow a variety of concurrent and mutually reinforcing freedoms in the economy – political, economic, social – and who pursue such a programme with vigour, dedication and personal example, are likely to create an environment in which there is rapid economic advancement and widespread improvement in standards of living.

New directions in leadership

New ideas about the nature of effective leadership are emerging from all directions. The traditional image of the 'blood-and-guts' leader who takes his or her organisation by the scruff of the neck and pulls it along by sheer force of personality is perhaps fading. More subtle behaviours are demanded of leaders in the new economy. This section offers a brief survey of two types of reflection on the future of leadership: one from organisational theory; and the other from behavioural studies.

Lessons from organisational theory

Peter Senge of MIT's Sloan School of Management first put forward the idea of the "learning organisation" in 1990: an organisation "where people continually expand their capacity to create the results they truly desire, where new and expansive patterns of thinking are nurtured, where collective aspiration is set free, and where people are continually learning how to learn together."[9] This thinking is founded on a straightforward premise: that the only sustainable competitive advantage for any organisation in the modern economy is the ability to learn faster than its competitors. This places great reliance on the idea that *human capital* is the most important resource held by an organisation: the ability to deploy new and evolving skills in flexible, high-performance teams is known to a key competency in the new economy. What applies to corporations applies almost identically to nations: leadership today is more about the skills needed to keep a country's 'teams' on a high-performance trajectory, and to keep refreshing the skills available.

The key to transforming any corporation or country into a learning organisation is leadership. A great mental leap is required to understand the role of leadership in the new economy. The traditional idea of good leaders – 'special' people who set the direction, make all the key decisions, and energise the troops – must, according to Senge and other management reformers, be altered significantly. As he puts it, our traditional idea is that "leaders are *heroes* – great men (and occasionally women) who "rise to the fore" in times of crisis." He goes further: "As long as such myths prevail, they reinforce a focus on short-term events and charismatic heroes rather than on systemic forces and collective learning. At its heart, the traditional view of leadership is based on assumptions of people's powerlessness, their lack of personal vision and inability to master the forces of change, deficits which can be remedied only by a few great leaders."[10]

In Senge's view, the new leader is responsible for ensuring that widespread learning takes place – as a designer, steward and teacher. Let us consider all of these in turn.

- *The leader as designer:* Senge tells us that this is a chord that goes back thousands of years. In Lao Tzu's famous phrase, the good leader is he, who when his work is done, the people say, "We did it ourselves". In other words, the designer creates the conditions that allow the people themselves to do the work, effectively and efficiently. This involves many disciplines, including the building of a *shared* vision and values, as well as organisational design – the linkages, reporting lines and inter-relationships – that will knit the organisation together into a coherent whole and allow it to deliver results.

- *The leader as steward:* The new leader must play a key role as the steward of the organisation's vision: in other words, he or she must safeguard, nurture and develop the 'big idea' for the future of the organisation. According to Senge, this involves listening and constant change – a willingness to bow before a bigger picture generated from a bigger mass of people. In this sense the leader is a humble guardian, holding something valuable in trust.

- *The leader as teacher:* Teaching, in leadership terms, should not be confused with the transfer of facts, or knowledge, or methods. It is about the more subtle role of fostering learning. An authoritarian leader imposes his or her own strategy or policy, and continually intervenes in decisions. A more subtle leader explains, clarifies and convinces. A good example used by Senge concerns America's Lyndon Johnson, who in his early years as president was very successful in selling the idea of a "Great Society" to the country at large, until there was very little perceived difference between his goals and the country's goals.[11]

These three 'new' roles are clearly a diversion from the traditional image of the larger-than-life leader, but they hold lessons for what is needed as the world economy evolves towards a focus on knowledge and learning rather than physical resources. Nelson Mandela, who is regarded in iconic terms across the world, reflects many of these attributes. A forceful but gentle personality, he engendered such trust that his diverse people were able to accept his role as steward of the vision for a new South

Africa, and as a teacher of the values of tolerance and acceptance. The design elements of the new South Africa – the institutional framework, the economic linkages – he left to a team of able deputies to develop in line with the vision.

Arguably even leaders like Lee Kuan Yew, widely perceived to belong to the authoritarian school, were able to transfer a strong personal vision to the country at large and nurture and refine this vision as events unfolded. Lee's vision, though forcefully expressed and implemented, was not at variance with the aspirations of the Singaporean people. This brings us back to the Galbraith quotation that opened this paper: a leader must connect with the abiding need of his people.

The presence of effective 'management teams' (at the level of a corporation or a country) does not diminish the role of leadership. Professor John Roberts of Stanford University is an international expert in economics and management who has lately preoccupied himself with organisational design.[12] He sees many roles for management: establishing a funding model, creating and staffing departments, putting together budgeting processes, managing costs, and many more. All of this is vital, but it is not enough. Leadership is needed to conceptualise the vision and strategy of the corporation (country), and leadership is needed to create and sell the basic organisational model that will deliver growth and development. Leaders must therefore be consummate communicators, able to convey complex models in clear and compelling ways so that others are inspired to embrace and understand them. Leaders also influence behaviour, by defining (and living) the values and social norms that shape culture.

A final thread from the world of corporate management concerns the very nature of leadership: is it a *function* or a *role*? In other words, is leadership concentrated in the hands of a small band of bosses, or is it a role that is spread throughout an organisation, at all levels? Modern organisational thought emphasises the latter approach. The complexity and unpredictability inherent in the modern world demands a great degree of agility and adaptability in organisations. This can only occur with a redefinition of leadership, which allows all individuals to exercise leadership within their spheres of influence. Unipolar, 'command-and-control' leadership therefore gives way to leadership to all levels.[13]

In this regard, it can be argued that in Kenya the ordinary citizenry has made a habit of waiting for leaders to "do something": fix the economy, build roads or clinics, or provide moral guidance. A more diffuse model of leadership is desirable, where each individual recognises his or her capacity to provide direction and set an example: at the level of the family, circle of friends, school, church or corporation. To understand one's own role in the destiny of one's country is a hugely self-empowering act. It builds personal confidence and harnesses the ideas and energy of millions (rather than a select few), and allows a 'bottom-up' approach that connects top leadership with the concerns of the greater mass. An enlightened Kenyan leader would seek to build the freedoms and institutional networks that achieve precisely this.

The leader as role model

"Values, good and bad, get transmitted. Human beings learn by example. We are mimics by nature. We are infected by the deeds of those around us. We are inspired by lives well lived; and polluted by ill-will in the atmosphere. And we pay special attention to those we regard as leaders. In the home, it's the parents; at the workplace, the top executives; and in society as a whole, we focus our gaze on politicians and celebrities."[14]

Most of history's great leaders have led by strong personal example. This is true of Lee and Thatcher, Mandela and Khama. It is true also of Hitler and Stalin, who caused great devastation in the world. The transmitting of values is a very powerful mechanism in any society, and it starts cascading down from the top. Mahatma Gandhi saw this very clearly, and would reply to anyone who asked him what his message to the world was: "My life is my message." This powerful statement encapsulates the essence of the role model: that people respond more deeply to observed behaviour, not to noble statements of intent.

This, perhaps more than anything, holds the key to the transformation of African economies. In Kenya we have had all the wrong examples set by leaders: personal aggrandisement; the building up large personal fortunes through patronage and corruption; an emphasis on opulence and the flaunting of the symbols of wealth; and ethnocentric intolerance. Arguably, much of the degradation of values that can be observed in the population at large has been caused by exactly this: the wrong example from the top.

A commitment to the values that will save Kenya – thrift, tolerance, integrity and hard work, to name but a few – demands a visible example set continuously and consistently from the top leadership of the country. Displaying large, luxurious offices and multi-million-shilling limousines – earned through a position, not performance – to the citizenry undermines the essence of what is needed to transform the country. The fact that a significant proportion of ministers are continually linked to corruption scandals plants the seeds of dishonesty in the observing population. A routine failure to turn up in parliament, or achieve demonstrable results in one's ministry, propagates the culture of lethargy that seeks overnight success rather than finding intrinsic value in work.

Leaders must not just live the values they uphold for the country, they must be seen to live them. There can be no doubt that the intellectually powerful, simply attired Prime Minister with visibly humble material needs – Manmohan Singh – is doing a great deal of long-term good for Indian society. Nelson Mandela taught tolerance and forgiveness to the new African ruling class by personal example. Margaret Thatcher worked famously long hours – and Britain followed suit.

This is not just a matter of the correct public relations and positive 'spin': leaders must actually believe in what they preach. George Van Valkenburg put it well: "Leadership is about doing what's right even when no one is watching." Other thinkers such as Lewis Lapham have advised that "Leadership consists not in degrees of technique but in traits of character; it requires moral rather than athletic or intellectual effort, and it imposes on both leader and follower the burden of self-restraint."

The rewards of fast-paced economic development will be difficult to come by in Kenya until we get the leaders who demonstrate, in their daily lives, the behaviours needed to achieve 'lift-off' for the country. If anything, this is a matter for civic education to enable voters to show the necessary discernment at the polls and select a new breed of leaders who 'become the change they want' for Kenya (to paraphrase Gandhi). Recent thinking on how behaviour gets transmitted in a community suggests, however, that positive change can be rapid and sustained when the correct transmission mechanisms are deployed.[15]

Conclusions

Amartya Sen's thesis about freedom being both the principal means and the primary goal of development places particular demands on leadership. A leader concerned with designing economic incentives and granting substantive freedoms to his people must rule with a light touch. He (she) must have the intellectual prowess to play a key role in designing a framework of incentives in the economy to reward the correct behaviours exhibited by economic agents. Yet he must also believe that development will come from the efforts and energy of the citizenry – not from the heavy hand of government. He must have the tolerance to allow free and full political debate and allow people to make political choices – even when this results in his own downfall. And this same leader must also understand that a great part of the country's development expenditure must be targeted towards collective goods (schools and universities, clinics and hospitals) that build future repositories of human capital for the country.

Organisation theory recommends that a leader should be prepared to be more a coach and a mentor, rather than a believer in rigid command-and-control hierarchies. He should be willing to design and to teach rather than decide unilaterally and preach unconvincingly. We also know that leaders are amongst the most effective transmitters of values and behaviour. Morally upright, hardworking leaders who emphasise performance and results over ostentation and showy flourishes are therefore a vital necessity for development.

Where are such people to be found? How is Kenya to develop such a breed? This chapter would be incomplete without attempting an answer. Do we wait for such a person to emerge, as the result of sheer good fortune or the workings of destiny? Can we do something that might create the groundwork for such an emergence? In this sense, the answer lies in all of us. By inculcating the necessary attributes and values in ourselves, we create the environment from which right-minded leadership can emerge. We must move ourselves away from the messianic model that requires that we await a Mandela or a Gandhi to deliver our salvation. Leaders are reflections of the people from which they emerge. Rather than construct the attributes of the 'perfect' leader and hope that such a person appears, we would be better served by living the necessary values ourselves.

We would also do well to take our focus away from personalities and towards institutions. The established economies of the first world are, arguably, able to withstand the emergence of the occasional poor leader simply because they are protected by strong institutions. America survived the illegal activities of Richard Nixon in the 1970s because its institutions – the legislature, judiciary and media – were able to provide a countervailing power and independent scrutiny. In Kenya, rather than waiting for leaders to create these institutions, we would be better served by creating institutions that require a certain type of leadership to run them.

Lee connected with his people's latent attributes of hard work and perseverance. He played the role of designer, building a strategy and a framework to take advantage of these inherent values. His key contribution was to inject the intellectual rigour needed to leverage these strengths in a complex and ever-changing global landscape. And by demonstrating these same values in his own personal conduct, he was able to reinforce the natural values found in his people. Creating such a virtuous circle is perhaps the most powerful work of a leader.

Equally, Margaret Thatcher allowed Great Britain to 'rediscover' its own talents and attributes, partly suppressed by long decades of state provision. These attributes – national pride, personal responsibility and a dogged refusal to lose – were easily surfaced when a leader who embodied them took centre stage. But the point is this: Thatcher did not need to invent these values, nor did she introduce them to her people. They were always present in the centuries-old national character of the British. Thatcher merely stimulated their resurgence, and crafted an economic strategy that allowed for full utilisation of their power. Britain has become a more entrepreneurial and more resilient nation as a result.

A final example: Seretse Khama, too, took advantage of national character traits: peacefulness, humility and very strong community spirit. His task was to design an economic framework to reflect these values in full. His framework emphasised a disdain for corrupt practices and prudent management of collective resources, and resonated deeply with his people. This ability to connect with the natural, embedded values of the citizenry is the perhaps the most important hallmark of a leader.

There is no reason to believe that we in Kenya lack the necessary attributes needed to take us to similar successes in the development race. What is true is that our leaders, far from reinforcing positive values, introduced a raft of negative traits: selfishness, a suspicious mindset centre on tribe, and a tendency to regard public funds as fair game for plunder. Over the decades, this poison has seeped into the well of our collective ethos. To cleanse the well, we need to look away from these leaders and towards ourselves, our families and communities. That is not an endeavour that will yield quick and tangible gains. But in doing this, we will be repairing the damaged fabric of ethical nationhood. Good leadership requires a good environment in which to do its good work. Providing that environment is within the grasp of every Kenyan.

Notes

[1] See Legovini, Arianna. "Kenya: A Macroeconomic Evolution Since Independence". www.ke.undp.org, 2002.

[2] See *Pulling Apart: Facts and Figures on Inequality in Kenya*. Nairobi: Society for International Development, 2004.

[3] Government of Kenya. *Economic Recovery Strategy for Wealth and Employment Creation*. Nairobi: GoK, 2003.

[4] See Bhagwati, Jagdish, *In Defence of Globalization*. New York: Oxford University Press, 2004: 64-66

[5] See, for example: Sen, Amartya. *Development as Freedom*. Oxford: Oxford University Press, 1999; Easterly, William. *The Elusive Quest for Growth*. Cambridge, Massachusets: MIT Press, 2001; and De Long, Bradford. *The Meaning of Economic Growth*. Draft 1.0, www.econ161.berkeley.edu, 1997.

[6] Many of the facts and figures quoted in this section can be found in: "Lee Kuan Yew". www.en.wikipedia.org, 2005; "Economy of Singapore". www.en.wikipedia.org, 2005; and McCarthy, Terry. "Lee Kuan Yew". *Time 100*, 23-30 August, 1999.

[7] A good summary of the career of Margaret Thatcher can be found in "Margaret Thatcher". www.en.wikipedia.org, 2005.

[8] Sen, Amartya. *Ibid*.

[9] Senge, Peter. *The Fifth Discipline*. New York: Doubleday Currency, 1990: 3.

[10] Senge, Peter. *Ibid*: 340.

[11] Sadly, Johnson's story did not end well. His misadventures in Vietnam made him lose his commitment to the truth and lost him much of his early popularity, to the extent that he was unable to stand for re-election in 1968.

[12] See Roberts, John. *The Modern Firm*. Oxford: Oxford University Press, 2004.

[13] "Hot HR Issues for the Next Two Years." The Conference Board of Canada, (August 2004).

[14] Bindra, Sunny. "The Power to Lead by Example", *Sunday Nation* (19 June 2005).

[15] For more on this, see Gladwell, Malcolm. *The Tipping Point*. London: Abacus, 2002.

About the Contributors

Tade Aina is the Representative, Ford Foundation Office of Eastern Africa.

Kimani Njogu is a Professor of Kiswahili and African Languages and Director of Twaweza Communications.

PLO Lumumba teaches at the Faculty of Law, University of Nairobi. Dr. Lumumba served as Secretary of the Constitution of Kenya Review Commission (CKRC).

Kibe Mungai is a human rights lawyer based in Nairobi and a member of the National Constitutional Executive Council.

Macharia Munene is a Professor of History and International Relations at United States International University (USIU).

Eric Aseka is a Professor of History at Kenyatta University.

Philomena Mwaura teaches in the Religious Studies Department at Kenyatta Univesity.

Mbugua Wa- Mungai teaches in the Literature Department at Kenyatta University.

Njeri Kang'ethe is a lawyer and journalist based in Nairobi.

Mark Ogutu teaches in the Business Administration Department at Kenyatta University.

Sunny Bindra is a consultant and newspaper columnist based in Nairobi.

Index

A

Aam Aadmi, 226
Academic Staff Unions, 9, 208
acclamation, 214
accountability, 21, 30, 56, 61, 159, 190, 217
activism, 8, 112, 214
African Charter on the Rights and Welfare of
    the Child (ACWRC), 146
affirmative action, 145, 160, 174
African Association of Political Scientists
    (AAPS), 4
African crisis, 126
African diaspora, 212
African Peer Review Mechanism (APRM),
    126, 212
African Union (AU), 4, 212
Afro Shiraz Party, 33
Agba Ekwe, 141
agentic, 163
Amnesty International, 74, 101
Association of Public Administration and
    Management (APAM), 4
Association of the Physically Disabled of Kenya
    (APDK), 169
Atumia ma Nzama, 132
AU Charter, 146
autarchic, 10
authoritarian, 10, 54, 57, 58, 71, 79, 80, 81,
    92, 93, 96, 212, 229, 230
authoritarianism, 60, 82, 83, 142, 143, 181,
    212, 227

B

baraza, 142, 156, 230
Berlin Wall, 78, 187
Bill of Rights, 31, 33, 39, 56
Black Power Movement, 109

C

Calmeadow Foundation, 204
cannibalism, 165
capital offence, 75, 82
capitalism, 10, 54, 55, 86, 137, 158
Catholic Church, 90, 186, 187, 190
Convention on the Elimination of all Forms of
    Discrimination Against Women
    (CEDAW), 146
central government, 27, 35, 36, 46
centralization, 28, 44
cerebral palsy, 172
Chama cha Mapinduzi (CCM), 33
change the constitution group, 69
charisma, 126, 182, 189
charismatic, 53, 127, 178, 179, 182, 187, 189,
    190, 228
Children's Act 2001, 148, 149, 151
citizenship, 6, 28, 36, 105, 108, 117
civic education, 126, 188, 230, 232
civil code, 53
civil service, 26, 34, 35, 56, 93, 156
civil society, 6-8, 11-13, 20, 22, 41, 42, 78,
    82, 91, 98, 102, 124, 129, 132, 133, 136,
    156, 171, 173, 177, 188, 191
civilization, 106, 108
class and national identities, 7
class structures, 17
cold war, 10, 104, 105, 107, 108, 109, 112,
    116, 118, 187
collective humanity, 3, 15
colonialism, 7, 17, 57, 58, 104-119, 140, 144,
    156
colour bar, 109
commission on one-party rule, 33
common law, 100, 140
communism, 41, 186
community based organization, 6, 22, 168

constituent assembly, 30, 32, 33
constitution, 25, 27-49
constitutionalism, 27, 30, 32, 34, 44, 46, 56, 57, 67
consumerism, 2
contract theorists, 7
corruption, 13, 41, 44, 47, 64, 87, 96, 114, 135, 137, 145, 176, 187, 188, 217, 219, 221, 226, 231
cosmology, 179
Council of Economic and Social Research in Africa (CODESRIA), 4
council of elders, 19, 132, 142
coup de tat, 28
Court of Appeal, 42, 75, 89
Convention on the Rights of the Child (CRC), 146
cross border conflicts, 1

D

dashiki, 109
de facto, 61, 62, 63, 70, 153
de jure, 26, 40, 70, 71
decentralization, 19, 30
decolonization, 4, 9, 57, 101
dehumanization, 182
democracy, 2, 4, 5, 8-13, 16, 22, 23, 26, 30, 31-34, 41, 47, 51, 56, 57, 60, 63, 65-67, 76-79, 81, 88, 94, 99, 102, 103, 181, 188, 190, 193, 216, 217, 226
democratic system, 1
liberal democracy, 2, 11, 13, 23, 34, 67
multiparty democracy, 8, 79, 88, 188, 226
parliamentary democracy, 57, 76
participatory democracy, 30, 31, 100
despotism, 57, 60
destooled, 180
devolution, 30, 43, 45, 161
dialogic, 15
diaspora, 104-118
dictatorship, 1, 8, 9, 13, 16, 26, 32, 53, 65, 66, 67, 79, 87, 125, 145

Dini ya Musambwa, 181
disabled, 163-175
diversification, 195, 212
diviner, 178
Donors Consultative Group (DCG), 80

E

ecology, 20
Economic Council of Canada (ECC), 199, 202, 204, 208, 212
Economic Recovery Strategy (ERS), 216
ecosystem, 197, 198, 200, 208, 209, 213
ecumenical, 158, 186
education, 42, 58, 59, 70, 98, 105, 106-108, 117, 126, 133, 135, 148-152, 160
Electoral Commission, 42, 47, 89
elitism, 106, 222
entrepreneurship, 195, 200, 209, 210, 212
environmental, 20, 140, 197, 198, 199, 201, 203, 208, 209
epistemological, 15, 235
equality, 27, 30, 50, 52, 53, 55, 156
equity, 89, 145, 200, 205, 209
Erastian, 187, 230
Eshina shia Abakofu, 132
ethnic cleansing, 1
  insularity, 3, 84
  nationalism, 45, 60, 185, 186
  rivalry, 26
  tension, 14, 132
ethnicity, 2, 4, 11, 18, 21, 22, 26, 64, 71, 102, 123, 124, 127, 135, 176
ethnicization, 18
evangelical, 140, 187
exclusion, 15, 126, 163, 164, 168, 170, 218

F

Forum for African Women Educationalists (FAWE), 152
femininity, 14
feminism, 161

feminist, 148
folklore, 139, 165, 173
Forum for the Restoration of Democracy
    (FORD), 41, 80
free markets, 216, 217, 224
freedom, 8, 9, 10, 12, 15, 26, 30, 52, 55, 59,
    66, 71, 75, 103, 113, 140, 148, 157, 222,
    226, 227, 232
freedom of speech, 6
    of assembly, 8

G

gender, 6, 14, 21-23, 31, 89, 125, 131, 139,
    141, 146, 148, 153-156, 160, 182, 190,
    192
genocide, 1
gerontocracy, 131
girl child, 148, 149, 165
global call to action against poverty, 158
globalization, 3, 12, 14, 15, 23, 135, 186, 234
gramscian, 124, 125

H

Harambee, 26, 69
hegemony, 124, 125, 128, 181
hermeneutics, 187
hero-worship, 26
heterogeneous, 6, 15
historicity, 17
homiletic, 188
homologous space, 165
House of Representatives, 35, 36, 39, 55
households, 6, 141, 215
human capital, 227, 228, 233
human rights, 11, 14, 21, 23, 31, 60, 63, 74,
    78-80, 83, 86, 98, 113, 125, 146, 48,
    159, 173, 176, 177, 185, 186, 188, 191,
    192
Human Rights Commission (HRC), 31, 171
hybrid, 15

I

International Covenant on Civil and Political
    Rights (ICCPR), 146
International Covenant on Economic, Social
    and Cultural Rights (ICESCR), 146, 148
ideology, 18, 26, 41, 51, 53, 86, 120-125, 127,
    128, 129, 131, 132, 135, 181, 187, 189
imagery, 173
incarnation, 188, 189
inclusion, 15, 72
indigenization, 11
indigenous knowledge, 10, 19
individualism, 5, 60
inflation, 10, 223, 224
instrumentalist theory, 64
Inter-Parties Parliamentary Group (IPPG), 88,
    91
intergenerational dialogue, 5, 12
International Monetary Fund (IMF), 14, 112
internationality, 7
Iron Curtain, 109

J

jua kali, 13
Judicial Service Commission (JSC), 36
judiciary, 27, 30, 34, 36, 40, 55, 56, 70, 75,
    160, 177, 233

K

Kabaka Yekka, 27
Kenya African Democratic Union (KADU),
    37, 61, 62, 64
Kambi, 132
Kenya African National Union (KANU), 35,
    37, 38, 39, 40, 41, 42, 45, 49
Kenya Gazette, 69, 102, 172, 175
kiama, 132, 142
kinship, 6, 7, 63, 131
kivaho, 131
knowledge systems, 15, 19

kokwet, 143
kyabasinga, 27

L

laissez-fairerism, 125
Lancaster House Conference, 34, 58
Law Society of Kenya (LSK), 41
leadership, 25-33, 50-54, 60, 70, 71, 73, 81-
    87, 94, 98, 99, 104, 105, 108, 113, 116,
    120-138
legislature, 27, 32, 34, 43, 46, 233
leitmotif, 130
Liberal Democratic Party (LDP), 98
liberalization, 80, 86, 102

M

machiavellian, 25, 62
magician, 178
mainline, 184, 186, 187, 191, 192, 193
majimbo, 35, 55, 64
majority rule, 6
Mama Amani, 154, 156
marginal social space, 164
marginalization, 10, 173
marxism, 10, 135, 136
masculinity, 14,
maskini wa Mungu, 169
materialism, 2, 5
matrilineage, 141
Mau Mau, 57, 58, 59, 107, 157
meritocracy, 135, 219
messianic, 225, 233
metalanguage, 11
micro-credit, 205
militarization, 21
minority rights, 6, 36
missiologists, 176
mlolongo, 76, 77
mobilization, 191, 211
monarchy, 6, 81, 141
movement political system, 31

mucii, 142
multinational corporations, 10, 221
multipartyism, 64, 79, 81-88, 91, 95, 98
musyi, 131
Mwakenya, 74, 75
mythology, 179

N

National Rainbow Coalition (NARC), 84, 93,
    98, 100, 147, 171, 188, 215, 219
National Assembly, 28, 34, 35, 39, 42, 69, 83,
    88-90, 93, 94, 102, 103
National Constitutional Conference, 43, 81
national infrastructure, 2
National Party of Kenya (NPK), 98
National Resistance Army (NRA), 29
National Resistance Movement (NRM), 29
nationalism, 193, 194
nativists, 115
natural justice, 72
National Council of Churches of Kenya
    (NCCK), 76, 90
New Partnership for Africa's Development, The
    (NEPAD), 4
nepotism, 64
Ngei Amendment, 66
Non-Governmental Organizations (NGOs), 6,
    165, 170
Njuri Ncheke, 132
Nobel Peace Prize, 157, 161
Nthi, 131
Nyakinyua, 142
Nyalali Commission, 34, 48
Nyayoism, 26, 77, 187
nyumba, 142
Nzama, 131, 132

O

Omugambi, 179
Omuruothi, 179
ontology, 129, 132, 137

Order of the Grand Warrior, 151
Organisation of African Unity (OAU), 108
Organisation of Afro-American Unity, 108,

P

Palestinian Liberation Organisation (PLO), 110
Pan-Africanism, 4, 19
paradigm shifting, 122
paralympics, 167
parliament, 4, 5, 23, 28, 29, 32-49, 58, 62-84,
    88, 90, 92, 93, 96, 100, 142, 157
    Parliamentary Select Committee, 66
    Parliamentary Service Commission, 92
    Parliamentary Standing Orders, 84
participation, 1, 2, 6, 11, 13, 16, 31, 43, 71,
    74, 110, 126, 139, 142-146, 154, 161,
    168, 184, 198, 202, 207, 208
partisan, 62, 94
patriarchal, 131, 141, 145
patrimonial, 6, 12, 124
patronage, 10, 18, 28, 58, 90, 172, 218, 231
Penal Code, 90
Pentecostals, 186, 188, 189
Persons with Disability Act 2003, 165, 172
petty bourgeoisie, 8
pluralism, 26, 80, 82, 83, 89, 96
plurilogic, 15
populism, 68
post-colonial, 7, 9, 50, 54, 61, 185, 186, 191
postmodern colonialism, 105, 113, 118, 119
power, 26-95
power, abuse of, 9, 18, 35, 43, 47, 57, 98, 101
    180, 214
presidential system, 31, 32
presidentialism, 81, 102
priest, 178, 179
primitive accumulation, 54
prisoners of conscience, 74
production, 10, 12, 17, 18, 23, 54, 106, 122,
    134, 196, 197, 219
Proverbs, 173, 192

provincial administration, 42, 43, 59, 80, 81,
    90, 150, 151
Public Service Commission (PSC), 34, 56, 75,
    76,

Q

Queen Mother, The, 141

R

racism, 1, 107, 109, 113, 116, 134
radicalization, 8
rainbow alliance front, 98
realpolitik, 145
referendum, 31, 36, 43, 47, 89, 143
reformer, 178
regionalism, (*majimbo*) *also majimboism* 35, 39
renaissance, 126, 127, 130, 139, 140
repatriation, 12
republican monarch, 67
Republicans, 86
residual power, 7
review commission, 42, 49, 171
revolutions, 8, 53
rite of passage, 150
roadside policy, 68
rural-urban migration, 1
Rural Women's Peace Link (RWPL), 155

S

saint, 178
secret ballot, 76, 77
sectarianism, 18, 47
Section 2A, 41, 70-82
security of tenure, 34, 40, 56, 75-82
sedition, 72, 76, 82, 90
seer, 178
senate, 35-39, 55, 62
separation of powers, 41, 53, 76
servanthood, 183, 189
Sixth Ordinary Session, 4, 23

slave trade, 2, 12
socialization, 3, 57, 191
sparkplug, 201
Special Branch, the 74
special schools, 164, 170, 174
state of emergency, 32, 34, 35
statist economy, 7
Statute Law, The, 102
Structural Adjustment Programmes (SAPs),
    9, 140
supra-ethnic, 123
sycophancy, 98, 99

T

taboos, 130, 170, 174
TANU, 33, 44, 46
technocentric, 197
The Big Lie Rule, 113
the eighth parliament, 96
theologians, 176
totalistic, 7
trade networks, 202
trans-ethnic association, 8
Transafrica, 100, 113
transparency, 31, 159, 217
tribalism, 59, 60, 124, 134, 135

U

Uganda Constitutional Commission (UCC), 30
uhuru, 48, 58, 60, 61, 64, 73
ujamaa, 26

UN Millennium Development Goals, 158
Uncle Toms, 109
underdevelopment, 17, 111, 127
United Nations Universal Declaration of
    Human Rights (UNDHR), 146
ungioyana na kionje gigutware ku?, 171
unilateral declaration of independence, 8
unipolar, 230
unitary state, 39
United Nations (UN), 107, 110, 114, 115,
    146, 155, 158, 162, 220
United People's Congress (UPC), 28
United States Information Agency (USIA), 109
universal discourse, 14
urbanization, 7, 19
Utui, 131

V

veto legislation, 35

W

Washington Post, The, 113, 119
walemavu, 169
wananchi, 69
Westminster, 27
Winter of Discontent, 222
World Bank, 10, 14, 41, 112, 156, 216,

Z

Zion Christian Church, 185

www.ingramcontent.com/pod-product-compliance
Lightning Source LLC
Chambersburg PA
CBHW021858020426
42334CB00013B/384